The Beloved Does Not Bite

In this new monograph, author Debra Dudek defines a new era of vampire texts in which vampires have moved from their iconic dark, feared, often seductive figure lingering in alleys, to the beloved and morally sensitive vampire winning the affections of teen protagonists throughout pop culture. Dudek takes a close look at three hugely-popular vampire series for young adults, drawing parallels between the TV series *Buffy the Vampire Slayer*, the *Twilight* Saga novels/films, and *The Vampire Diaries* TV series/book series. By defining a new era of vampire texts and situating these three series within this transition, *The Beloved Does Not Bite* signals their significance and lays the groundwork for future scholarship on the flourishing genre of paranormal romances for young adults.

Debra Dudek is an Associate Professor in the School of Arts and Humanities at Edith Cowan University, Australia.

Children's Literature and Culture
Jack Zipes, *Founding Series Editor*
Philip Nel, *Current Series Editor*

For a full list of titles in this series, please visit www.routledge.com.

Canon Constitution and Canon Change in Children's Literature
Edited by Bettina Kümmerling-Meibauer and Anja Müller

Fictions of Integration
American School Desegregation and the Legacies
of Brown v. Board of Education
Naomi Lesley

New Directions in Children's Gothic
Debatable Lands
Edited by Anna Jackson

More Words About Pictures
Current Research on Picture Books and Visual/Verbal
Texts for Young People
Edited by Perry Nodelman, Naomi Hamer, and Mavis Reimer

Childhood and Pethood in Literature and Culture
New Perspectives on Childhood Studies and Animal Studies
Edited by Anna Feuerstein and Carmen Nolte-Odhiambo

Origin Narratives
The Stories We Tell Children about Immigration
and Interracial Adoption
Macarena Garcia Gonzales

Italian Children's Literature and National Identity
Childhood, Melancholy, Modernity
Maria Truglio

The Beloved Does Not Bite
Moral Vampires and the Humans Who Love Them
Debra Dudek

The Beloved Does Not Bite
Moral Vampires and the Humans Who Love Them

Debra Dudek

Routledge
Taylor & Francis Group
NEW YORK AND LONDON

First published 2018
by Routledge
711 Third Avenue, New York, NY 10017

and by Routledge
2 Park Square, Milton Park, Abingdon, Oxon OX14 4RN

Routledge is an imprint of the Taylor & Francis Group, an informa business

Library of Congress Cataloging-in-Publication Data
CIP data has been applied for.

ISBN: 978-0-415-78826-7 (hbk)
ISBN: 978-1-315-22542-5 (ebk)

Typeset in Sabon
by codeMantra

for Jake
beloved monster, slayer of that

Contents

List of Figures

Acknowledgments

I acknowledge the University of Wollongong for providing me with Study Leave to write a substantial portion of this book, and The Centre for Research in Young People's Texts and Cultures (CRYTC) at the University of Winnipeg for the space in which to do so.

Some of the ideas in this manuscript originally appeared in "The Beloved That Does Not Bite: Genre, Myth, and Repetition in *Buffy the Vampire Slayer*" published in *Seriality and Texts for Young People: The Compulsion to Repeat.* Eds. Reimer, M., Ali, N., England, D., Unrau, M.D., Dennis Unrau, M. Palgrave Macmillan, 2014. Grateful thanks to Palgrave Macmillan for kind permission to reproduce those ideas here.

My sincere thanks go to the following people—without you, this book would not have been possible. Seriously.

Friends and colleagues at those two UOWs I acknowledge above, whose enthusiasm and support for this project never wavered, even when I did.

Children's literature colleagues for listening at conferences to early versions of some of these chapters and for asking twisty questions.

The editorial team at Routledge—Jennifer Abbott, Elizabeth Levine, and Erin Little—and Assunta Petrone at codeMantra. Special thanks to Phil Nel, who heartily believed in this project from the beginning, who relentlessly pushed topic sentences to the front of paragraphs, and who enthusiastically supported my anecdotes.

Sharon Crozier-De Rosa, Sarah Sorial, and Frances Steel for the many after-work drinking, brainstorming, and ranting sessions.

Anne Brewster for imparting theatre-night wisdom.

Nicole Markotić for introducing me to *Buffy*, for providing junk food buffets at the viewing marathons, and for inviting me to test some early ideas on her students.

Suzette Mayr for epic beach rambles, for Cheezel and red wine indulgences, and for persistently trying to find me new female television heroes.

Michéle Manaigre for yoga talks, dog walks, and cellular love.

Catherine Gerbasi for passion and beauty and hugs that stretch across oceans.

The gorgeous Garmans—Jake, Eli, and Iris—for talking stories, probing questions, and for teaching me to see differently.

My Dudek family—John, Marilyn, Dawn, Ross, Wendy, Lukas, and Liam—who encouraged me to completion. Special thanks to my Mom and Dad, who put up with me for seven months, who watched scenes from films and TV episodes, and who listened to songs over and over again, and to Dawn for her help with the images and for permitting her stunning painting to adorn the cover of this book.

Introduction
The Beloved Cycle: A New Vampire Sub-genre

While working on this book, I spent some time at my parents' cottage in the Canadian wilderness. I would re-emerge for meals and talk to my parents about what I was writing and about how I was trying to work through my thoughts about love and how love exists in *Buffy the Vampire Slayer*, the *Twilight* saga, and *The Vampire Diaries*. One night, my mother turned to me and said, "Do you believe vampires are real?" I looked at her with a perplexed expression on my face, so she continued, "The way you talk about vampires and love, it seems as though you think they are real." I kept her question in mind while I wrote because it reminded me that television shows and films and the characters who inhabit those stories insinuate themselves into the fabric of our lives. They whisper to us and perform risky feats of love we may fear for ourselves. Nina Auerbach in *Our Vampires, Ourselves* proclaims, "what vampires are in any given generation is a part of what I am and what my times have become" (1). If I believe Auerbach's claim, which I do, then my mother's question is not so absurd: perhaps the reality of these vampires is they exist in me.

As an avid fan of *Buffy*, I initially resisted thinking about the show academically, so I could enjoy my not-so-secret obsession with Buffy and Angel privately. As more and more vampires appeared in television and film, however, and as I watched the vampire genre shift, I started thinking more about why my pleasure attached itself so firmly to the Buffy-and-Angel pairing. Angel left Buffy after three seasons to move to Los Angeles for his own show, and Riley seemed a poor substitute. I enjoyed the sparring sexiness of Buffy's messed-up relationship with Spike (except for one horrible episode in Season Six), but I really wanted Buffy and Angel crossover episodes. Then, with the publication of *Twilight* and its subsequent massive fan base, teenage male vampires became hot stuff. They moved out of the darkness and into the daylight, and in those hallowed halls of American high schools, human girls fell in love with vampire boys. As a reflection upon these changes in the vampire genre, *The Beloved Does Not Bite* responds to the questions: what does it mean to love a vampire and to be a vampire who loves? Although this book deals specifically with how particular vampires love and are loved, these questions and their answers translate across species and stories.

I test questions about how love initiates a moral response in three of the most popular and influential series, all of which pitch towards a young adult audience—*Buffy the Vampire Slayer* (*BtVS*); the *Twilight* saga (*Twilight*); and *The Vampire Diaries* (*TVD*)—and argue that a new era in the vampire genre exists: the Beloved Cycle, in which the vampire, who does not bite to kill, becomes the beloved. Drawing on Rick Altman's semantic/syntactic framework, I claim this generic shift signals an ideological and affective move from sympathy to love. At the core of my analysis sits the claim that moral thought and action in these three series begins with reciprocal, sustained romantic love between a male vampire and a female human. In other words, this love between a vampire and a human inspires them to reflect upon what it means to be good and to act in ways that promote good.

Good Monster Love

Love stories pulse at the heart of many fictions, but *paranormal* romances test the extremes to which love extends to an absolute other who embodies good and evil. In *Seduced by Twilight: The Allure and Contradictory Messages in the Popular Saga*, Natalie Wilson questions the popularity of the *Twilight* saga and suggests, following Tania Modleski, "romances increase in popularity during socially tumultuous times" (14). Wilson believes, "*Twilight* vampires speak to our cultural need to come to terms with not only teenage sexuality but also shifting political and religious power structures" (18). More specifically, she points to Edward as

> a monster perfectly fitting for our post-9/11, anxiety-ridden age. He holds out the nostalgic promise that love can conquer all—even terrorist-like Volturi vampires. With his impervious body like a living shield, he suggests we need not worry about terror alerts. His intellect and wealth speak to our desires to know all the secrets of existence while living a life of privilege not hampered by worry over the end of oil, the rising cost of electricity, nor the weakening dollar. His ultimate overcoming of prejudice (for humans and wolves) makes him a good fit for a world we like to consider post-racial. Further, his capacity to love with every ounce of his being functions as a comforting salve in our era of ubiquitous infidelity, divorce, dysfunctional relationships, and domestic violence.
>
> (35)

While not all her points apply to Angel, Stefan, and Damon, as well as Edward, Wilson does usefully acknowledge how Edward serves as a sometimes conflicted floating signifier for peacekeeper, lover, capitalist, and activist. Wilson's final point about Edward's "capacity to love with every ounce of his being" comes closest to the core of my study, but I extend her description of Edward's all-encompassing love to foreground this love as a feature in each of the vampire-human relationships. I suggest such love should not be dismissed as a "nostalgic promise that love can conquer all" but rather should be embraced as a premise for living a good life. The appeal of men who articulate and act upon their emotions cannot be overestimated. That such men (albeit undead vampires who look like men) may be living in communities and not buried in a coffin or perched in a mansion, offers hope we, too, may recognize and be recognized by them.

This ability to recognize and be recognized and therein to act morally stems, in part, from an ability to determine between evil and good, even, and perhaps especially, when they exist in the same being. As philosopher Richard Kearney argues in his book *Strangers, Gods and Monsters*, monsters can teach people about what he calls "the enigma of evil" (100). To discuss the function of monsters in narrative, Kearney draws on the work of structural anthropologist Claude Lévi-Strauss, summarizing his argument as follows: "By telling stories about monsters we provide symbolic resolutions to enigmas—those of our origins, time, birth and death—which cannot be solved at the level of our everyday historical experience. In short, monster myths offer imaginary answers to real problems" (233). This idea of offering imaginary answers to real problems exists at the core of *BtVS*: Buffy often encounters both demons and humans who embody and challenge notions of what it means to be good and to be evil. Whether the problem be a cyber-stalker, an abusive boyfriend, a power-hungry mayor, or a bullying pack of demonic hyenas, each episode or story arc presents Buffy with a dilemma that must be—and is—solved. In the *Twilight* saga, the real problems begin when Bella enters into a potentially abusive relationship and escalate when figures of the law threaten her family's safety. In *The Vampire Diaries*, the back-story of the Civil War infiltrates the present to show the real perils of a community divided against itself. In each series, love—platonic, familial, and/or romantic—initiates the imaginary answers to these problems.

Monsters as metaphors for real problems find their most imaginative answers in the expansive seven-season Buffyverse, which allows for a complex consideration of the monster-as-metaphor trope. As Giles reminds Buffy in the series pilot, the Hellmouth upon which Sunnydale rests contains all manner of demons including "zombies, werewolves, incubi, succubi, everything you've ever dreaded was under your bed, but told yourself couldn't be by the light of day. They're all real!" ("Welcome to the Hellmouth" 1001). In the *Twilight* saga, however, the metaphor narrows to focus on the interactions between humans, vampires, and werewolves only, and more specifically on one family of vampires and one community of werewolves. The storyworld of *TVD* likewise concentrates on the interrelations between a small group of beings—humans, vampires, werewolves, and witches—which, arguably, allows for a more sustained and deeper dissection of the historical dynamics that inform the nature of good and evil in that body politic.

All three series deal with a form of evil for which the vampires eschew responsibility, at least at the site of their becoming undead. Useful for this analysis of metaphorical morality, Kearney's discussion of evil in Western discursive genres identifies four types of evil: mythological, scriptural, metaphysical, and anthropological. The nature of evil these three series examine concerns the mythological, in which "considerations of moral choice are inextricably linked to cosmological cycles of fate and destiny. Evil is basically *alienation*—something predetermined by forces beyond us" (84). Both Buffy's predetermined role as the slayer and Angel's lack of choice concerning his vampiric state suggest fate and destiny are at work. Angel's original change from a rather foppish human into an evil vampire was not something he chose, and neither was Edward's. The vampiric origins of the Salvatore brothers initiate with their love for Katherine, but through the use of generations of doppelgängers, for instance, *The Vampire Diaries* suggests fate and destiny inform their love, too, which still places them within the mythological notion of evil. More generally, vampires are evil creatures made so through no wrongdoing of their own, and, indeed, the human back stories of many of the feature vampires in the three series—such as Drusilla, Spike, the Cullens, Damon, and Caroline—highlight their inherent innocence and purity or their trusting gullibility.

Such beloved vampires waft into our lives to provide a metaphor for how we might negotiate Otherness with a loved one. As popular culture critic Douglas Kellner argues in "*Buffy, The Vampire Slayer* as Spectacular Allegory: A Diagnostic Critique," "allegory uses symbolic representation to comment on, interpret, and provide a vision of a historical moment." He suggests, *BtVS* can be read

> as an allegory about contemporary life with its monsters as metaphors for societal difference and threats, and Buffy and her friends' special powers can be read as metaphors for how knowledge, skill, and courage can help solve problems and dispatch evil. Classically, monsters like vampires symbolize predatory sexuality; werewolves connote bodily energies and forces exploding out of control; witches signify traditional female powers, including sexuality, which threaten rational patriarchal order; while a wide range of demons signify various sorts of deviance and threats to contemporary order and security.
>
> (6)

He continues, "Allegory, more than metaphor, points to a complex structure and polysemic depth of meaning in an artefact that demands levels of interpretation. It is allegory, then, that provides the structure and levels of meaning for the series as a whole, as well as holding together the various story arcs and narrative sequences" (7). Kellner's claim, then, brings metaphor into the arms of allegory, at least in the case of *BtVS*. Neither the *Twilight* saga nor *TVD* builds the comprehensive and intricate storyworld that exists in *BtVS*, but, in this book, I am less concerned with the structure of the Buffyverse and more compelled by the intimacies that permeate that world. These vampires may be metaphors for "predatory sexuality" as Kellner claims, but sexuality lures their lovers towards bliss, and in their mutual vulnerability, they strive for perfection, for a moral existence that makes them worthy of love.

Part of mutual vulnerability means opening oneself to the intimacies of a beloved—both emotionally and physically—and vampires invoke a permeability that opens the entire body to their touch, or at least to their teeth. Vampires, as Auerbach proclaims, "inhere in our most intimate relationships; they are also hideous invaders of the normal. I am writing about vampires because they can be everything we are, while at the same time, they are fearful reminders of the infinite things we are not" (6). I agree vampires enter into our intimacies and reveal our nightmares of the normal, but these vampires, all of whom appear after the publication of Auerbach's book, are not "hideous invaders"; they enthrall us with their beauty and tempt us towards the promise of an exceptional life. If they remind us of the "infinite things we are not," then perhaps we should be grateful for this reminder, so we might continue to strive to act from a place of love that leads to a more just life.

The Horror of Love

Buffy the Vampire Slayer, the *Twilight* saga, and *The Vampire Diaries* blend horror and teen romance to create a Beloved Cycle in the vampire genre, which features a beloved vampire who does not bite to kill. This genre characteristic allows for an investigation of how love can form the basis of moral action, but it also implies love can be horrific. In this section, I outline the philosophical concepts that inform my analysis throughout the book. I begin with a summary of relevant points in Noel Carroll's *The Philosophy of Horror* and then delineate how the works of two canonical philosophers of love illuminate this precarious balance between morality and horror: Iris Murdoch's *The Sovereignty of Good* and Martha Nussbaum's *Love's Knowledge: Essays on Philosophy and Literature*, and *Upheavals of Thought: The Intelligence of Emotions*.

Noel Carroll's influential book *The Philosophy of Horror: Or, Paradoxes of the Heart* moves from an analysis of what he calls the emotion of "art-horror"—which he defines as an emotion informed by horror and disgust, by monsters who are both a threat and are impure—to a philosophical treatise on why people consume horror. The two main questions he addresses are: "1) how can anyone be frightened by what they know does not exist, and 2) why would anyone ever be interested in horror, since being horrified is so unpleasant?" (8). The presence of a monster functions as the main component in his classification of the horror genre, but in order to distinguish between horror and other stories that include monsters, such as fairy tales and myths, he considers the reactions of characters in the story when they encounter the monster: "In works of horror, the humans regard the monsters they meet as abnormal, as disturbances of the natural order" (16). While the series I analyze do not fit into this category of art-horror, primarily because the monsters strive for purity, or at least morality, this process of looking to the human characters for emotional cues provides an important methodology for my own work. In the three vampire series under consideration, the main female characters—Buffy, Bella, and Elena—move from fearing to loving a monster while other characters may never move beyond a feeling of fear, or do so tentatively. Because the stories focus on the reactions of the main characters and their changing responses, the affective responses of audiences ideally align with these young women.

Even more relevant to my argument is Carroll's connection between horror and emotions and how the genre appeals to its viewers: his eponymous paradox of the heart. He states, "horror appears to be one of those genres in which the emotive responses of the audience, ideally, run parallel to the emotions of the characters. Indeed, in works of horror the responses of characters often seem to cue the emotional responses of audiences.... The characters in works of horror exemplify for us the way in which to react to the monsters in the fiction" (17). What I find most intriguing and confronting about this claim are the contradictory cues the audience must navigate in vampire stories within the Beloved Cycle. In the three series I examine, the main characters love men who not only have the potential to kill them—for this possibility holds true for all women—but they have witnessed their beloveds kill others, so they know the possibility for harm has moved from consideration to action. In *BtVS*, Buffy's own superhuman strength quells our uneasiness, but in the cases of Bella and Elena—at least before they, too, become vampires—we must learn to trust their belief that their lovers will not cause them physical harm. In other words, we, too, must believe love initiates moral action.

Of course, Angelus, Spike, Damon, and some of the Cullen clan, hover at the edges of this belief, pecking at our complacency like the portentous crows that punctuate the plots. They signal to us that lovers can morph into killers or sadists as quickly as they can fly across a room. We cringe when Angelus gleefully breaks Jennie Calendar's neck; when Spike attempts to rape Buffy; when Jasper's bloodlust for Bella wins over his control; and when Damon forces Elena to drink his blood so she will not die. For me, the pit in my belly reminds me I need to re-evaluate my connection to these characters and to guard against contentment.

Carroll locates feelings of fear and disgust on the monster himself, but with these vampire beloveds, while the possibility of wrong actions may produce such feelings, it is rarely the presence of the monster himself that brings them about. When Damon rips the heart out of Mason's chest, my stomach heaves in disgust; when he stakes Rose as an act of mercy, I cry; and when he and Elena kiss, I hug my pillow in bliss. All these feelings attach to Damon, a monster and a beloved, which complicates an easy alignment of vampire with monster to be feared.

Carroll classifies these emotional states, these flashes of feeling—these "upheavals" to use Nussbaum's term—as "occurent" rather than "dispositional," which he claims are more akin to a personal characteristic, such as envy. He also attributes both physical and cognitive dimensions to these emotional states. He argues,

> [b]roadly speaking, the physical dimension of an emotion is a matter of felt agitation. Specifically, the physical dimension is a sensation or a feeling. An emotion, that is, involves some kind of stirring, perturbation, or arrest physiologically registered by an increase in heartbeat, respiration, or the like. The word "emotion" comes from the Latin "emovere" which combines the notion of "to move" with the prefix for "out." An *emotion* originally was a *moving* out. To be in an emotional state involves the experience of a transition or migration—a change of state, a moving out of a normal physical state to an agitated one, one marked by inner movings. To be an occurrent emotion, I want to claim, involves a physical state—a sense of a physiological moving of some sort—a felt agitation or feeling sensation.
>
> (24)

I quote from Carroll at length here because this sense of being moved occurs both at the level of character identification, as per Carroll's theory, but also through the use of music, as I argue in Chapter 3.

Furthermore, I want to put more pressure on how being emotionally moved occurs physically but also how these movements prompt ideological shifts, or at least moral considerations. Carroll characterizes his theory as a "cognitive/evaluative theory"—as Nussbaum does hers—in order to merge emotion with evaluation: "an occurrent emotional state is one in which some physically abnormal state of felt agitation has been caused by the subject's cognitive construal and evaluation of his/her situation" (Carroll 27). Here, Carroll wants to eliminate the criticism that might point to a physical reaction being the only indication of an emotional experience. Instead, he urges a theory that insists upon not only the physical feeling but also the attachment of feeling to belief. For instance, the pit in my stomach does not always signify despair; sometimes this same pit dissolves into bliss. In order for me to understand my pitfall,

I must evaluate my situation. Does the pit tell me I hold my breath in a state of dread as I watch Angel open his eyes in disbelief as Buffy sends him to hell with a sword in his belly and/or does it indicate joyful anticipation as Elena and Damon kiss without waking up and finding it a dream?

This focus on feeling and belief returns us to Carroll's first question about how anyone can be frightened by a creature who does not exist. Since my concerns relate less to fear and more to love, I reshape Carroll's question to address how anyone can be moved by watching or reading about the love between a vampire and a human. While I do not pretend to understand the frenzy that has surrounded fan identification with Team Edward or Team Jacob, or why these three series secure such massive audiences, their popularity urges me to look more closely in order to question what they say about love and about our beliefs for justice.

In asking how people can be afraid of a monster they know does not exist, Carroll suggests we should think of such a monster as a thought rather than as a belief in the monster himself:

> let us say that the particular object of art-horror—Dracula, if you will—is a thought. Saying that we are art-horrified by Dracula means that we are horrified by the thought of Dracula where the thought of such a possible being does not commit us to a belief in his existence. Here, the thought of Dracula, the particular object that art-horrifies me, is not the actual event of my thinking of Dracula but the content of the thought, viz., that Dracula, a threatening and impure being of such and such dimensions, might exist and do these terrible things. Dracula, the thought, is the concept of a certain possible being. Of course, I come to think about this concept because a given book, or film, or picture invites me to entertain the thought of Dracula, that is, to consider the concept of a certain possible being, viz., Dracula. From such representations of the concept of Dracula, we recognize Dracula to be a threatening and impure prospect, one which gives rise to the emotion of art-horror.
>
> (29)

This concept of monster as thought draws me in because I want to privilege thinking—in these three series about monsters—as containing the possibility for moral action. That is, I want to say thought itself can be a moral action.

Though vampires have traditionally been viewed as amoral or evil, it has become broadly accepted that twenty-first century sympathetic vampires follow a moral code. As Catherine Spooner summarizes in "*Gothic Charm School*; or, How Vampires Learned to Sparkle," "They appeal to a moral imperative and a sense of decorum that are not just about preserving the social contract but also a kind of self-fashioning—even, perhaps, soul-making" (150). *The Beloved Does Not Bite* sinks its teeth into this moral imperative in order to draw forth the flavor of this ethics. These concepts of ethics and morals connect and, at times, overlap, especially as moral actions inform a larger ethics. Philosophers such as Bernard Gert, for instance, connect morality to ethics: "What 'morality' is taken to refer to plays a crucial, although often unacknowledged, role in formulating ethical theories." For example, where once the female vamp "came to represent the attraction and danger of modernity, luring men into forsaking traditional values in favour of modern ambitions, prioritising technological progress, financial gain and sexual liberation" ("The Undead," Abbott 100), now the male vampire harkens back to the Victorian gentleman in the case of *Twilight* or to Southern chivalry in *The Vampire Diaries.* These vampires' actions seem more outward facing, more selfless, as they strive to act righteously.

This striving for right action can be understood within a framework of either descriptive or normative morality. Morality, Gert says, can be used "descriptively to refer to some codes of conduct put forward by a society or some other group... or accepted by an individual for her own behavior" or "normatively to refer to a code of conduct that, given specified conditions, would be put forward by all rational persons." Overall, *The Beloved Does Not Bite* looks at normative criteria for morality, which invites viewers to test their own responses to specific situations rather than to accept an already-established code of conduct. For instance, when Angel leaves Buffy and Edward leaves Bella, they act morally because they want their beloveds to flourish, and these acts invite us to ponder whether under similar circumstances we might act the same way.

Such moral actions connect to a broader ethics of love. To define such an ethics of love, I turn to Murdoch's *The Sovereignty of Good* and two books in which Nussbaum develops her theory of emotions: *Love's Knowledge*; and *Upheavals of Thought.*[1] I follow both philosophers' assertions that emotions—and especially love-based emotions—play an important role in moral considerations about what it means to live well. In short: to live well means to love well and to love well means to focus one's attention towards particular others who are key to one's own flourishing. Murdoch opens her argument with the assertion that love is a central concept in morals (29). She builds upon this argument with the claim that moral activity can take place as a thought process even if it is unobserved by others. Indeed, I warily concede that one type of moral activity is my own private contemplation of what these series' philosophical scenarios tell us about love's role in living a just life. I am not saying the characters act justly all the time or even most of the time. I do contend, however, their dilemmas provide thought experiments, or, to recall Kearney's stance, they extend imagined answers to real problems.

In tandem with my assertions that these series enact moral dilemmas in order to rehearse for us our own possibilities for just action, they also represent this very process of contemplation as a moral act. Much of Damon's moral activity takes place in private or is erased when Damon compels people to forget his words. Furthermore, often these scenes end an episode and are underpinned by musical lyrics that invite a re-evaluation of a character, and therein resonate long after the final musical note fades. These structural repetitions reverberate throughout the series and position the viewer as compassionate confidante. For instance, although Damon articulates his moral dilemmas or reveals his tenderness to the audience, Elena and Stefan rarely witness these thoughts and actions. Instead, they encourage him to try to be a better man, to overcome his imperfections.

Damon's imperfections—and Elena and Stefan's love for Damon despite his imperfections—feature as the strongest example of love's complexities. Both Murdoch and Nussbaum advocate for a notion of love that strives for a virtuous life in an imperfect world. Nussbaum repeatedly asserts that in this very striving we perform loving and moral action (*Upheavals* 469, 626, 711), which Murdoch connects to ideas of the Good:

> Love is the tension between the imperfect soul and the magnetic perfection which is conceived of as lying beyond it.... And when we try perfectly to love what is imperfect our love goes to its object *via* the Good to be thus purified and made unselfish and just.... Love is the general name of the quality of attachment and it is capable of infinite degradation and is the source of our greatest errors; but when it is even partially refined it is the energy and passion of the soul in its search for Good, the force that joins us to Good and joins us to the world through Good.
>
> (100)

Nussbaum shies away from words such as "Good" and "purity," preferring instead concepts of striving, ambivalence, and mystery, but a common ground between their philosophies hinges upon an acceptance of imperfection as key to love.

I focus primarily on Nussbaum's notion of romantic/erotic love (*Upheavals* 65), which I distinguish in this book from familial, sibling, or fraternal love. Nussbaum sees erotic or romantic love as core to her project and defines such love as follows:

> Erotic love involves an opening of the self toward an object, a conception of the self that pictures the self as incomplete and reaching out for something valued.... erotic love is characterized as involving an intense attachment to and longing for a particular

> person; this attachment may transform itself to take on other more general objects, but its beginning lies in personal attachment. Erotic love also involves characteristic ways of viewing the beloved person, who is seen as radiant and wonderful, and also as necessary for the lover's happiness. Finally, the beloved person is also seen as independent – as uncontrolled and unpossessed, not simply a part of the lover, or submissive to his will.
>
> (*Upheavals* 460, 470)

Although all aspects of this definition resonate throughout this book, *The Beloved Does Not Bite* fleshes out three main ideas: love includes opening oneself to another; love begins with a personal attachment and then expands out from the couple; and the lover views the beloved as radiant. Chapter 3 focuses most specifically on opening oneself, of making oneself vulnerable to the beloved, especially through the kiss. Chapter 6 highlights the expansion of love from the couple to the community, especially when the community is called upon to protect itself from an outside force. All three series draw upon images of radiance, with the radiance of angels occurring again and again in Angel's name and Bella's repeated comparison of Edward to an angel (see for examples *Twilight* 19, 262, 341, 452–453). More specifically, as the *Vampire Diaries* novels state, Elena's name means "light," and, of course, Edward himself radiates light, as does Bella once she becomes a vampire. As Buffy implies about Angel's radiance, "when he's around... It's like the lights dim everywhere else" ("Angel" 1007), and Spike literally radiates and becomes light in the final battle against The First, which I discuss in Chapter 6.

Vampires who love and are loved test the idea that emotions imply weakness and human frailty in a world in which humans seem to seek immortality, and erotic love relies upon acknowledging and even embracing one's emotions, including love, sadness, and guilt. Nussbaum argues,

> human beings appear to be the only mortal finite beings who wish to transcend their finitude. Thus they are the only emotional beings who wish not to be emotional, who wish to withhold these acknowledgments of neediness and to design for themselves a life in which these acknowledgments have no place. This means that they frequently learn to reject their own vulnerability and to suppress awareness of the attachments that entail it.
>
> (Nussbaum, *Upheavals* 137)

The three series offer worlds in which human beings *have* transcended their finitude through vampirism, and for the most part, they suggest such transcendence sucks. Angel laments he and Buffy cannot share a human life in which they grow old together and die; Edward refuses to turn Bella into a vampire because he worries that being a vampire entails living without a soul, without a human core; and Stefan longs to be human again, although he would sacrifice his humanity so Elena could transform back into a human.

Since Buffy belongs to a line of slayers, which presumably will continue *ad infinitum*, and Bella and Elena both become vampires, the narrative shifts its focus from ideological assumptions about mortality to debates about the importance of accessing and embracing their emotions. Nussbaum asks,

> how and whether ethical agents can live with the facts of their own interdependence and incompleteness – venturing out into the world and engaging evaluatively with it – without being stifled by shame, disgust, and hate. The Stoics recommended *apatheia*, the emotionless condition, because they thought that no non-Stoic life could be free of these reactive emotions and the evils they bring. The possibility of a non-Stoic ethics, in which there is some positive role for the guidance of emotions, depends on our answering their question differently.
>
> (*Upheavals* 300–301)

The Beloved Does Not Bite engages with precisely this idea of answering the question differently because emotions—and particularly love-based emotions—frequently guide moral and immoral action. Furthermore, the three series, and in particular *The Vampire Diaries*, demonstrate the dangers of *apatheia* and suggest the absence of emotions, especially guilt, links to evil.

Murdoch traces this idea of a heroic demon back through philosophical discourse to a place where evil and good, mortal and immortal collide. She points to Kant's man-god, to his abolishment of God and replacement with man: "this man is with us still, free, independent, lonely, powerful, rational, responsible, brave, the hero of so many novels and books of moral philosophy.... In fact Kant's man had already received a glorious incarnation nearly a century earlier in the work of Milton: his proper name is Lucifer" (78). The vampire heroes of these three series draw on this tradition of the fallen man-god, who then transforms into the brooding Byronic hero (see Auerbach), a precursor to the romantic vampire beloved. As Nussbaum says about Heathcliff in *Wuthering Heights*, "To one who loves totally, no defense can exist. The other is in oneself and is oneself. For to allow one's boundaries to be porous in this way is not to be the self that one was, and in society is. It is, indeed, to be an alien and a gypsy, to give up on the hard shell of self-sufficiency with which all of these characters protect themselves" (*Upheavals* 608–609). Both vampire and human characters struggle with this dilemma between being self-sufficient or being porous and open to the pain and fear that often accompanies love.

While emotions other than love—such as grief and fear—may be considered as impetus for moral action, many of these emotions have their origin in love. Indeed, Nussbaum names fear and grief as love-based emotions connected to perception:

> What distinguishes fear from hope, fear from grief, love from hate—is not so much the identity of the object, which might not change, but the way in which the object is seen. In fear, one sees oneself or what one loves as seriously threatened. In hope, one sees oneself or what one loves as in some uncertainty but with a good chance for a good outcome. In grief, one sees an important object or person as lost; in love, as invested with a special sort of radiance.
>
> (*Upheavals* 28)

These wavering emotions directed towards the same being resonate throughout the three series, and especially in the fraught relationship between Elena and Damon, as Elena cycles through each emotion in her determination to see through the monster he performs to the man she glimpses.

In these series, looking frequently figures as a precursor to and indicates a development of love as an impetus for moral choices. Both Murdoch and Nussbaum emphasize metaphors of sight in their theories of love and ethical action, and moments of looking, or what Murdoch calls "attention," are fundamental to the way the three series portray loving relationships between characters. Murdoch borrows the word "attention" from Simone Weil, in order "to express the idea of a just and loving gaze directed upon an individual reality. I believe this to be the characteristic and proper mark of the active moral agent" (33). Buffy, Bella, and Elena look and are looked upon, and in these observations, moral predicaments and solutions occur. For instance, when Bella looks at Edward and sees a being of sublime beauty and Jacob looks at him and judges him to be a cold killer, then Edward as a mutual object of attention provides a focal point for moral considerations. Similarly, both Edward and Jacob observe Bella and arrive at different determinations for the type of action that should occur, and these deliberations and debates suggest the possibility of a multiplicity of choices.

Nussbaum's three normative criteria for love—compassion, reciprocity, and individuality—offer a guide for considering love as a potential basis for moral action (*Upheavals* 478–481). As I discuss more fully in Chapter 5, compassion relies on the perception the beloved suffers from no wrongdoing of his own and his existence expands her own sense of well-being. Reciprocity defies notions of love as ownership and instead proclaims mutual concern. As Nussbaum argues, Donald Winnicott's observations of what he calls "subtle interplay" (*Upheavals* 196) are one nuance that indicate a reciprocal, mutual love. Finally, when Nussbaum underlines individuality as foundational to love and moral action, she takes on philosophers who claim particular loves work against ethical evaluations because they predispose us to favor those we love. I return to this point because it looks like Angel takes his love for Buffy and puts it to work for a broader social good, whereas Edward, Stefan, and Damon place Bella and Elena's safety above all else.

Furthermore, *The Vampire Diaries*' relentless recycling of characters through the use of doppelgängers and "shadow selves" tests this criterion of individuality and its attendant requirement of what Nussbaum calls "qualitative distinctness" (480). *TVD* goes to great lengths to show Elena is not the same as Katherine who is not the same as Amara, even though they all look the same. As Damon huffs, "You want doppelgänger blood? I've got doppelgängers coming out of my ears!" ("Death and the Maiden" 5007). In other words, perhaps their blood satisfies the requirements of a witch's spell, but when it comes to love, each woman remains separate and distinct. If, as Nussbaum claims, "the wish of love is to reveal the self and to be seen..." (*Upheavals* 462), then Buffy, Bella, and Elena wish to open themselves to their vampire beloveds so they can be seen and known and loved.

Sympathetic Vampires

The beloved vampires with which this book engages evolve out of sympathetic vampires of earlier narratives, and the primary difference hinges upon the dynamic of sustained, mutual love between a human and a vampire. Although sympathetic vampires demonstrate an ability to love and be loved, this relationship is fleeting and more akin to erotic desire without sustained love. My work acknowledges sympathetic aspects of contemporary vampires but departs from critics such as Joan Gordon, Milly Williamson, Patrick Day, Veronica Hollinger, and Tim Kane, who highlight the transformation of the vampire from an evil bloodsucker to a sympathetic bloodabstainer. Instead, my work on these Beloved Cycle narratives contends love rather than sympathy is the main emotion that motivates the affective pull toward these vampires. Although not central to their argument, Gordon and Hollinger's introduction to *Blood Read: The Metaphor of the Vampire in Contemporary Culture* (1997) offers one of the earliest acknowledgements of this invitation to sympathy:

> In large part, the domestication of the vampire has come about through a shift in perspective from which the horror tale has conventionally been told. Following Mary Shelley's unusual narrative technique in *Frankenstein* (1818), although adapting it to their own purposes, many writers now narrate their horror stories from the inside, as it were, filtering them through the consciousness of the horrors that inhabit them. Not surprisingly, the impact of this shift

> from human to "other" perspective works to invite sympathy for the monstrous outsider at the same time as it serves to diminish the terror generated by what remains outside our frame of the familiar and the knowable.
>
> (2)

In his book, *The Changing Vampire of Film and Television* (2006), Kane picks up on this idea of the sympathetic vampire and argues these representations of vampires align along three temporal periods, each of which highlight one aspect of the vampire: the "Malignant Cycle," which extends from 1931–1948 and features vampires as killers without compassion (21); the "Erotic Cycle," which runs from 1957 to 1985, and figures vampires who are less murderous and more sensual, who seduce their victims with a kiss before attacking (43–44); and the "Sympathetic Cycle," which begins in 1987 and continues to 2003, the date *Underworld* was released, the most recent film he analyzes. Abbott, too, marks the 1970s Hammer films as precursors to the sympathetic vampire that finds its fullest contemporary realizations in *Bram Stoker's Dracula*, *Buffy the Vampire Slayer*, *The Vampire Diaries*, and *Twilight* ("The Undead" 110). These earlier analyses of sympathetic vampires show us the ancestors of the undead characters who emerge in the new Beloved Cycle.

These beloved vampires emerge from a long history of sympathetic vampires who both frighten and entice women. While Kane suggests the Sympathetic Cycle of film and television vampires begins in 1987 with *The Lost Boys* and *Near Dark*, Maria Lindgren Leavenworth and Malin Isaksson look to Anne Rice's novels for the genealogy of contemporary sympathetic vampires. In their chapter "Single White Females and Sympathetic Vampires: The Canons," they summarize Erik Marshall's contention that Francis Ford Coppola's 1992 film *Bram Stoker's Dracula* recasts the vampire as cultural other and as a threat to romance because of how the film alters the female characters from victim to participant:

> If Coppola can be said to powerfully have influenced the contemporary stress on eternal, fated romance and on the depiction of the main vampire as impossible to resist, then Anne Rice's depictions of Louis and Lestat, predominantly in *Interview with the Vampire* (1976) and *The Vampire Lestat* (1985) are the most influential contemporary predecessors for the sympathetic vampire, in turn harkening back to John Polidori's Ruthven in *The Vampyre* (1819) and Lord Byron's Darvell in "A Fragment of a Novel" (1819).
>
> (33)

In other words, the fear-inducing vampire perhaps always contained aspects of the now unquestioned—although not always readily accepted—heartthrob.

Despite the sympathetic vampire's two-hundred-year history, Leon Hunt, Sharon Lockyer, and Milly Williamson imply it—at least in its current fullest form—emerges as a modern figure. In their introduction to *Screening the Undead: Vampires and Zombies in Film and Television* (2014), they assert, "the sympathetic vampire, whose interior experience of suffering and pain... is a significant modern generic convention, represents a dramatisation of distinctiveness, individuality and significance at a cultural moment marked by anomie and social dislocation.... The differing sympathy-inducing performances of the sympathetic vampire make it a figure of empathy for diverse audiences" (7). Later in the collection, Williamson writes even more emphatically in her own chapter "Let Them All In: The Evolution of the 'Sympathetic' Vampire": "It is now a truism to suggest that the vampire is no longer a monster dramatising the fear of the Other, but has been rendered sympathetic, knowable, a figure of empathy" (71). Williamson cites Varney in "Varney the Vampyre" as a tortured vampire, who invokes feelings of sympathy due to his suffering (71–72). Williamson's work comes closest to mine in her brief acknowledgement of *Buffy the Vampire Slayer* as "enormously influential" in "spawn[ing] a new and highly lucrative industry of paranormal romance" (75–76), which bred the *Twilight* saga as arguably its most popular offspring.

However, my work shows the main vampires of these three series move beyond the sympathetic vampire to become the beloved, and not simply a lover or one who can love fleetingly. For instance, although Kane argues Angel belongs to the "Sympathetic Cycle" of vampires, a vampire who is more human than beast, while still retaining the erotic nature of his predecessors in the "Erotic Cycle" (88–89), I extend this analysis to argue Angel embodies aspects of all three cycles, as he fluctuates between his "good" sympathetic self, Angel, and his "evil" malignant and erotic self, Angelus. Buffy, therefore, experiences the torment of loving and trusting Angel and fearing the return of his predatory impulses. As I demonstrate, Edward in the *Twilight* saga contains aspects of this blend, but with more focus on the erotic and sympathetic, and *The Vampire Diaries* uses the Salvatore brothers, Damon and Stefan, to embody malignant, erotic, and sympathetic characteristics. Ultimately, however, Angel, Edward, Damon, and Stefan combine these characteristics to become the beloved and to love compassionately, reciprocally, and individually.

One need only consider the yearning for love and family that permeates *The Lost Boys*, *Near Dark*, and *Interview with the Vampire* to see the sympathetic vampire arises most overtly in tandem with his domestication. Passionate love embraces familial love as one way to extend romance into a broader social context. This gesture informs significant action in its most extreme form when beloveds are called upon to defend their communities, as I discuss in Chapter 6. While critics have delved into the family dynamics of *BtVS* and the *Twilight* saga, they look more to broader family structures than to the role lovers play in those structures. Williamson, for instance, flags family and youth as two parallel sites that arise out of *BtVS* to influence later paranormal romances and also nods to *Near Dark* and *The Lost Boys* as precursors to "a cycle of sympathetic vampire fiction in which youth and the broken family emerge as significant themes" (75). Whereas these two films signal a return to the family, *BtVS* deviates from this model because "families remain incomplete and unstable, and romance operates outside of marriage and the ties of the family" (76). Alternatively, Williamson argues, in *Twilight* "the vampires seem to represent the patriarchal family and a return to conservative family morals and gender politics" (78). In their discussion of the *Twilight* saga, *True Blood*, and *The Vampire Diaries*, Lindgren Leavenworth and Isaksson state, "The nuclear family, once thought to offer protection, is fractured in all three canons and its destruction seems to be a prerequisite for the female protagonists' encounters and relationships with vampires who come to stand in for the protection the family originally provided" (31). Although critics cover a range of responses from celebrating the diverse family affiliations in *Buffy* and disparaging the *Twilight* saga for its seeming return to conservative values, I argue all three series challenge notions of the nuclear family. The *Twilight* saga goes the furthest in its focus on the heterosexual couple as the nucleus of family, but more importantly for my study, the Cullen clan functions as an extended—not nuclear—family. *BtVS* posits the Scooby Gang as extended family, and *TVD* exterminates the nuclear family to focus on its remnants, such as the relationships between siblings. Most radically, the Stefan-Elena-Damon trio resists being slotted easily into a privileged site of the stable heterosexual couple.

Although young vampires feature in such family narratives, Young Adult fictions themselves have rarely been considered part of the vampire canon, depriving us of the opportunity to work across modes for a fuller understanding of vampire narratives. One edited collection and the research website to which it is attached, however, acknowledge the prevalence of YA fictions in maintaining the seeming immortality of vampire narratives and in participating in the creation of the sympathetic vampire. In their edited collection—"the first book-length study to analyse and comment on this new strand of sympathetic vampire as it appears in the twenty-first century" (2)—*Open Graves, Open Minds: Representations of Vampires and the Undead from the Enlightenment to the Present Day* (2013), Sam George and Bill Hughes address both the value of continuing to analyze vampire narratives and the inclusion of vampire texts for young people into this canon:

> a concern for such popular and widely disseminated narratives, and the longevity of its central figure, is worth analysing in its own right....

> Some vampire fictions have a stylistic competence and ingenuity and a certain daring that raises them above many contemporary 'literary novels'. Often, intriguingly, it is among the Young Adult novels of the undead that these are to be found.... perhaps [because] reader expectations are less ossified and commercial constraints less determining. (6)

Open Graves, Open Minds casts the sympathetic, vampire lover as the main figure who drifts through the edited collection, as the essays—including the excellent introduction—draw out the precursors to this figure and reflect upon its contemporary embodiments.

Before *Open Graves, Open Minds* considered the development of a YA vampire genre, only Rob Latham focused his vampire study on young people and youth cultures. However, *Consuming Youth: Vampire, Cyborgs, and the Culture of Consumption* (2002) focuses not on love, but—as its title suggests—contends that vampires and cyborgs underscore youth's "ensnarement in the norms and ideologies of consumption, rather than ... more conventional measures of identity rooted in the structures of family life" (1). More than a decade after the publication of Latham's book, young vamps—and by this term, I mean vampires who were turned when they were young—have returned to family life for their identities but reconfigure what family means. In each series, the young vampire and human lovers use their love for each other as a reason for making ethical decisions about how to act justly for themselves, their families, and the communities in which they live. These lovers rework the stereotype of the emotional, irrational teenager and commit themselves to romantic relationships that have the potential to last forever, especially in the *Twilight* saga and *The Vampire Diaries*, in which human girls eventually become vampires. As a starting point for living well, young beloved vampires mostly keep their fangs in their gums, so they can kiss their lovers without killing them.

Moreover, these young couples commit to each other more fully than their parents did. Buffy's parents are separated—or as Buffy says, "my parents weren't exactly the paragon of stay-togethery-ness" ("Conversations with Dead People" 7007)—and Buffy's mother Joyce engages in a number of ill-fated, or indeed humorously-adolescent relationships ("Ted" 2011 and "Band Candy" 3006). Bella's parents are divorced, and although her mother remarries, and her father eventually has a romantic relationship, we rarely gain insight into the specifics of these relationships. Elena's parents are dead, and the relationship between her substitute parents—Elena's Aunt Jenna and her partner Alaric—dies when Jenna does, therein leaving Elena orphaned symbolically again.

As Beloved Cycle narratives, these three series shift the vampire genre to focus on the committed, monogamous relationship between a vampire and a human, reviving the emphasis on love that stretches back to early reviews of the most canonical vampire narrative, *Dracula*. As Margaret Carter (1988) notes in her eloquent synthesis of thirty years of vampire scholarship, the book was a romance:

> Stoker's masterpiece received virtually no academic attention before 1956, except for brief references connected with studies of vampirism in folklore. One of Montague Summers's sources, Dudley Wright, confines himself to the remark, "Mr. Bram Stoker has made the vampire the foundation of his exciting romance *Dracula*" (186). Summers's monumental *The Vampire: His Kith and Kin* concludes with a chapter entitled "The Vampire in Literature." Here Summers devotes three pages to *Dracula* of which he acknowledges "there is no sensational romance which in modern days has achieved so universal a reputation" (333).
>
> (2)

Most early academic engagement with *Dracula* categorizes it as a romance, the very category that becomes the core of negative academic criticism about the *Twilight* saga.

That *Dracula* follows conventions of the romance genre implies Dracula himself can love. *The Beloved Does Not Bite*, however, focuses more on the point that a vampire can both love and *be* loved: in the Beloved Cycle, this reciprocity makes moral choices possible. Tracing the trajectory of vampiric love from Stoker's novel through to *Twilight*, Lindsey Scott hinges her discussion on Dracula's claim in the novel, "I too can love. You yourselves can tell it from the past. Is it not so?" (Stoker qtd. in Scott 118). Scott argues,

> the declaration that a vampire too 'can love' serves less as a rebuke from the Count to his audience and more as a question that Stoker poses to his readers, readers who are, more than likely, familiar with the stories of other literary vampires... When Gary Oldman's Dracula announces with steely conviction, 'Yes, I too can love', the remainder of Stoker's passage is replaced by the words: 'and I shall love again'.... in the broader context of the myth's metamorphosis, this additional sentiment instinctively pre-empts the next phase of the vampire's evolution: *'And I shall love again.'*
>
> (118, 124)

Scott convincingly demonstrates the intertextual and metatextual references to Dracula—and then Edward's—ability to love, which pulses through Stoker's novel, Coppola's film, and Hardicke's *Twilight*. I extend the vampire's capabilities from one who loves to one who also opens himself to be a beloved, for in this reciprocity exists a deep humanity attached to a core of ethics.

Though many critics see a focus on the love story as a weakness, especially in the *Twilight* saga, this approach overlooks the ways in which these works' explorations of love and desire complicate neat moral categories. Wilson, for instance, argues, "Our world may be far from the post-racial, post-feminist utopia some claim, but it can at least be post-*Twilight* if we, as critical readers of our culture, refuse the seductive message that falling in love with a sparkly vampire will solve all our problems" (7). She continues, "*Twilight* validates patriarchal capitalism and suggests that married monogamy creates a stable society while at the same time bolstering readers' worth by feeding longstanding beliefs such as 'true love conquers all'" (18). As I demonstrate in this book, Wilson's reading simplifies a complex imperative. Falling in love may not "solve all our problems" but neither should love be dismissed as irrelevant to living a good life.

Indeed, critics' tendency to censure and mock Bella for her potentially dangerous love and desire for Edward has the unfortunate consequence of misunderstanding the novels' more nuanced, complex examination of compassion. Carrie Anne Platt's essay in *Bitten by Twilight* stands as an example of such criticism:

> Although the Twilight series is progressive in its recognition of the reality of adolescent female sexuality, the sexual politics of the saga are decidedly conservative. Far from being sexually empowered, Bella is rendered a perpetual victim of her own uncontrollable desires, desires that get her into more and more trouble as the series progresses. The overall ideological message is clear: to be young, female, and sexual is to court danger, destruction, or even death. (80)

If we are to believe Platt, Bella's troubles seem to hinge upon making bad decisions that put herself and her family at risk. However, in the same collection, Margaret Toscano takes a more generous, although still problematic, approach by focusing on how Bella's love challenges Mormon ideas about morality: "Meyer does not simply put love before reason; she also shows the convolutions that healthy and unhealthy needs and loves can take by revealing how irrational love can lead to compassion, while rational dispassion, as exemplified by the ancient Italian vampire clan, the Volturi, can lead to control" (26). I flesh out this connection between love and compassion more fully in Chapter 5, although I refute this characterization of love as irrational.

Problematically, this love clings primarily to the heterosexual couple in all three series but especially in the *Twilight* saga and *TVD*, which, in turn, infuses the series with a culture of heteronormativity. Wilson argues such heterosexual romance sidelines other forms of right action:

> Continuing through to *Gossip Girl* and *Vampire Diaries* and graduating on to the likes of *True Blood* and *Sex and the City*, we learn that everyone from burgeoning pop divas to clairvoyant waitresses place primary importance on romantic desire. This cultural indoctrination into the "love is everything" mantra conditions us to fixate on heterosexual romance and to seek pleasure via imagining our (and others') romantic lives. The pleasure of such projections are heightened via the message that we can become different, better selves through successive relationships.
>
> (58)

While I agree a fixation with heterosexual romance problematically normalizes only one type of pleasure, Wilson overstates the case that romantic love overshadows all other responsibility and understates the ability of love to encourage striving for a better self. As I shall demonstrate, in *BtVS* justice begins with the love between Buffy and Angel but it expands to embrace friendship and duty.

Moreover, Bella's love for her fetus, which she understands as her unborn child, rises above her love for herself and for Edward. In the end, Bella's decision not to terminate her pregnancy leads to her own death and rebirth as a vampire. This scene became the focus of heated debates when the movie first appeared, as critics engaged with its arguably "pro-life" message alongside the tragic death of Savita Halapannavar, who died when doctors in Ireland refused to abort her fetus while she suffered a miscarriage. However, as Noah Berlatsky points out, the film is too complicated to be reduced to a straightforward "pro-life" propaganda piece: "I think it's a mistake to see Bella's narrative solely as a pro-life fantasy, and I think it's a mistake to dismiss as unwitting dupes those who think that there's something worthwhile in her story.... Bella's transformation from human to vampire is in part a metaphor for her transition from woman to mother—a transition accomplished in fear, pain, terror, and love." I can see both sides of this debate, but I believe it is worth thinking about Bella's decision in terms of the narrative arc of the saga and to recall the Preface of *Twilight* when Bella offers to die in place of her own mother. In other words, Bella's position suggests she will sacrifice herself to protect the lives of many others and not only the life of her fetus, which she reiterates to Renesmee in *Breaking Dawn* when she gives Renesmee a locket that says she loves her more than her own life.

Perhaps more radically, *The Vampire Diaries* does supplement heterosexual romantic love with fraternal love. Flashbacks show the closeness between Damon and Stefan before they both fall in love with Katherine, and this intimacy informs their actions throughout the series as they repeatedly save each other's lives, or act selflessly in order to benefit the other. Additionally, the show titillates with the suggestion of what fans call the "Defan" bromance, and much of the promotional material plays with this idea by featuring Elena as the slim body that separates Stefan and Damon's kiss. Although the rhetoric of their relationship features hate rather than love, as Damon says, love and revenge "aren't mutually exclusive" ("History Repeating" 1009), a point I analyze in more detail throughout this book and especially in Chapter 2 via a scene in which Stefan and Damon stab each other with a letter opener. Such moments of penetration occur throughout the series as the brothers stake each other in gestures of love and/or anger.

Love and revenge are not mutually exclusive because, as the series indicates, quite different registers of affect often coexist in the same character. In revealing who threatens the social order, monsters also convey who helps sustain it, and how threat and sustenance are not always easy to disentangle. Although *The Vampire Diaries* compellingly supplements romantic with fraternal love, other types of love—such as between parents and children and platonic friendships between men and women—suffer for the sake of romantic love. Stefan kills and feeds on his father in order to complete his vampiric transformation; Elena's adoptive parents die in a car crash; Caroline's father tortures her; Bonnie and Matt's parents appear and disappear throughout the series; and Tyler's parents are murdered. While absent parents are a staple of YA fiction because this absence provides space for the maturation of the protagonists, the sheer volume of tragic parent-child relationships in this series points to a larger ideological strain. On the one hand, these parents represent inflexible ideas about maintaining the status quo and therefore need to be replaced by a generation that respects and, indeed, embraces difference; on the other hand, their deaths occur in order to allow heterosexual romance to flourish. I am not saying this flourishing in itself is a problem, but I do worry because heterosexual romantic relationships seem to be the *only* possibility for lovers, unlike, for instance, in *BtVS* where the same-sex romances between Willow and Tara and later Willow and Kennedy fill the screen.

My stance aligns most closely with Williamson who, in her examination of the *Twilight* saga, separates love from the irrational. Williamson sketches a connection between Romanticism and the *Twilight* saga and suggests, "what we see in the *Twilight Saga* is homage to the philosophy of passionate love born of the late eighteenth-century Romantic movement. For Bella, significance and meaning come through passionate love, and this love justifies any action, with a grandiosity borrowed from Romanticism—including her own death" ("Let Them All In" 83). She continues,

> passion is ultimately endorsed *because* it gives meaning; it transforms insignificance into significance. Perhaps this can account for the enormous popularity of these books and films among young

> women and adolescent girls. The coupling of passion and meaning are a significant and pleasurable contrast to the fetters affecting the ability to act meaningfully for young women and girls and the difficulty in finding the occasions for significant action in a cultural moment which promises the democratic possibility of achievement for all, but doesn't deliver it.
>
> (84)

Williamson gestures towards a link between passion and significant—or what I call right—action; *The Beloved Does Not Bite* looks closely and invites a closer look at how love initiates significant action across *Buffy the Vampire Slayer*, the *Twilight* saga, and *The Vampire Diaries*. Furthermore, it demonstrates how love between two people extends out from the couple and into a larger community, suggesting the "democratic achievement for all," to which Williamson alludes.

In order to do this work of looking closely and inviting a closer look, I select significant episodes or passages to show how love and right action occur in specific moments, which then pulse through the rest of the narrative. The series occur across different mediums—television, film, novels, comic books—but the screen versions feature most in this book. This emphasis on the visual frequently aligns with the shape of action and the pull of emotion. Forgiveness, however, is often granted through a speech act, which may rely more upon the verbal than the visual. In the sections which analyze the *Twilight* saga, I acknowledge how novelistic techniques translate into filmic ones, and my analysis tends to tilt towards the latter. Overall, I pay special attention to the screen versions of these series, in order to bring to the foreground an emphasis on the visual, on looking, which forms the core of the ethics of love I develop throughout the book.

My sharply focused close readings of exemplary episodes yoke to my theoretical emphasis on looking closely, in order to perform the intense looking that permeates the series themselves and to model a practice I advocate in the classrooms in which I teach. I move in a space between distance and proximity, between an analysis of genre conventions and close-readings of specific scenes. This movement invites readers who are familiar with the series to see a scene differently or to return to the series to look again. For readers unfamiliar with these vampire stories, I hope the flow between episodic summary and close attention piques your curiosity and nudges you towards the narratives. This methodological movement seems particularly apt for an examination of screen vampires, for as Ken Gelder argues in his Preface to *New Vampire Cinema*, "simultaneity of remoteness and closeness or proximity turns out to be important to vampire films as both a theme (the vampire's distance from/closeness to the victim is the thing that instills the narrative with suspense) and the means by which the genre perpetuates itself as a genre" (v). Gelder writes here about physical distance and proximity, and I certainly address this physicality, but I also emphasize emotional closeness, as the vampire and human beloveds resist their emotional pull towards each other and also give in to it.

An erotics of looking and kissing sutures a viewer to these ethical acts emotionally through the screen and pulls cinematic genre conventions into play. The development of this ethical erotic draws upon the work of Robert Sinnerbrink, who advocates for an acknowledgement of and openness to the "immersive experience of the cinema—the relinquishing of one's engaged perception, thought, and action in favour of a sensuous receptivity, affective engagement, and reflective openness towards virtual cinematic worlds" (35). He further outlines features of what he calls "romantic film-philosophy":

> first is that it avoids assuming that there is a readymade conceptual framework or theoretical approach that should be applied to a film to reveal its meaning or, alternatively, which the film is supposed to illustrate. The second is a sustained receptiveness to what film aesthetically discloses; an engagement with the aesthetic elements of film, the reflection it inspires, and to the way film resists immediate translation into theoretical argument. This kind of responsiveness to film's forma of aesthetic disclosure, its distinctive ways of thinking, might involve, for example, consideration not only of its narrative aspects but its audiovisual rhythms, hermeneutic ambiguities, and capacity to both enact and evoke affective forms of thought.
>
> (38)

By doing this type of reflection, the "film is thus allowed to show rather than tell; to reveal rather than be reduced; to think rather than be analysed" (40). Instead of applying a specific theory to a film, Sinnerbrink suggests one should "draw upon the ways in which certain films disclose either what is intolerable, traumatic, or disturbing in our world today... or to experiment with the aesthetic disclosure of alternative ways of thinking and feeling, acting and being, in our relations with nature and culture" (43). Through the use of music, song lyrics, lighting, and camera angles and distance, for examples, these three vampire series represent and create emotional responses that lure us in to thought experiments about how we might act when faced with an ethical dilemma in which we negotiate a horror-filled world.

I pair Sinnerbrink's romantic film-philosophy with the methodologies of Vivian Sobchak and Heather Love in order to develop a practice of close-reading that couples film and literary studies. In her article "Close but not Deep: Literary Ethics and the Descriptive Turn," Love advocates an approach that combines description and close reading. Responding to a "broadly sociological rejection of traditional literary methods" (373) that takes its most extreme form in Franco Moretti's notion of *distant reading*, Love refuses to reject close reading, which she claims "is at the heart of literary studies" (373). Instead, she suggests a model of "close attention" that relies on "description rather than interpretation" and therein avoids "the metaphysical and humanist concerns of hermeneutics" (375). Love's emphasis on a combination of description and close reading enthralls me because it draws attention to the text, to *seeing* what exists on the screen or page, to looking and listening closely. While I agree with Love's emphasis on closeness, I hesitate to claim my descriptions do not relate to interpretation via my own human experience. As I describe the way the light falls on half of Damon's face, as I describe the music that breathes into Elena's bedroom, as I describe the tender touch of a hand on a cheek, I attempt to show you what I see, what the texts invite me to see.

Of course, such a practice requires a careful hand. As Love notes while explaining the critic's "observer" role (via the work of Bruno Latour and Erving Goffman), "This approach leaves no room for the ghosts of humanism haunting contemporary practices of textual interpretation. It also leaves little room for the ethical heroism of the critic, who gives up his role of interpreting divine messages to take up a position as a humble analyst and observer" (381). Love's characterization of the critic as observer couples comfortably with Sinnerbrink's closing paragraph in which he eschews the philosopher's "theoretical mastery." Instead, he suggests, "The romantic critic or theorist thus becomes a kind of translator, or better, a 'medium' or mediator between different media of thought: cinematic and philosophical, aesthetic and conceptual, poetic and political" (44). Analyst, observer, translator, mediator—I embrace these roles in order to describe vampires whose actions waver between the unsavory and the delectable. Description, however, still operates as a form of analysis: I describe what I want you to see and hear, with the hope you will join me, not by coercion but perhaps because of curiosity. Short of watching these series with you, and pointing to certain scenes, I hope to bring them to you on these pages.

While my descriptive sentences cannot do what film or television does, they aspire to evoke an embodied response elicited by these visual media. Like Vivian Sobchak's description of watching the scene in *The Piano* when Baines touches Ada's leg through the hole in her stocking, so the descriptions of these vampire series seek to draw forth an experience of both watching the series and responding to them:

> I had a carnal interest in and investment in being *both* "here" *and* "there," in being able *both* to sense *and* to be sensible, to be *both* the subject *and* the object of tactile desire.... I want to emphasize that I am not speaking metaphorically of touching and being touched at and by the movies but "in some sense" quite literally of our capacity

> to feel the world we see and hear onscreen and of the cinema's capacity to "touch" and "move" us offscreen.
>
> (66)

Sobchak's description of her feeling of watching this scene exemplifies Sinnerbrink's "sensuous receptivity" and "affective argument" and connects Carroll's notion of being moved by art-horror. I, too, try to open myself to such viewings and to share these moments with you, not to seduce you but to call attention to the affective pull the screen represents and invites.

The structure of this book follows loosely the structure of the series themselves. Season One of *Buffy* and *The Vampire Diaries* and the first novel and film of the *Twilight* saga establish the relationships between the moral vampires and their potential beloveds. These relationships initiate through an acknowledgement of male beauty and grow through looking and then kissing. The second texts in the series complicate the relationships: Angel turns into Angelus; Edward leaves Forks; Stefan becomes addicted to human blood; and Damon almost dies. These complications lead to and reveal love as the beloveds must make moral judgments about right action. Some of these significant acts, however, lead to suffering that invites compassion and forgiveness. Finally, these deeply loving relationships that have been established over time radiate out from the couple to affect and protect the larger community. *The Beloved Does Not Bite* can be read as an overall story about how love begins, grows, and, at times, ends, but each chapter also stands on its own. The series both enable and resist a linear reading, for the beautiful messiness of love rarely arranges itself in a straight line.

Chapter 1 traces the generic shift that transforms sympathetic vampires into beloved vampires, and outlines the semantic and syntactic changes across the three series. It also provides a brief summary of the series, with special attention to the beginning sequences of each pilot episode.

Chapter 2 shuns the claim "beauty is only skin deep" to show how beauty initiates, sustains, and enhances the relationship between beautiful vampires and their human beloveds. A semantics of male beauty portrays the vampire beloved's body as both immortal and vulnerable, and in each series, the vampire's naked flesh reveals his vulnerability: Angel's naked torso functions as a metaphor for his tormented soul; Edward's beauty invites a comparison to the sublime; Stefan's liminal nudity characterizes his repressed urges; and Damon's exposed and eroticized chest initiates a consideration of his heart. By focusing on the beautiful male body, these three series establish male beauty and female desire as a combination that coheres into love.

In Chapter 3, I establish looking as necessary to loving. This chapter traces moments of "really looking," to use Murdoch's phrase. It begins with analyses of the beloveds looking across distances at each other and then proceeds to discuss how the gaze draws the other in. I argue that looking brings the beloved closer and leads to the kiss, a more intimate form of opening oneself to the beloved. The chapter takes its title from a discussion between Angel and his ex-lover, Darla. Darla asks Angel about Buffy and says, "Did you think she'd understand? That she would look at your face—your true face—and give you a kiss?" ("Angel" 1007). While Buffy screams when she first sees Angel's vampire face, by the end of the same episode, they move from looking across the bar at each other to kissing long and hard enough to sear Buffy's cross necklace into Angel's bare chest.

Chapter 4 asks "What does it mean to love and to act morally?" and links love and moral action to the pain and suffering that occurs through leaving. This chapter charts how leaving and letting go become gestures of love, which hook moments of open vulnerability to intense suffering that occurs in and after scenes of leaving. These departures signal not the end of love but evidence of its gravity. The three series represent leaving as a misguided but necessary step toward a fulfilling erotic love.

Nussbaum claims compassion as a necessary component of love, and argues, "compassion pushes the boundaries of the self further outward than many types of love" (*Upheavals* 300). Chapter 5 outlines how the three series link compassion and forgiveness to love and to a love-based justice. This outward push of the self takes its most extreme form when, possessed by the ghosts of two past lovers, Angel and Buffy re-enact a scene of these two lovers' deaths, with Buffy in the role of the killer seeking forgiveness. This chapter expands upon intimate scenes of compassion and suggests such reversals and rehearsals offer models for broader gestures of compassion and forgiveness that extend beyond the couple.

Chapter 6 responds to a question Stefan asks himself as he contemplates how he should respond to Damon's actions early in Season One of *The Vampire Diaries*: "but how do I stop a monster without becoming one?" Angel, Edward, Stefan—and at times, Damon—all choose not to kill humans because they believe such action to be wrong, but they rarely hesitate to kill another monster if the death serves a larger purpose. More radically, Damon—once a soldier in the Civil War—justifies killing anyone as long as that death will protect Elena and/or the larger community. Each series provides a seemingly-ethical rationale for killing: *BtVS* exists within a context of saving the world; the *Twilight* saga frames its defense within a familial structure; and *TVD* stands as a metonym for a divided America in need of protection from itself. In each series, discourses of war and scenes of battles suggest ethical love emanates out from the romantic couple to a larger concept of the greater good.

The Conclusion carries the analysis of the ideological and affective implications of these vampire series to other paranormal romances and to futuristic dystopias for young adults. In dystopian trilogies, such as *The Hunger Games* and *Divergent*, and more explicitly in *Matched* and

Delirium, romantic love challenges and often overturns an authoritative power structure. Paranormal romances also do this work. For instance, since 2007 more than ten different YA series about fallen angels have been published, and in each of these series, the love between angel and human defies a higher power. Moreover, zombies shuffled into popularity with a YA audience via the *Generation Dead* series and the critically-acclaimed *Warm Bodies* film and books. In all these series, a human or part-human being falls in love with a beautiful—if slightly cold or rotting—monster as though to spite skeptical critics and to prove the adage that love can conquer all.

Note

1 Nussbaum continues to develop her theory of emotions in *Political Emotions: Why Love Matters for Justice* (2013), and she returns to some of the issues she discusses in *Love's Knowledge* and *Upheavals of Thought.* Her main argument in *Political Emotions* extends her previous work more fully into the public arena, as she contemplates what she calls "political love" (22). While I find this work extremely important and engaging, it extends beyond the scope of my current project.

Works Cited

Abbott, Stacey. "The Undead in the kingdom of shadows: the rise of the cinematic vampire." *Open Graves, Open Minds: Representations of Vampires and the Undead from the Enlightenment to the Present Day.* Eds. S. George and B. Hughes. Manchester: Manchester, UP, 2013. 96–112. Print.

"Angel." *Buffy the Vampire Slayer: The Complete First Season on DVD.* Writ. David Greenwalt. Dir. Scott Brazil. Twentieth Century Fox, 2001. DVD.

Auerbach, Nina. *Our Vampires, Ourselves.* Chicago: U of Chicago P, 1995. Print.

Altman, Rick. "A Semantic/Syntactic Approach to Film Genre." *Cinema Journal* 23.3 (Spring 1984): 6–18. Print.

"Band Candy." *Buffy the Vampire Slayer: the Complete Third Season on DVD.* Writ. Jane Espenson. Dir. Michael Lange. Twentieth Century Fox, 2002. DVD.

Berlatsky, Noah. "*Twilight* is not simply a pro-life fantasy." *The Atlantic.* 17 November 2012. Electronic.

Carroll, Noël. *The Philosophy of Horror: Or, Paradoxes of the Heart.* New York: Routledge, 1990. Electronic.

Carter, Margaret L, ed. *Dracula: the Vampire and the Critics.* Ann Arbor, MI: UMI Research Press, 1988. Print.

Collins, Suzanne. *Catching Fire.* London: Scholastic, 2010. Print.

———. *The Hunger Games.* London: Scholastic, 2009. Print.

———. *Mockingjay.* London: Scholastic, 2011. Print.

Condie, Ally. *Crossed.* New York: Penguin, 2011. Print.

———. *Matched.* New York: Penguin, 2010. Print.

———. *Reached.* New York: Penguin, 2012. Print.

"Conversations with Dead People." *Buffy the Vampire Slayer: Season Seven Collector's Edition*. Writ. Jane Espenson and Drew Goddard. Dir. Nick Marck. Twentieth Century Fox, 2002. DVD.

Day, William Patrick. *Vampire Legends in Contemporary American Culture: What Becomes a Legend Most*. Lexington: UP of Kentucky, 2002. Print.

"Death and the Maiden." *The Vampire Diaries*. Writ. Rebecca Sonnenshine. Dir. Leslie Libman. CWTV. 14 November 2013. Television.

Gelder, Ken. *New Vampire Cinema*. London: British Film Institute, 2012. Print.

George, Sam and Bill Hughes. *Open Graves, Open Minds: Representations of Vampires and the Undead from the Enlightenment to the Present Day*. Manchester: Manchester UP, 2013. Print.

Gert, Bernard. "The Definition of Morality." *The Stanford Encyclopedia of Philosophy* (Fall 2012 Edition). Ed. Edward N. Zalta. Electronic.

Gordon, Joan and Veronica Hollinger, eds. *Blood Read: The Vampire as Metaphor in Contemporary Culture*. Philadelphia: UPenn, 1997. Print.

"History Repeating." *The Vampire Diaries*. Writ. Bryan M. Holdman and Brian Young. Dir. Marcos Siega. CWTV. 12 November 2009. Television.

Hunt, Leon, Sharon Lockyer, and Milly Williamson, eds. *Screening the Undead: Vampires and Zombies in Film and Television*. London: I.B. Tauris, 2014. Print.

Kane, Tim. *The Changing Vampire of Film and Television: A Critical Study of the Growth of a Genre*. Jefferson, NC: McFarland & Co, 2006. Print.

Kearney, Richard. *Strangers, Gods, and Monsters: Interpreting Otherness*. New York: Routledge, 2003. 1–20. Print.

Kellner, Douglas. "*Buffy, the Vampire Slayer* as Spectacular Allegory: A Diagnostic Critique." 1–21. https://pages.gseis.ucla.edu/faculty/kellner/essays/buffy.pdf. Electronic.

Latham, Rob. *Consuming Youth: Vampires, Cyborgs, and the Culture of Consumption*. Chicago: U of Chicago P, 2002. Print.

Lindgren Leavenworth, Maria and Malin Isaksson. *Fanged Fan Fiction: Variations on Twilight, True Blood, and The Vampire Diaries*. Jefferson, NC: McFarland, 2013. Electronic.

Love, Heather. "Close but not Deep: Literary Ethics and the Descriptive Turn." *New Literary History* 41 (2010): 371–391. Print.

Marion, Isaac. *The New Hunger*. New York: Atria/Emily Bestler, 2013. Print.

———. *Warm Bodies*. New York: Atria/Emily Bestler, 2010. Print.

Meyer, Stephenie. *Breaking Dawn*. New York: Little Brown, 2008. Print.

———. *Eclipse*. New York: Little Brown, 2007. Print.

———. *New Moon*. New York: Little Brown, 2006. Print.

———. *Twilight*. New York: Little Brown, 2005. Print.

Murdoch, Iris. *The Sovereignty of Good*. 1970. New York: Routledge, 2013. Print.

Nussbaum, Martha C. *Love's Knowledge: Essays on Philosophy and Literature*. New York: Oxford UP, 1990. Print.

———. *Political Emotions: Why Love Matters for Justice*. Cambridge, MA: Harvard UP, 2013. Print.

———. *Upheavals of Thought: The Intelligence of Emotions*. Cambridge: Cambridge UP, 2001. Print.

Oliver, Lauren. *Delirium*. Sydney: HarperCollins, 2011. Print.
———. *Pandemonium*. Sydney: HarperCollins, 2012. Print.
———. *Requiem*. Sydney: HarperCollins, 2013. Print.
Platt, Carrie Anne. "Cullen Family Values: Gender and Sexual Politics in the Twilight Series." *Bitten by Twilight: Youth Culture, Media, and the Vampire Franchise*. Eds. Melissa A. Click, Jennifer Stevens Aubrey, and Elizabeth Behm-Morawitz. New York: Peter Lang, 2010. 71–86. Print.
Roth, Veronica. *Allegiant*. Sydney: HarperCollins, 2013. Print.
———. *Divergent*. Sydney: HarperCollins, 2011. Print.
———. *Insurgent*. Sydney: HarperCollins, 2012. Print.
Scott, Lindsey. "Crossing Oceans of Time: Stoker, Coppola and the 'New Vampire" Film." *Open Graves, Open Minds: Representations of Vampires and the Undead from the Enlightenment to the Present Day*. Eds. S. George and B. Hughes. Manchester: Manchester UP, 2013. 113–130. Print.
Sinnerbrink, Robert. "Re-enfranchising Film: Towards a Romantic Film-Philosophy." *New Takes in Film-Philosophy*. Eds. Havi Carel and Greg Tuck. Basingstoke and New York: Palgrave Macmillan, 2011. 25–47. Print.
Smith, L.J. *Vampire Diaries*. Books 1 & 2. *The Awakening* and *The Struggle*. 1991. London: Hodder, 2009. Print.
———. *Vampire Diaries*. Books 3 & 4. *The Fury* and *The Reunion*. 1991. London: Hodder, 2009. Print.
Sobchack, Vivian. *Carnal Thoughts: Embodiment and Moving Image Culture*. Berkeley: U of California Press, 2004. Print.
Spooner, Catherine. "*Gothic Charm School*; or, How Vampires Learned to Sparkle." *Open Graves, Open Minds: Representations of Vampires and the Undead from the Enlightenment to the Present Day*. Eds. S. George and B. Hughes. Manchester: Manchester UP, 2013. 146–164. Print.
"Ted." *Buffy the Vampire Slayer: The Complete Second Season on DVD*. Writ. Joss Whedon and David Greenwalt. Dir. Bruce Seth Green, 2002. DVD.
Toscano, Margaret M. "Mormon Morality and Immortality in Stephenie Meyer's Twilight Series." *Bitten by Twilight: Youth Culture, Media, and the Vampire Franchise*. Eds. Melissa A. Click, Jennifer Stevens Aubrey, and Elizabeth Behm-Morawitz. New York: Peter Lang, 2010. 21–36. Print.
Warm Bodies. Dir. Jonathan Levine. Summit, 2013. Film.
Waters, Daniel. *Generation Dead*. New York: Hyperion, 2008. Print.
———. *Kiss of Life*. New York: Hyperion, 2009. Print.
———. *My Friends are Dead*. OMZ, 2016. Print.
———. *Passing Strange*. New York: Hyperion, 2010. Print.
"Welcome to the Hellmouth." *Buffy the Vampire Slayer: The Complete First Season on DVD*. Writ. Joss Whedon. Dir. Charles Martin Smith. Twentieth Century Fox, 2001. DVD.
Williamson, Milly. *The Lure of the Vampire: Gender, Fiction, and Fandom from Bram Stoker to Buffy*. London: Wallflower Press, 2005. Print.
———. "Let Them All In: The Evolution of the 'Sympathetic' Vampire." *Screening the Undead: Vampires and Zombies in Film and Television*. Eds. Leon Hunt, Sharon Lockyer, and Milly Williamson London: I.B. Tauris, 2014. 71–92. Print.
Wilson, Natalie. *Seduced by Twilight: The Allure and Contradictory Messages of the Popular Saga*. Jefferson, NC: McFarland & Co, 2011. Print.

1 From Killing to Kissing

Tracing the Syntactic Redetermination

Buffy, the *Twilight* saga, and *The Vampire Diaries* conform to and build upon other texts within the "Sympathetic Cycle" by drawing on a range of genres including horror, romance, teen drama, action, and comedy. While Kane argues genre pastiche is typical of the films and televisual texts within the sympathetic cycle (88), the genre pastiche *BtVS* exemplifies and the *Twilight* saga and *The Vampire Diaries* expand moves beyond Kane's study. Since the publication of Kane's book in 2006, the syntax and semantics established in *BtVS* can be seen in numerous other teen film and televisual series, including the *Twilight* films and *The Vampire Diaries* and other paranormal romances for teens and adults, such as *Teen Wolf, Bitten*, *Warm Bodies*, *True Blood, Moonlight*, and *Blood Ties*. *BtVS*, however, is the first vampire series that moves teenage protagonists from sympathizing with to falling in love with vampires, successfully merging teen drama, romance, and horror. In *BtVS*, most vampires are still evil monsters who have to die, but, when Buffy falls in love with Angel and Angel with Buffy, a new syntax begins.

In this new cycle of the vampire genre, these vampire-human lovers offer moral guidance about how to live and love well and how to act ethically because of this love. In other words, the semantic and syntactic elements of this genre precipitate an ideological and affective shift from fearing and/or sympathizing with a vampire to loving him. Following Rick Altman's methodology, *The Beloved Does Not Bite* attends to semantic and syntactic elements of this new Beloved Cycle and connects these elements to the ways in which the three series offer "imaginary answers to real problems"—to borrow from Kearney's work—via a love-based justice in which emotional evaluations allow for a reconsideration of what it means to act ethically; or as Gordon and Hollinger state, monsters "help us construct our own humanity, to provide guidelines against which we can define ourselves" (5).

I borrow this terminology of *syntax* and *semantics* from genre and film critic Rick Altman because it provides a useful framework for analyzing the conventions that recur across these three teen vampire series. Altman defines semantic and syntactic views as follows:

> we can as a whole distinguish between generic definitions which depend on a list of common traits, attitudes, characters, shots, locations, sets, and the like—thus stressing the semantic elements which make up the genre—and definitions which play up instead certain constitutive relationships between undesignated and variable placeholders—relationships which might be called the genre's fundamental syntax. The semantic approach thus stresses the genre's building blocks, while the syntactic view privileges the structures into which they are arranged.
>
> ("Semantic" 10)

Both syntactic and semantic approaches define a genre through the repetition of elements across and within texts. For instance, Angel's character draws upon the semantics of previous vampires—his face changes from human to monster, he wears a long black coat, he lurks in the shadows.

More significantly, Angel introduces a new semantic element: the vampire who does not bite to kill. This semantic element combines with the syntax of his relationship with Buffy, which becomes a precursor to contemporary vampires and vampire-human long-term romantic relationships, such as Edward and Bella in the *Twilight* saga and Stefan and Elena and Damon and Elena in *The Vampire Diaries*. These series have flourished and, after sixteen years, sired new offspring—such as *The Vampire Diaries* spin-off show *The Originals*—which substantiates my claim the vampire genre has moved from the Sympathetic Cycle to a Beloved Cycle. As Altman observes, "[j]ust as individual texts establish new meanings for familiar terms only by subjecting well known semantic units to a syntactic redetermination, so generic meaning comes into being only through the repeated deployment of substantially the same syntactic strategies" ("Semantic" 16).

In recent vampire televisual series, the semantic unit of a vampire trying to behave ethically by resisting his vampirism undergoes syntactic redetermination in two main forms. One syntactic redetermination transfers the new semantic element of the vampire seeking redemption onto the syntax of the *film noir* genre, which is established in the series *Angel* and continues into relatively short-lived television shows for adult viewers, such as *Moonlight* and *Blood Ties*. Another syntax, much more successful and seemingly durable, and the one upon which this book focuses, follows the romantic relationship between a guilt-ridden male vampire and an exceptional female human. These examples include *True Blood* for adult audiences and *The Vampire Diaries* and the *Twilight* saga for teen viewers.

The pilot episode of *Buffy the Vampire Slayer* ("Welcome to the Hellmouth" 1001) both draws from and refuses characteristics of the horror genre and anticipates the series continued genre blending, with a focus on romance. The episode opens with a scene in which a young dark-haired man and a blonde woman break into a school, looking for a place in which they can be intimate. The man enters first, holding the hand of the woman, who appears unsure. They hear a noise, and she asks, "What was that?" He says, "Some *THING*," and makes spooky gestures with his hands. She hits him playfully, and they continue into the school. They appear to be looking for a deserted place where they can make out. The woman, seemingly skeptical and fearful, says, "Are you sure that we're alone?" He replies in the affirmative and reaches for her. She says, "Good," as she turns around and grabs him. He screams as she plunges her vampire fangs into his neck. Recognizable elements of horror permeate this scene: the deserted building, the young blonde woman, the sparsely lit atmosphere, and the suspenseful music. The "horizon of expectation," to use Hans Robert Jauss's term, leads to a conclusion that sees at least the blonde girl, if not the couple, murdered by some lurking serial killer. Instead, the blonde girl opens her maw to reveal herself as the serial killer, and the ground shifts on the genre.

The Vampire Diaries similarly employs and overturns techniques from the horror genre, again interweaving aspects of romance. The television series opens with Stefan's voiceover saying, "For over a century, I have lived in secret. Hiding in the shadows. Alone in the world. Until now. I am a vampire. And this is my story." The action then shifts to a young man and woman—seemingly a couple—driving in a car along a deserted road. Suddenly, a figure appears in the middle of the road. The man brakes, but the car slams into the figure, whose body tumbles over the back of the car. The man emerges from the car to see if the person he hit is still alive. The figure on the road suddenly sits up and grabs the man. The camera zooms in to a close-up to show an open mouth with fangs. We hear the sound of biting. The scene ends with the woman running screaming down the road and then being lifted into the air by some unseen force.

The next scene opens with an image of the back of a man's head looking into some bushes. The same voice that opens the episode continues to tell his story: "I shouldn't have come home. I know the risk. But I had no choice. I have to *know* her." The camera pulls back to a long shot, and we see the man, who we later learn is Stefan, stands on the roof of a house. He jumps off the roof and lands effortlessly, and the setting transfers to a bedroom where a young woman sits on a bed and writes in a book. We hear what we presume to be her voice sharing the words she writes: "Dear Diary. Today will be different. It has to be. I will smile. And it will be believable. My smile will say, 'I'm fine. Thank you. Yes, I feel much better. I will no longer be the sad little girl who lost her parents. I will start fresh. Be someone new. That's the only way I'll make it through.'" Thus, within the first three minutes of the first episode, the main characters and their personalities emerge, although viewers remain unsure about the seeming disconnect between the vampire who tells his story and the vampire who kills the young couple in the car. Later, the show reveals Damon murdered them, but the visual ambiguity and the verbal tension remain until Damon makes an appearance three-quarters of the way through the first episode. This dialogic format between Stefan and Elena interrupted by Damon's actions reverberates throughout the first two episodes and reaches its choral climax when Elena and Stefan either say the same words at the same time, such as at the end of the first episode, when they both say that they are looking for "someone alive" or when the voices narrating their individual diary entries sound like an intimate conversation.

While *Twilight* deviates from these overt vampire references in its opening moments, both the book and the film introduce the main narrative with a suggestive romance/horror beginning. The novel starts with the following short Preface:

> I'd never given much thought to how I would die—though I'd had reason enough in the last few months—but even if I had, I would not have imagined it like this.
>
> I stared without breathing across the long room, into the dark eyes of the hunter, and he looked pleasantly back at me.
>
> Surely it was a good way to die, in the place of someone else, someone I loved. Noble, even. That ought to count for something.
>
> I knew that if I'd never gone to Forks, I wouldn't be facing death now. But, terrified as I was, I couldn't bring myself to regret the decision. When life offers you a dream so far beyond any of your expectations, it's not reasonable to grieve when it comes to an end.
>
> The hunter smiled in a friendly way as he sauntered forward to kill me.
>
> (2)

Bella's self-reflective moment connects love and death, and although the hunter's identity as a vampire remains undisclosed until the final chapters, Bella's confrontation with her own death indicates this romance has teeth.

Moreover, the passage demonstrates Bella's perceived connection between love and moral action, for the decision that leads her to this moment occurs because the "hunter" threatens the life of Bella's mother. Bella believes her choice to die in order to save a loved one is a worthy sacrifice, and we see this decision made over and over again throughout this saga and the other two series. Buffy dies twice to save other people, both known and unknown, and Elena and her friends repeatedly sacrifice themselves so their loved ones can live, most notably when Elena dies and becomes a vampire in order to save Matt and when Bonnie dies and becomes a ghost in order to bring Jeremy back to life.

To return to *Twilight*, the visual metaphor that accompanies the voiceover in the opening scene of the film shifts Bella's love-based decision to die in place of her mother to Bella's position as a vulnerable and hunted being, thus linking love with vulnerability. The film begins with Bella's voiceover and no images: "I've never given much thought to how I would die...." In the pause after this sentence, the sound of gentle music and bird chirps enter, and the black screen becomes a close-up of a lush green forest. The camera travels over moss-covered logs and finds beneath them a watering hole with a deer drinking from it. As Bella's voice returns, the camera closes in on the face of the deer, so Bella and the deer become one: "But dying in place of someone I love... seems like a good way to go." The following chase scene places the viewer in the role of the hunter, until a blue jacket flits past in the foreground. As the deer leaps over a fallen tree and the music crescendos, a man reaches out and grabs her. A sudden cut to a blue sky shifts the scene, and Bella's voice and face appear: "So I can't regret the decision to leave home." The rest of her voiceover provides the backstory to leaving Phoenix and moving to Forks, but none of the novel's references to her immanent death appear. Instead, the film represents Bella as the hunted and the viewer as the hunter, or at least complicit in the hunt, part of the pack.

The series unite horror conventions with romance generally but with *Romeo and Juliet* specifically. Besides the overt story of the "star-crossed lovers" and their "death-marked love" (*Romeo and Juliet* "Prologue") that transcends their death and unites warring families, *Romeo and Juliet* also introduces some of the semantic elements in the Beloved Cycle overall: love at first sight, a problematic love triangle, night as the friend of love and sunrise as its enemy, and the blurring of lines between life and death. Perhaps mentioning all three series draw breath from *Romeo and Juliet* seems obvious, but the second part of the *Twilight* saga, *New Moon*, relies so heavily upon this intertext it would be remiss of me not to address it. The book opens with an epigraph from the play that aligns with Edward's concern that his kiss/bite will kill Bella: "These violent delights have violent ends / And in their triumph die, like fire and powder, / Which, as they kiss, consume" (*Romeo and Juliet*, Act II, Scene VI). Arguably the most tragic of teen love stories, *Romeo and Juliet* suggests teenagers can and do love deeply, and although the lovers themselves do not benefit from their actions, their love leads to larger justice for their community. These three vampire series rewrite this love and demonstrate how being marked by death does not necessarily mean the end of life and love.

All three series, then, signal from the beginning a link between love and death, between romance and horror. In relation to conventions of vampire narratives specifically, for the most part, *BtVS* leaves the semantics of the vampire intact: they can be killed by sunlight, a wooden stake to the heart, and beheading; crosses repulse them; they cannot enter a home without being invited in; they feed on human blood to survive; and they feel no guilt and indeed find pleasure in killing. The core of the genre redetermination lies in the fact that one vampire, Angel, has a soul, which means he feels guilt for all his past transgressions and now lives to help Buffy rid the world of evil. When Angel first presents himself to Buffy, he says, "I know what you're thinking; don't worry, I don't bite" ("Welcome to the Hellmouth" 1001). Angel's articulation of this phrase "I don't bite"—and his actions that support his utterance—establishes Angel's separation from the normalized discourse of the vampire who bites and initiates a new semantic unit of the vampire who does not bite humans to kill them. Instead, the bite becomes a metaphor for connection between a human and her beloved vampire. Both Buffy and Elena encourage the bite to help their lovers survive, and in *Twilight*, Edward must suck poisonous vampire venom out of Bella after James—the hunter mentioned in the opening scene—bites her.

This semantic shift of the vampire who does not bite to kill leads to the syntactic redetermination of the genre: the erotic love between a vampire and a human. In order to facilitate this romance, another semantic change occurs in the *Twilight* saga and *The Vampire Diaries*: sunlight does not kill vampires. In a now somewhat laughable narrative device, all vampires in the *Twilight* saga can live in the sunlight, but they need to stay out of the sun because the sunlight makes their skin sparkle, which means people who see them will know they are not human. As I discuss in Chapter 2, Edward's sparkly skin seems sublime to Bella, but translates so poorly onto a celluloid medium I doubt any other writer or director will resuscitate this aspect of Meyer's vampires. Over in Mystic Falls, vampires generally burn to death in the sunlight, but Stefan, Damon, Caroline, and Katherine—and then Elena—all have rings made by one of the Bennett witches that allow them to move in the daylight, and the Originals maintain special vampire powers due to their status as the first and oldest vampires.

Perhaps one of the most significant syntactic additions into the Beloved Cycle originates from the romantic triangle in which two male monsters love the same female human. In her article "Virtuous Vampires and Voluptuous Vamps: Romance Conventions Reconsidered in Stephenie Meyer's *Twilight*," Lydia Kokkola claims the *Twilight* saga combines conventions of adult romance and problem teen novels in order to allow for more radical relationships—such as the threesome—to sit alongside the notion that sexual relations between teenagers still have problematic outcomes, such as pregnancy: "Meyer's deployment of triangular relationships draws on a long tradition in adult romances, but it is remarkably rare in the more conservative, adolescent romance genre" (169–170). Kokkola argues this position about the genre blending convincingly, but I suggest these radical relationships predate the *Twilight* saga and are less rare in the adolescent paranormal romance genre. The *Vampire Diaries* novels published in the early 1990s feature the Stefan-Damon-Elena/Katherine threesome, and *BtVS* plays with several threesomes, including Angel-Buffy-Spike, Angel-Buffy-Riley, Angelus-Drusilla-Spike, and the implied threesome that features Angel, Buffy, and Angelus.

These threesomes allow for a moral consideration about how a love-based justice does not align easily with a single moral action. For instance, although Buffy loves Angel and believes an aspect of Angel exists in Angelus, she still sends Angel/Angelus to hell with one phallic thrust of her sword. In the *Twilight* saga, Edward and Jacob set aside their mistrust of each other in order to protect Bella, and in *TVD*, Damon repeatedly calls attention to Stefan's morality, such as when he states in "Haunted," Stefan "walks on a moral plane waaaay out of our eyeline" (1007). This invisibility of Stefan's moral plane, however, leads to a compelling debate about love, moral considerations, and visibility. Arguably, Damon's struggle to be "the better man," as Elena frequently implores of him, carries more moral weight because his contemplations stem from a place of love and seem connected to an "endless aspiration to perfection which is characteristic of moral activity" (30), to use Iris Murdoch's words, whereas Stefan's decisions seem relentlessly inviolable.

Set alongside these threesomes are platonic friendships between men and women, which reveal an emotional complexity that precedes the romance between the beloveds but also functions as a means of demonstrating the particularity of the romance. Buffy and Xander's friendship brings out a jealous side of Angel, as does the friendship between Jacob and Bella for Edward. The loving friendships between Stefan and Lexi and then Damon and Rose expose Stefan and Damon's capacity to love and to act morally. Problematically, however, once these friendships serve this purpose, they vanish from the narrative except as spectral reminders, literally when both Rose and Lexi reappear for a brief time as ghosts. Stefan meets Lexi when he first becomes a vampire and seeks to quench his insatiable thirst without concern for doing so in an undetectable way. Lexi teaches him being a vampire does not mean being without love or acting selfishly. When Damon stakes her in order to cover up his own killings ("162 Candles" 1008), he says he does so for the "greater good" ("History Repeating" 1009), but this assertion rings false unless the greater good means Damon himself can continue to live in Mystic Falls undetected.

A single instance of the elimination of a platonic friendship between a male and a female might not register, but when Damon stakes Rose as an act of mercy in Season Two ("The Descent" 2012), Rose's deeply moving death seems metaphorically laden. Rose symbolizes a life lived without romantic love, so from her deathbed she seeks to enlighten Damon about the value of this type of love. As a 500-year-old vampire who sacrifices romantic for platonic love, she—and her five-episode story arc—functions as a cautionary tale about the cost of shutting off one's emotions. Although the details of this story arc exceed the scope of this book, Damon's words to Rose, "Caring gets you dead, huh?" encapsulate the connection between love and death, and the notion that death seems a fair price to pay for love.

The final aspect of syntactic redetermination in the Beloved Cycle that bears mention here concerns the presence of werewolves in the diegesis of the *Twilight* saga and *The Vampire Diaries*. In *Buffy the Vampire Slayer*, the Buffyverse contains all manner of demons, and werewolves, such as Willow's boyfriend Oz, exist as part of that fabric. In the *Twilight* saga, however, it seems only humans, vampires, and werewolves coexist, and in *The Vampire Diaries*, this triumvirate expands to include witches. This inclusion of werewolves enables a discussion about racial/species difference, which extends the love-based justice that begins with vampire and human pairings to include the love and solidarity between vampires and werewolves, a point I discuss in more detail in Chapter 6.

The Series and Their Lovers

The Beloved Does Not Bite emphasizes the development of the enduring relationships between the primary lovers—Buffy and Angel, Bella and Edward, Elena and Stefan, and Elena and Damon—in *Buffy the Vampire Slayer*, the *Twilight* saga, and *The Vampire Diaries* in order to outline the generic similarities between the way the series establish and sustain love as a claim for justice. At the time of finishing this book in December 2016, *Buffy* and *The Vampire Diaries* series have not ended, which makes overall conclusions about the resolution of their storylines impossible.[1] *The Beloved Does Not Bite* focuses mainly on the first half of these two television series because these seasons establish the primary relationships that are then put under different types of challenges in subsequent seasons, while still maintaining the founding principle of love as an impetus for living justly. In this section, I outline key elements in the storylines of each series, in order to provide a context for the rest of the chapters.

Buffy the Vampire Slayer seems destined not to die. The character of Buffy the Vampire Slayer first appeared in 1992 in a film of the same name. While the film achieved modest attention, it was not until the film's writer and creator, Joss Whedon, revamped his idea as a television series that Buffy became a household name. After airing on television for seven seasons from 1997 to 2003, Seasons Eight through Eleven continue in comic-book form. *The Beloved Does Not Bite* focuses on the television series, which circulates around the idea that Buffy, a normal high school girl, discovers she is "the vampire slayer, one girl, in all the world, a chosen one. One born with the strength and skill to hunt the vampires, to stop the spread of evil" ("Welcome to the Hellmouth" 1001). Her friends—known as the Scooby Gang—include Willow, a witch; Xander; and her Watcher, Giles. In Season One, Angel appears as Buffy's almost-boyfriend who mostly lurks and warns her of impending dangers. In the backstory, we learn Angel spent the first half of his 240 vampire years living without remorse, without a soul. Known as Angelus during this time, The Master calls him the most "vicious creature ever," the vampire with the face of an angel ("Angel" 1007). Then, a gypsy clan curses Angel and returns his soul to him, which condemns him to an eternity of penitence for his past evil deeds. Only a moment of "true happiness" will undo the curse, and just over half way through Season Two, this moment arrives: Buffy and Angel make love for the first time ("Surprise" 2013), and when Angel awakens, he finds "the pain is gone," and so is his soul ("Innocence" 2014). The final eight episodes of Season Two follow Buffy as she tries to come to terms with the loss of Angel and the return of Angelus.

For most of the first three seasons, Angel exists as the only beloved vampire. Other vampires are one-dimensional killers and evil demons, although some of Spike's dialogue anticipates the development of his character into a sympathetic, and arguably beloved, vampire. After Angel leaves *BtVS* at the end of Season Three, the remaining four seasons develop Spike's character as he seeks to become—and sometimes succeeds in becoming—Buffy's lover. I focus primarily on the first three seasons and the relationship between Buffy and Angel because their love for each other forms the generic basis for the relationship between Bella and Edward in the *Twilight* saga and between Elena and Stefan and Elena and Damon in *The Vampire Diaries*.

The *Twilight* saga begins as a series of four books written by Stephenie Meyer—*Twilight* (2005), *New Moon* (2006), *Eclipse* (2007), and *Breaking Dawn* (2008)—that were adapted into five movies released in theatres between 2008 and 2012, with *Breaking Dawn* divided into two separate films. Like Buffy, Bella Swan moves to a new town and a new high school after the divorce of her parents. Where Buffy moves from Los Angeles to Sunnydale, California to live with her mother, Bella moves from Phoenix, Arizona to Forks, Washington to live with her father, who serves as the town's sheriff. Bella stumbles around school, her clumsiness seemingly one of her most endearing features. When she sees the sublimely beautiful Edward Cullen, she finds herself irresistibly drawn to him. The first two books and films develop their tumultuous relationship. He resists her because his thirst for her puts her in danger, but her desire and determination to be with him—and to become a vampire so she can spend eternity with him—prevail.

After Edward leaves Bella early in *New Moon*, the series plays up the romantic tension between Edward and the werewolf Jacob Black. Like Angel, Edward and his vampire family make an ethical choice to live as "vegetarians" feeding on animals and not humans. This decision makes them somewhat unique amongst vampires—only one other vampire community lives without feeding on humans—and it also provides the foundation for a truce with the local indigenous community, the Quileutes, many of whom shape-shift into wolves. The possibility of an Edward-Bella-Jacob threesome dissipates when Jacob imprints upon the unfortunately named Renesmee, the human/vampire hybrid daughter of Bella and Edward. When a wolf imprints upon another being, the love connection binds the two irrevocably. Because Jacob somewhat-creepily bonds to a thankfully accelerated-aging baby, the vampire and werewolf communities set aside their animosity in an act of solidarity against the threatening Volturi, who want to kill Renesmee because they fear she will expose the vampires, which is a transgression punishable by death. The saga ends with the Volturi standing down from battle after the Cullens convince them Renesmee poses no threat.

Written by L.J. Smith and first published in 1991 as four horror/romance novels for teens, *The Vampire Diaries* finds new life eighteen years later as a television series, presumably drawing on the renewed interest in visual representations of the interactions between high school humans and vampires *BtVS* and *Twilight* revive. Having finished half its eighth season and the third season of its spin-off show *The Originals* in December 2016, the television series—like the books—focuses on the relationships between the human-turned-vampire Elena Gilbert, and the vampire brothers Stefan and Damon Salvatore. While the primary love story initially features Elena and Stefan, bad-boy brother Damon also loves Elena, and she often finds herself drawn to him. Elena finally confesses her love to Damon in the finale of Season Four, so their relationship as a couple develops throughout Seasons Five and Six, until Elena symbolically dies in the final episode of Season Six, returning from the dead only in the final episode of the series.

Unlike the *Twilight* saga in which the films and books align fairly faithfully, *The Vampire Diaries* draws from the novels only the barest character sketches. The main characters remain the same, but the plot of the television series barely brushes against the novels. In Season Two, Katherine—Elena's doppelgänger—returns to try to seduce Stefan away from Elena, and Klaus threatens the well-being of the community, but the similarity stops there. Instead, the television series creates a storyworld in which the past and present actions of characters invite a reflection upon what it means to be human, and the characters themselves—and especially the vampires—often ruminate upon their condition. If *BtVS* translates the complexities of the world into metaphors that allow for a deeper understanding of the demons that haunt humans, and the *Twilight* saga privileges the family as the site for social action, then *TVD* plumbs the depths of human emotion and suggests being human means being able to love.

The show highlights the premise that vampires have the ability to turn off their emotions and creates multiple scenarios to test the limits of love and its connection to moral action. Season One provides the backstory: in 1864, the brothers Stefan and Damon Salvatore both loved and were loved by the vampire Katerina Petrova, who they knew as Katherine Pierce. The brothers tell Katherine she must choose between them, but she refuses and instead begins the process of turning both of them into vampires so the three of them can live together and love each other forever. In order to become a vampire, a human must be bitten by a vampire, drink vampire blood, die, and then drink human blood, so when Stefan and Damon are killed for being vampire sympathizers, they need only drink human blood to complete the transformation. Stefan drinks from and kills his father and then convinces Damon to drink from a young woman. Damon's resistance and Stefan's insistence shape the future of their relationship because Stefan forever feels guilt for Damon's vampirism and Damon blames Stefan for the loss of Katherine's love, after she seemingly kills herself because they refuse her terms to live in a loving threesome.

Season One begins with Stefan and Damon's return to Mystic Falls in 2009, and history threatens to repeat itself when they both fall in love with Elena, a Petrova doppelgänger. The main tensions circulate around the love/hate relationship between the brothers, the love they both feel for Elena, and the way Elena feels about them. Both the novels and the television series employ dual focalizing techniques and a switch between first and third person points of view in order to provide the inner-thoughts of and connection between Elena and Stefan and to cast Damon as the evil, unknowable outsider, a convention now accepted as part of contemporary vampire narratives. As Michelle J. Smith states, "The inclusion of vampire and human points of view has a different outcome in the postmodern Gothic in that greater understanding of, and sympathy for, the vampire's perspective make long-term loving relationships between humans and vampires possible" (200). The novel opens with an entry from Elena's diary in which she writes about feeling afraid and lost, and then shifts to a third-person perspective in which she reflects upon her feelings: "Since when had she, Elena Gilbert, been scared of meeting people? Since when had she been scared of *anything*?" (3). Elena's admission of her feelings and then her angry denial of them parallel Stefan's uncertainty and vulnerability three pages later when the narrative changes to his thoughts:

> For a moment he wondered again, if he should just give it all up. Perhaps he should go back to Italy, back to his hiding place. What made him think that he could rejoin the world of daylight?
>
> But he was tired of living in the shadows. He was tired of the darkness, and of the things that lived in it. Most of all, he was tired of being alone.
>
> (6)

Both Elena and Stefan express their self-doubts in a question-and-answer structure, which provides a rhetorical connection between them. Elena's opening address—"Dear Diary"—and the third person point of view invite readers to take up the position of confidantes, into whose ears Elena and Stefan whisper their publicly unexpressed emotions.

The television series, the main focus for this book, continues this structure that couples Elena and Stefan and marginalizes Damon, at least for most of the first season. In the televisual medium, Damon's marginalization wobbles because the viewer bears witness to his struggles and his striving toward goodness and to his ability to be hurt. Damon's love is more emotionally coded, more visceral, and connects more exclusively to Elena, whereas Stefan's desire to know her results in a more controlled and measured love, a love based on his will. Nussbaum is right when she says, "Romantic love is not something that is governed by the will. It is, instead, something with respect to which we are, at least in part, passive. It seems that we can't choose to fall in love with someone; it simply happens to us. And we can't altogether govern the way in which, or the goodness with which, it will happen" (*Love's Knowledge* 336). Even though Stefan says he has no choice but to return to Mystic Falls because he has to "know her," he returns with intention to know Elena and to love her. His love and the way he engages with Elena seem governed by his will, which imposes a barrier between him and Elena.

While Elena and Stefan function as a romantic couple for the first three seasons, the relationship between Elena and Damon moves from platonic friendship to romantic love, and the numerous dreams and mistaken identities between Elena/Katherine and Damon provide the possibility and titillation for their eventual romance. Damon's love, as well as the moral decisions he makes based upon his love, provides a complex and nuanced exemplar for a love-based justice. Even when Stefan shuns his moral compass, his descent into depravity appears as an aberration rather than an inherent aspect of his personality. As I do with *BtVS*, I focus primarily on the first three seasons of *TVD*, which provide the foundation for how love between a human and a vampire grounds moral action. When Elena becomes a vampire at the end of Season Three, the series still considers love and emotions to be core to living well, but Elena's newborn vampire proclivities extend beyond the focus of this book.

The overall plots of these three series connect less to events and more to relationships. Many people die—some of them become the living dead, and some just stay dead—humans behave monstrously, and monsters love beautifully, but as Jason Mitchell states about soap operas in his "Film and Television Narrative" entry for the *Cambridge Companion to Narrative*, serial dramas "prioritize relationships over events; when a major event happens in a soap opera, the question of 'what happens?' is often secondary to 'how does it affect the community of relationships?'" (164). In *Buffy*, the *Twilight* saga, and *TVD*, forbidden kisses, longing glances, painful separations, and sensuous dreams become momentous occasions. And, it all begins with looking at a beautiful male body...

Note

1 With serendipitous timing, *The Vampire Diaries* eighth and final season ended on 10 March 2017, exactly 20 years after the first episode of *Buffy the Vampire Slayer* aired. The season finale, "I Was Feeling Epic," maintains the dynamics *The Beloved Does Not Bite* examines, especially in relation to erotic and fraternal love as a basis for right action: Stefan sacrifices his life, so Elena and Damon can experience a full life together. Stefan explains his actions to Elena: "Damon wanted to sacrifice everything to save you, to save this town. ... Tonight I saw a side of Damon that I hadn't seen in a while. The older brother I looked up to. The son who enlisted in the Civil War to please his father. The Damon I knew when I was a boy. I wanted that Damon to live. And I wanted you to have an opportunity to get to know him. He's the better man. He's the right man." The closing montage shows Damon and Elena holding hands and then separating as a symbol of their deaths, Elena to rejoin her family, and Damon to embrace Stefan into the closing credits.

Works Cited

"162 Candles." *The Vampire Diaries.* Writ. Kevin Williamson and Julie Plec. Dir. Rick Bota. CWTV. 5 November 2009. Television.

Altman, Rick. "A Semantic/Syntactic Approach to Film Genre." *Cinema Journal* 23.3 (Spring 1984): 6–18. Print.

———. *Film/Genre.* London: British Film Institute, 1999. Print.

Angel: The Complete Series. Creators David Greenwalt and Joss Whedon. 20th Century Fox, 2007. DVD.

"Angel." *Buffy the Vampire Slayer: The Complete First Season on DVD.* Writ. David Greenwalt. Dir. Scott Brazil. Twentieth Century Fox, 2001. DVD.

Bitten. Creator Daegan Fryklind. Entertainment One. 2014–2016. TV Series.

"The Descent." *The Vampire Diaries.* Writ. Sarah Fain and Elizabeth Craft. Dir. Marcos Siega. CWTV. 27 January 2011. Television.

Gordon, Joan and Veronica Hollinger, eds. *Blood Read: The Vampire as Metaphor in Contemporary Culture.* Philadelphia: UPenn, 1997. Print.

"Haunted." *The Vampire Diaries.* Writ. Andrew Kreisberg and Brian Young. Dir. Guy Ferland. CWTV. 29 October 2009. Television.

"History Repeating." *The Vampire Diaries.* Writ. Bryan M. Holdman and Brian Young. Dir. Marcos Siega. CWTV. 12 November 2009. Television.

"I Was Feeling Epic." *The Vampire Diaries.* Writ. Julie Plec and Kevin Williamson. Dir. Julie Plec. CWTV. 10 March 2017. Television.

"Innocence." *Buffy the Vampire Slayer: The Complete Second Season on DVD.* Writ. and Dir. Joss Whedon. Twentieth Century Fox, 2002. DVD.

Jauss, Hans Robert. "Theory of Genres and Medieval Literature." *Towards an Aesthetic of Reception.* Trans. Timothy Bahti. Brighton: Harvester P, 1982. 76–109. Print.

Kane, Tim. *The Changing Vampire of Film and Television: A Critical Study of the Growth of a Genre.* Jefferson, NC: McFarland & Co, 2006. Print.

Kearney, Richard. *Strangers, Gods, and Monsters: Interpreting Otherness.* New York: Routledge, 2003. 1–20. Print.

Kokkola, Lydia. "Virtuous Vampires and Voluptuous Vamps: Romance Conventions Reconsidered in Stephenie Meyer's *Twilight*." *Children's Literature in Education* 42 (2011): 165–179. Print.
Meyer, Stephenie. *Breaking Dawn*. New York: Little Brown, 2008. Print.
———. *Eclipse*. New York: Little Brown, 2007. Print.
———. *New Moon*. New York: Little Brown, 2006. Print.
———. *Twilight*. New York: Little Brown, 2005. Print.
Mitchell, Jason. "Film and Television Narrative." *Cambridge Companion to Narrative*. Ed. David Herman. Cambridge: Cambridge UP, 2007. 156–171. Print.
Moonlight: The Complete Series. Creators Ron Koslow and Trevor Munson. Warner Home Video, 2011. DVD.
Murdoch, Iris. *The Sovereignty of Good*. 1970. New York: Routledge, 2013. Print.
Nussbaum, Martha C. *Love's Knowledge: Essays on Philosophy and Literature*. New York: Oxford UP, 1990. Print.
The Originals. Creator Julie Plec. Alloy. 2013-. TV Series.
"Pilot." *The Vampire Diaries*. Writ. Kevin Williamson and Julie Plec. Dir. Marcos Siega. CWTV. 10 September 2009. Television.
Shakespeare, William. *Romeo and Juliet*. New York: Penguin, 2005. Print.
Smith, L.J. *Vampire Diaries*. Books 1 & 2. *The Awakening* and *The Struggle*. 1991. London: Hodder, 2009. Print.
———. *Vampire Diaries*. Books 3 & 4. *The Fury* and *The Reunion*. 1991. London: Hodder, 2009. Print.
Smith, Michelle J. "The Postmodern Vampire in 'Post-race' America: HBO's *True Blood*." *Open Graves, Open Minds: Representations of Vampires and the Undead from the Enlightenment to the Present Day*. Eds. S. George and B. Hughes. Manchester: Manchester UP, 2013. 192–209. Print.
"Surprise." *Buffy the Vampire Slayer: The Complete Second Season on DVD*. Writ. Marti Noxon. Dir. Michael Lange. Twentieth Century Fox, 2002. DVD.
Teen Wolf. Creator Jeff Davis. MGM. 2011-. TV Series.
True Blood. Creator Alan Ball. HBO. 2008–2014. TV Series.
Twilight. Writ. Melissa Rosenberg. Dir. Catherine Hardwicke, 2008. DVD.
The Twilight Saga: Breaking Dawn—Part 1. Writ. Melissa Rosenberg. Dir. Bill Condon, 2011. DVD.
The Twilight Saga: Breaking Dawn—Part 2. Writ. Melissa Rosenberg. Dir. Bill Condon, 2012. DVD.
The Twilight Saga: Eclipse. Writ. Melissa Rosenberg. Dir. David Slade, 2010. DVD.
The Twilight Saga: New Moon. Writ. Melissa Rosenberg. Dir. Chris Weitz, 2009. DVD.
Waters, Daniel. *Generation Dead*. New York: Hyperion, 2008. Print.
———. *Kiss of Life*. New York: Hyperion, 2009. Print.
———. *My Friends are Dead*. OMZ, 2016. Print.
———. *Passing Strange*. New York: Hyperion, 2010. Print.
"Welcome to the Hellmouth." *Buffy the Vampire Slayer: The Complete First Season on DVD*. Writ. Joss Whedon. Dir. Charles Martin Smith. Twentieth Century Fox, 2001. DVD.

2 "Doesn't He Own a Shirt?"
Beauty and Justice

Plato allowed to the beauty of the lovely boy an awakening power...
—Iris Murdoch, *The Sovereignty of Good* (1970), p. 86

I remember the first time I saw a beautiful vampire. 1987. *The Lost Boys*. I was in my musician groupie phase, so vampires who looked like rock stars appealed to me. Even though he played one of the sidekicks, Billy Wirth with his long dark hair and chiseled cheek bones made an impression. I understood Michael's dilemma, why he might be drawn to David and his group of fun-loving, living-on-the-edge friends. Sexy and dangerous, they lived by a code of loyalty, and if a few people died along the way, well, that was life, so to speak. Even though IMDb lists the genre of the film as a blend of comedy/horror, I remember being deeply moved by David's death, by the choral music cresting in the background, by the way death softened the hard lines of David's face, in a way neither funny nor fearful.

I waited another 7 years for more beautiful vampires to appear, and appear they did in Neil Jordan's *Interview with the Vampire*. Ignoring Tom Cruise's Lestat, my sister and I focused on Antonio Banderas as Armand and Brad Pitt as Louis and remembered the washboard abs we saw in *Thelma & Louise* lay hidden beneath Louis's blousy white shirts. Three years later, with the appearance of Angel in *Buffy the Vampire Slayer*, I enjoyed a weekly fix of a sexy, sensitive, funny vampire. I kept pace with Buffy as she fell in love with Angel, and in the closing scene of the "Angel" episode (1007), when Buffy and Angel embrace long enough for Buffy's cross to brand itself into Angel's chest, my friends and I sighed because we understood love meant pain, too.

This chapter shuns the claim "beauty is only skin deep" to show how beauty initiates, sustains, and enhances the relationship between beautiful vampires and their human beloveds. A semantics of male beauty—and particularly the face and torso—portrays the vampire beloved's body as both immortal and vulnerable, and in each series, the vampire's naked flesh reveals his vulnerability: Angel's wounded torso functions as a metaphor for his tormented soul; Edward's beauty invites a comparison to the sublime; Stefan's liminal nudity characterizes his repressed urges; and Damon's exposed and eroticized chest initiates a consideration of his heart. By focusing on the beautiful male body, these three series establish male beauty and female desire as a combination that coheres into love.

Beauty, historically more often associated with women and nature, now aligns with men, and in particular with supernatural men. Vampires from novels find their onscreen embodiments in the lean-bodied, pretty-faced Brad Pitt, David Boreanaz, Robert Pattinson, Paul Wesley, and Alexander Skarsgård leaving their on-screen beloveds and their off-screen fans mesmerized. While it may not be difficult to sketch a tall, blonde, broad-shouldered, smooth-chested, lean-hipped standard of these actors, my objective here is not to define an aesthetics of beauty but rather to outline its philosophical and ethical components, primarily through the work of Iris Murdoch and Elaine Scarry.

While I focus primarily on male beauty and on female attraction to male beauty, I acknowledge a recognition of beauty occurs both ways. An acute pleasure of these three series exists, however, because beautiful men strut and suffer for women, a syntax rarely—if ever—seen on television prior to *Buffy*. Women comment on and react to male beauty in ways the male vampires do not articulate overtly about their female human beloveds. In her essay "At Stake: Angel's Body, Fantasy Masculinity, and Queer Desire in Teen Television," Allison McCracken notes about Angel,

> Of all the characters' bodies in *Buffy*, Angel's body is the most displayed and eroticized. He reverses the usual spectacularization of the female body by functioning early on as Buffy's *homme fatal*, a mysterious stranger she first describes as "gorgeous," and whose body becomes the object of her gaze and that of others. Angel's bare chest is displayed prominently and often in the series as both an aesthetic and an erotic object.
>
> (120)

The *Twilight* saga offers similar titillation through Jacob, but only rarely displays Edward's glittery chest. Stefan and Damon, on the other hand, return to the erotic, tortured aesthetic Angel introduces.

Although my next chapter describes and analyzes the significance of looking to establishing an ethics of love, this chapter argues the female human gazes upon the male vampire's beauty and therein creates a dynamic of reciprocity between beholder and beheld. I demonstrate how the visual texts invite the viewer's gaze and represent the female gaze to challenge critics who posit women as powerless watchers and watched. For instance, in *Ways of Seeing*, John Berger famously proclaims, "Men act and women appear. Men look at women. Women watch themselves being looked at" (47). Although Berger writes in this passage about European oil paintings, the dynamic holds for contemporary film and television. In a strikingly similar formulation, Laura Mulvey structures "Woman As Image, Man as Bearer of the Look" and argues in her seminal article "Visual Pleasure and Narrative Cinema,"

> In a world ordered by sexual imbalance, pleasure in looking has been split between active/male and passive/female. The determining male gaze projects its fantasy onto the female figure, which is styled accordingly. In their traditional exhibitionist role women are simultaneously looked at and displayed, with their appearance coded for strong visual and erotic impact so that they can be said to connote *to-be-looked-at-ness.*
>
> (19)

Mulvey's essay continues to influence contemporary film studies, and several critics employ her theory to discuss the *Twilight* saga, which constitutes most of the analysis to date about the beautiful eroticism of vampires in the three series upon which I focus.

Critics articulate a broad range of responses regarding Bella's gaze as either powerful and agentic or disempowering and deluded. Sara Wasson and Sarah Artt, for instance, draw upon Mulvey's theory in order to argue for a liminal space for the female heterosexual viewer as "ambivalent agent, not just victim" (181). They divide their essay into two sections firstly to examine why the *Twilight* saga has "generated such a vast popular appetite among women for the sight of another woman being progressively mutilated" and secondly to discuss "the films' recurring fascination with looking at the body of a man, the female spectator's gaze simultaneously tempted and defensively obscured by the glitter of vampire skin" (181). Wasson and Artt suture these two ideas together to stitch Bella's broken body to a desire to be seen, cherished, and sexually satisfied: "Although Bella repeated declares that she hates attention, there is a particular kind of beholding to which she is not at all averse: a rapt, transfixed gaze at her many wounds... Bella's extraordinary catalogue of wounds is thus not only a symbol of deferred sexual penetration—rather, the wound is an intensity that gives the female character substantial power over the male protagonists..." (182, 183). They argue, the "litany of marble metaphors, its relentless sensual deferrals, its staged tableaux and its suspended narrative structure all exemplify masochistic textual form" (186). *The Beloved Does Not Bite* aligns with critics who see Bella's gaze as telescoping her desire, although it pays more attention to the wounded, vulnerable male body than to Bella's injuries, and it extends this analysis back from the *Twilight* saga to consider the female gaze in *Buffy* as well as forward to *The Vampire Diaries.*

I agree, for instance, with Kim Edwards who, in her article "Good Looks and Sex Symbols: the Power of the Gaze and the Displacement of the Erotic in *Twilight*," posits, "the real object of desire in (and beyond) the text is Edward, and thus the implied male authority of the gaze in fetishising an image as sexual stimulant is reclaimed by Bella, and by extension, her empathising audience" (29). Alternatively—and less convincingly—in "Romance and the Female Gaze: Obscuring Gendered Violence in *The Twilight Saga*," Jessica Taylor attempts to provide both a scathing criticism and a hesitant defense of the saga's gendered power dynamics. Initially, she slams the saga's portrayal of the naturalization and normalization of patriarchal dominance "as a desirable state for women" (396), and then she ends the article by trying to understand the saga's huge popularity by casting men as the objects of Mulvey's *to-be-looked-at-ness*: "Lingering descriptions within the texts, coupled with the casting of photogenic actors to perform the roles in the film adaptations, positions the audience to desire the powerful and potentially violent male body, rather than to fear it" (397). Rather than simply and problematically reversing Mulvey's theory to apply to women looking at men, Taylor draws on Germaine Greer's argument that women can gaze upon boys—categorized as males not old enough to shave—but not men because boys cannot refute their objection. Taylor suggests Edward and Jacob fit Greer's category of boy because of the smooth, hair-free appearance of their bodies: "If Greer is right, and the possibility of the female gaze rests upon the presence of a 'non-masterful' boy, then the threat of the violent but visually desirable 'boys' of *The Twilight Saga* is reduced in a similar manner to Mulvey's original discussion of the male gaze reducing the threat of the female body" (398). While I appreciate Taylor's attempt to give a balanced analysis of the *Twilight* saga and to try to account for the popularity of the saga by creating a space in which female viewers can gaze safely upon beautiful boys, her account does not hold. If the main problem with the saga exists in the patriarchal dominance—that is, the mastery—of Edward and Jacob over Bella, then it does not hold that they can also be non-masterful boys due to their hairlessness.

Other writers also shape their criticism around the ambiguity of Bella's character, particularly about how Bella's overall narrative favors an abstinence story about not having sex until marriage while her everyday experiences focus on her overwhelming longing for Edward's touch. In "Beauty and the Beautiful Beast: Stephenie Meyer's *Twilight* Saga and the Quest for a Transgressive Female Desire," for instance, Fleur Diamond acknowledges both the conservative and transgressive elements of Bella's desire, but persuasively suggests the *Twilight* saga and other examples of Young Adult supernatural fiction perform "a symbolic task in articulating that 'missing discourse' of female desire" (43). Diamond quotes Deborah Tolman's work on female desire, which acknowledges the double bind that finds women sexualized but also alienated from their own sexuality. Girls learn to "look at, rather than experience, themselves, to know themselves from the perspective of men, thereby losing touch with their own bodily feelings and desires" (Tolman qtd. in Diamond 44). Refreshingly, Diamond argues, "Beneath the overt subscription to Christian tenets of chastity before marriage and complementary heterosex lies an erotic that is surprising for its barely repressed ferocity and capacity for transgression. *Twilight*'s sub-text is one young woman's pursuit of a ferocious sexuality for herself" (46). This chapter supplements Diamond's claim and suggests Buffy, Bella, and Elena all pursue their own sexuality but also their sexuality exists in and initiates a loving relationship based on reciprocity.

This reciprocity figures in all three vampire series, and it begins with a perception of beauty. As Elaine Scarry argues in *On Beauty and Being Just*, "the moment of perceiving something beautiful confers on the perceiver the gift of life; and now we begin to see that the moment of perceiving beauty also confers on the object the gift of life. The pacific quality of beauty comes in part from the reciprocal, life-granting pact" (69). Although Bella repeatedly comments upon Edward's beauty, it is worth remembering she embodies beauty in her very name. As Elena's name means light, so Bella emanates beauty in her name and perceives it in Edward, and together they breathe new life into each other, even when they both cease to draw breath. Similarly, when Angel watches Buffy for the first time and then decides to help her—therein granting himself the gift of life, or at least purpose to his life—Whistler says to Angel, "God, jeez, look at you. She must be prettier than the last Slayer" ("Becoming, Part 1" 2021).

The bodies of vampires—the way they look, the way they draw the gaze, the way they move, the way they dress, the way they die—display human fears about our own bodies and about our desire for the bodies of our potential beloveds. In an era in which men are slowly being represented as emotionally vulnerable, each of the three series disrobes the male body from the waist up in order to draw attention to its beauty and to disclose each vampire's vulnerabilities, especially in the region of their hearts. As Stacey Abbott in *Celluloid Vampires* says of an earlier time period, "the vampire body became the site upon which our concerns and anxieties about the body in the 1980s were projected. They became physical, despiritualized, out of control, and when they die, they explode in an excess of all that we expel" (124). Natalie Wilson in *Seduced by Twilight* extends Abbott's work to suggest the Cullen vampires embody 21st century preoccupations with the body: "What better way to stave off aging, weight gain, and bodily harm than to become a living (not-breathing) statue?... *Twilight* reveal[s] an obsession with the body beautiful—a timely obsession given our cultural context of bodily discipline and 'improvement' (35). I do not disagree with Wilson, but I want to focus more attention on how *BtVS*, the *Twilight* saga, and *TVD* display the beautiful male body, especially partially unclothed.

In these three series, the male vampire body draws the desiring gaze and acknowledges the body's vulnerability—regardless of its immortality. Speaking about mortal beings rather than physically impermeable bodies, Richard Dyer and later Natalie Wilson link the unclothed male body to vulnerability, and this position still applies to the vampire body in its emotional rather than physical vulnerability. Dyer argues popular fiction hardly depicts semi-naked white men until the 1980s because nakedness reveals vulnerability and a lack of protection (qtd. in Spooner 146). Wilson takes up this point and claims in the *Twilight* saga Edward rarely features without clothing while Jacob repeatedly bares his body: She cites the meadow scene and the moment when Edward nearly exposes himself in Volterra as scenes of "extreme vulnerability" (92). On the other hand, Catherine Spooner reads the moment Edward reveals his sparkling body to Bella not as making himself vulnerable but as demonstrating his inaccessibility:

> Edward is presented as exotic, marvelous, eminently consumable—a rare and precious object, a work of art rather than a man. He is, however, oddly asexual.... Edward as spectacle draws the female gaze, but also repels it. He reflects rather than absorbs light. His glittering skin is a focus for female desire while also simultaneously denying its satisfaction. The ultimate commodity, Edward's scintillating, sculptural body leaves only the desire for more.
>
> (149)

As I will show throughout this chapter, this concept of nakedness and simultaneous vulnerability and inaccessibility/impenetrability holds throughout all three series, but in *TVD* especially, Stefan and Damon's naked chests and arrowed hipbones also taunt and tempt Elena and the viewers through whom her desire resonates.

Angel, Edward, Stefan, and Damon's bodies display as both vulnerable and impenetrable most often when their bodies become spectacles of pain. Steve Neale in his 1983 essay, reprinted as the prologue to *Screening the Male: Exploring Masculinities in the Hollywood Cinema* takes Mulvey's notion of scopophilia as it applies to the female body and asks if it transfers to the male body during scenes of male combat:

> We are offered the spectacle of male bodies, but bodies unmarked as objects of erotic display. There is no trace of an acknowledgement or recognition of those bodies displayed solely for the gaze of the spectator.... We see male bodies stylized and fragmented by close-ups, but our look is not direct, it is heavily mediated by the

> looks of the characters involved. And those looks are marked not by desire, but rather by fear, or hatred, or aggression.
>
> (18)

This analysis holds to a certain extent in the three series, and especially in the *Twilight* saga and *The Vampire Diaries*, in which much of the minor combat takes place between male vampires. I distinguish here between minor combat and major battles, the latter of which are the main focus of my final chapter. Major battles—such as between the Mayor and the students of Sunnydale High School; and between the Cullen allies and the Volturi—include a larger cast of characters, all of whom pitch in to fight the good fight. Minor combat or skirmishes take place episodically, usually between only one or two characters. Fetishistic scopophilia, in *BtVS*, however resists such easy alignment with a gendered look because often Buffy fights male vampires, or as in the opening scene of the "Angel" episode I discuss shortly, both Angel and Buffy provide the spectacle.

A focus on the male vampires' beauty underpins a larger ethics about right action without detracting from the pleasure of looking. To borrow from Iris Murdoch in *The Sovereignty of Good*, beauty "is an occasion for 'unselfing'" (82) and "is the only spiritual thing which we love by instinct.... a perfection of form which invites unpossessive contemplation and resists absorption into the selfish dream life of the consciousness" (83). I take "unselfing" here not to mean letting go of oneself but rather as a movement towards an Other without ownership, a movement that initiates contemplation and resists solipsism. An overt articulation of this contemplative moment occurs in *Twilight* when Bella first sees the Cullens and names them as "devastatingly, inhumanly beautiful. They were faces you never expected to see except perhaps on the airbrushed pages of a fashion magazine. Or painted by an old master as the face of an angel" (18). Revealingly, Bella equates beauty with being angelic, a discursive gesture back to *Buffy*, which also anticipates later paranormal romances that feature angels, as I discuss in my Conclusion.

Murdoch's "unselfing" and Simone Weil's "radical decentering" inform Scarry's work on the importance of beauty to justice. She summarizes her position as follows: "beauty, far from contributing to social injustice... or even remaining neutral to injustice as an innocent bystander, actually assists us in the work of addressing injustice, not only by requiring of us constant perceptual acuity—high dives of seeing, hearing, touching—but by... more direct forms of instruction" (62). This instruction, or beauty's "call" to use Scarry's phrasing (109), takes the following shape: I see something beautiful—whether it be a person, a poem, a sunset—and my perception of such beauty fills my vision and calls me to it. In this instance, this beautiful being becomes the center of my world, and my daily concerns, distractions, solipsism, move aside, so I can attend to and be present in this moment. Because of this beautiful being, I want to make such beauty accessible to all, and I want to be a good person in the face of this beauty. Beautiful things provide both a state of bliss and a feeling of being moved to the side, of being not the main focus of attention. Scarry suggests bliss in laternalness may not in itself be a source of justice, but it prepares us for working towards justice in the world.

I recognized this power of beauty in a conversation with a close friend of mine about how she makes her marriage work. When I asked her how she overlooks the faults of her beloved, she responded, "I can't help it because she's so good looking." This conversation resonates with me because I was, at the time, stunned by her response. I anticipated an answer that would bestow upon me some wisdom—and maybe even practical advice—about how to look the other way, about how, for instance, cleanliness is less important than sharing similar beliefs, or about how you look at the big picture of life with your beloved rather than obsessing about little details. What does it matter that my lover leaves clothes on the floor on the very spot from which they drop from his body? It all clicked into place for me when I saw a man whose beauty distracted me so completely from my troubles that when I nearly tripped over his shorts on the floor outside the bathroom, instead of thinking, "why can't you pick up your shorts?" I thought, "this beautiful man is naked somewhere beyond those shorts." Now, a pair of shorts on the floor is different from "Oh, this beautiful man who I desperately desire and whose very presence puts me in a state of bliss is a vampire, who may want to kill me," but the two situations illuminate how a pull to beauty can overwhelm or supersede allegedly rational reasons for repulsion (or attraction). Once we have already been unselfed and radically decentered, the degree of the perceived obstacle does not matter. A bite to the neck may as well be a pair of shorts on the floor, for all it matters at this stage.

And how does this consideration of beauty move us towards justice? Certainly, our wooziness may distract us from any purpose. However, as Scarry argues, beauty can also call us to attend to its fairness. She yokes beauty to justice through the etymological equivalence of fairness as beauty and as justice (90–92): "beautiful things give rise to the notion of distribution, to a lifesaving reciprocity, to fairness not just in the sense of loveliness of aspect but in the sense of 'a symmetry of everyone's relation to one another,'" a concept of fairness she borrows from John Rawls (95). Symmetry functions in several ways: it describes beauty itself; it exists in the symmetrical reciprocity between perceiver and perceived; and it distributes and provides access to beauty amongst everyone. When Angel's beautifully symmetrical face appears for the first time in *BtVS*, symmetrically placed in the center of the frame, it invites a closer look, a desire to see the details of his beauty without the blue light obscuring his features ("Welcome to the Hellmouth" 1001). In this act of looking, which feels like the welcome to which the title of the episode alludes, we attend to little else: "At the moment one comes into the presence of something beautiful, it greets you. It lifts away from the neutral background as though coming forward to welcome you—as though the object were designed to 'fit' your perception" (Scarry 25). Angel comes forward to welcome us all as we walk with Buffy towards the mouth of hell and hope to save the world, or at least to change it for the better.

Underscoring the gaze's ability to elicit both vulnerability and desire, Scarry suggests a position that strives for equal power and equal vulnerability between perceiver and perceived. Although Mulvey and others write specifically about visual mediums and the apparatus by which the gaze functions, Scarry's point of view best illuminates the dynamic between gazer and gazed upon: "surely what we should wish is a world where the vulnerability of the beholder is equal to or greater than the vulnerability of the person beheld, a world where the pleasure-filled tumult of staring is a prelude to acts that will add to the beauty already in the world—acts like making a poem, or a philosophic dialogue, or a divine comedy; or acts like repairing an injury or a social injustice" (75). Scarry outlines three ways beauty links to justice: through the object itself; through the perceiver of beauty; and through the impulse to create. The second of these three possibilities foregrounds a relationship between beauty, looking, and love, and therefore features most fully in this chapter.

The perceiver of beauty becomes protector in an attempt to preserve the beautiful, as each series demonstrates when the female lover protects her vampire beloved. Discussing this responsibility of the beholder in her essay "The Passion of the Material," Vivian Sobchak articulates a connection between ethics and aesthetics grounded in the fleshly body and the material world. She names this intertwining of world and flesh as passionate, which she links to suffering, being acted upon, and devotion to others. Though torture seems an unlikely example, for Sobchak, its severity makes legible the affective links between suffering and passion: "the very task of the torturer is to provoke and intensify the body-subject's re-cognition of their existential vulnerability as a merely objective 'thing'" (288). She theorizes passion as containing an understanding of our own vulnerability to be acted upon and as a responsibility towards others to protect against their suffering. She argues this latter aspect of passion can be defined "as an *active devotion* to others and the objective world, as an intense, driving, and overmastering feeling that emerges and expands beyond our conscious will yet acts on us, nonetheless, from *within*. Thus, like suffering, passionate devotion is in excess of our volition; but, unlike suffering, it is within our agency" (288). I draw upon these ideas in my analysis of the suffering male vampire body and the response it generates in his female human beloved. The tortured body of the vampire beloved becomes a crucial site of ethical action, especially in *Buffy* and *The Vampire Diaries.* When Angel and Stefan are captured and tortured, Buffy, Elena, and Damon reveal their active devotion.

Angel's Beautiful Face and Tortured Body

> I suppose some girls might find him good looking... if they have eyes ("The Pack" 1006).
>
> —Buffy to Willow about Angel

Many of the key semantic and syntactic elements that reverberate through the *Twilight* saga and *The Vampire Diaries* appear first in an extended way in *Buffy the Vampire Slayer.* Beautiful, tortured vampires who provide a flash of flesh appear in other texts—such as *Interview with a Vampire*—but not to the same extent as Angel. Angel's shirtless torso features throughout the first three seasons of *BtVS*, offering a spectacle that directs the gaze to his beauty and often to his pain. Following Scarry who says, "Beauty always takes place in the particular" (*On Beauty and Being Just* 18), I pay particular attention to the scenes that establish Angel's beauty—located first in his face and then on his torso—as an impetus for Buffy's just action, especially as she moves from appreciating and acknowledging his beauty to trying to protect it.

Angel's beauty as object of the gaze permeates the first five episodes, as characters—both female and male—cast their eyes upon him. McCracken argues Angel challenges patriarchy and heteronormativity because "his body is a fantasy space *within the text* as well as outside it, a body to be literally inscribed with girl, queer, and gay desires" (120). She affixes this idea about literal inscription on Angel's wounded body, which I develop later in this chapter, but before his body displays its permeability, it also functions as a discursive site that calls to characters. When Xander first sees Angel, he splutters to Willow, "Well, he's buff! She never said anything about him being buff!... He's a very attractive man! How come *that* never came up?" ("Teacher's Pet" 1004). Similarly, when Angel walks past Cordelia in the Bronze, she exclaims, "Oooo! Hello salty goodness. Pick up the phone. Call 911. That boy is gonna need some serious oxygen after I'm through with him" ("Never Kill a Boy on the First Date" 1005). Both Xander and Cordelia's comments establish Angel's beauty as cause for attraction and consumption. Xander says Angel is attractive, but, tellingly, he also gives him an abbreviated version of Buffy's name, therein aligning Angel and Buffy.

As McCracken points out, Angel's body functions as a fantasy site inside and outside the text. If the two episodes cited above establish

Angel's beauty within the text, his first appearance in the series also calls to viewers outside the text, for Angel appears to the viewer before any of the characters see him. Angel's first appearance in the first episode follows the horror trope in which a female walks down an empty street followed by a shadowy figure. In this case, Buffy turns a corner and finds herself in an alley. Seemingly frightened, she looks up and the figure rounds the corner, his face hidden by darkness but limned by light. He wears a dark suit and a white button-down shirt, his neck and the top of his chest revealed. He enters the alley tentatively and walks full frontal towards the viewer. The camera pulls closer as he walks forward, his face still hidden. As he moves down the alley, the frame washes in blue light and we see his face. High cheekbones, stylish hair, a strong jaw—his face seems soft not threatening. He continues walking slowly, looking around him. The camera pulls back to reveal Buffy in a handstand on an iron bar above the alley. Angel steps into the light. Buffy swings down, knocks him to the ground, and places a foot on his chest. We finally see his face from Buffy's perspective: the blue light did not hide his attractiveness, but Buffy seems unmoved, more concerned about him as a foe than as an object of beauty. "Why are you following me?" she asks, her foot still firmly planted on his chest. "I know what you're thinking," he responds. "I don't bite." Buffy relents, steps back, and her eyes move down his body and back up again. He moves into full light, as he stands up and brushes himself off.

In this scene, Buffy establishes herself as the perceiver, as the one with more power, even as they scope each other. A stronger white back light makes Angel's white shirt gleam, and the velvet of his black jacket seems slightly over-dressed for stalking. As Buffy and Angel talk, they exchange positions, him standing where she stood and she where he did, so he moves back into the darkness. He answers all her questions but reveals little—he wants what she wants, to kill them, to kill them all; she is standing at the mouth of hell, which is about to open. He warns her not to turn her back, to be ready for the Harvest. He holds knowledge she did not know she lacked. He reaches into his jacket, warns her she needs to be ready, and tosses her a small black box. As they part, his eyes move back into shadow, and his face divides into a dark side and a lit side, a technique *TVD* later employs. His eyes remain cloaked in darkness, so the gaze focuses on his slightly too-red lips, his chiselled jaw, a high cheek bone. Buffy opens the box. Inside rests a large silver cross on a chain. When, in the next scene, Buffy responds to Giles's question about the identity of the mysterious man in the alley who told her about the Harvest, she characteristically grumbles, "This guy. Dark, gorgeous in an annoying sort of way.... I really didn't like him" ("Welcome to the Hellmouth" 1001). The way Angel's face presents to the viewer, however, invites none of this annoyance, unless being annoyed functions as a euphemism for a somatic feeling of being unsettled—or agitated, to use

Carroll's word—of one's body being alerted to and moving out towards another's presence.

Buffy's defensiveness continues in the second episode when they next see each other. When she asks his name and he tells her, she responds, "Angel. It's a pretty name" ("The Harvest" 1002). Buffy articulates her recognition that his name matches his face five episodes later when Giles and Buffy research Angel's history. They find him described in the Watchers' diaries as "the one with the angelic face," to which Buffy replies, "They got that right" ("Angel" 1007). More might be suggested by Angel's name when we return to Scarry's ideas about the immortality and immutability of beauty. She cites Augustine's musings in *De Musica* in which he speaks about how such an eternal and immutable rhythm comes from God (98). I do not suggest a Christian framework for reading beauty, but I do want to complicate Angel's name, his beauty, his immortality, and the role he plays in Buffy's education about fairness in a world where a line between good and evil cannot be drawn easily.

Although Buffy spars with Angel verbally, keeping her guard up, the camera brings them closer to each other. In the first episode, the shot/reverse shot keeps them at medium distance from each other, but in their second conversation, the camera closes in on their faces, bringing them into close proximity visually. When Buffy explains to Angel she has to go into the tunnels because she has a potential friend down there and then retorts, "Do you know what it's like to have a friend?" the camera is close enough to see Angel's face change from his wise-cracking expression to a look of sadness. In this moment, Buffy, too, drops her defenses, and says softly, "That wasn't supposed to be a stumper." They hold each other's gaze for a heartbeat, and then he provides her with intelligence about where the vampires will be. She disappears into the tunnels, and he whispers "good luck" to her departing back, an intimate moment spoken to Buffy but heard by only the viewer.

The growing intimacy and reciprocity between Buffy and Angel continues over the next several episodes, and it often starts as an expression of concern for each other's wellbeing after a moment of seeing—of perception, to use Scarry's terminology. The first time Angel and Buffy see each other after Buffy stops the Harvest from freeing the Master, Angel comes to the Bronze to warn her about another vampire terrorizing the town ("Teacher's Pet" 1004). The episode is framed by two encounters between Buffy and Angel that take place at the Bronze: one at the beginning of the episode and the second at the end. In the first meeting, Buffy sees Angel across the room, framed in the doorway. She goes to him, and says, "Well, look who's here. I'd say it's nice to see you, but then we both know that's a big fib." Buffy continues to taunt Angel about his cryptic warnings and sudden appearances and disappearances. He does not engage with her teasing and instead notes, "You're cold," which Buffy takes as a statement about her verbal ferocity rather than her physical state. Shrugging out of his black leather jacket and putting it around Buffy's shoulders, Angel replies, "No I mean you *look* cold." Shot over Buffy's shoulder, the camera shows Angel's torso, now clothed in only a thin white muscle shirt that highlights the width of his shoulders and the musculature of his arms. It also reveals three deep gashes in Angel's left arm, which Buffy also notices. She leans towards him, as though to touch his arm, but he pulls back and she resists the touch, asking instead what happened. Angel replies noncommittally, "I didn't pay attention." The scene continues with a few more witty and nonchalant questions from Buffy and Angel's trademark tips for how to slay the vampire who left its claw marks on Angel's arm.

The scene I describe above foregrounds for the first time Angel's physical vulnerability and even passivity, for we do not bear witness to the fight but see only evidence of it written on Angel's body. As McCracken astutely notes in her discussion of the eroticization of Angel's body, it invites attention because of its penetrability, and "its simultaneously hard and soft features invite viewers to linger over the erotic possibilities of the passive male" (119). As Buffy teases Giles earlier about his role as watcher, and her role as slayer, so far Angel's role suggests a sphinx-like all-seeing passivity. Unlike Edward's marble hardness or even Stefan and Damon's fast-healing flesh, Angel's skin bears the marks of battles, and bids Buffy and the viewer to pay attention. Even his explanation about the event, "I didn't pay attention," instructs both audiences: pay attention, look closely.

In the second encounter, Buffy sits alone at the bar wearing Angel's leather jacket, as she has been throughout the episode, a visual metaphor for Angel's embrace and protection. A medium shot shows her in profile, and as Angel approaches her, the viewer watches him walk into center frame, but Buffy does not see him until he leans on the bar beside her. She turns her head, so we see her in an over-the-shoulder shot, looking up into Angel's face. A reverse shoulder shot means we now share Buffy's vantage point. A small smile softens Angel's face as he speaks with Buffy, but she remains slightly aloof, trying to pry information from him about who he is and how she might contact him. Ever mysterious but now slightly flirty, Angel avoids her questions with a playful, wry smile—a smile akin to the one Damon later makes his trademark—and moves to the other side of her along the bar. She offers to give him his jacket back, but he declines and says it looks better on her. Angel's admission about Buffy's appearance seems as intimate as touch, as does the way they hold each other's gaze before he moves off into the crowded bar. Buffy watches him go, sees as he turns once to look back at her over his shoulder, and for the first time, Buffy admits her attraction to him and to us as she utters a soft, "Oh boy," with its multiple levels of meaning signifying both his beauty and her pull to him: Oh boy, you are a beautiful man; Oh boy, am I in trouble.

Episode Seven ("Angel") moves from Buffy and Angel acknowledging their attraction to each other to acting upon it. This pivotal episode provides Angel's backstory, and it sets the scenes for Buffy and Angel's first kisses, which I discuss in detail in the next chapter. Before Angel and Buffy kiss each other, however, Angel bleeds for Buffy, and his wound foreshadows his torture at the hand of Drusilla, as I show in the next section. His wound also invites Buffy's touch and leads to the first spectacle of Angel's naked torso. As McCracken argues, Angel's body is "a fantasy construct, a classical body but also a Christ-like, feminine one that is open, vulnerable, and subject to bleeding" (123). Immortal, angelic, but also Christ-like, Angel's wound on the side of his body in this scene bleeds through his white t-shirt, an injury not unlike the place where Christ bled from his side after being speared by a soldier. Angel, too, suffers a tear from a spear when one of The Three breaks off an iron window bar and thrusts it into Angel's side.

After being attacked by The Three, who the Master has sent to kill Buffy, and sensing they cannot defeat them, Buffy helps Angel to his feet and they run back to her house. Once safely inside, Buffy sees the blood on Angel's shirt and directs him to take off his jacket and shirt, so she can bandage his wound. They walk together into the kitchen, Buffy moves to the counter to open a first aid kit, and Angel—his back to Buffy, his face to the viewer—lifts his t-shirt over his head. The titillating medium shot frames Angel's naked chest from the nipples up, and then swings to Buffy's point-of-view, so the muscled V of his back fills the screen. Buffy comments on his "nice tattoo," and then moves in front of him to dress his injury. An intimate two-shot positions Buffy's face next to Angel's naked chest, his erect nipple conspicuously and sensually in the foreground, as he gazes down at her (Figure 2.1). The next thirty-second scene uses a shot/reverse shot to follow their flirtatious looks and speech thick with sexual tension. Buffy's heavily-lip-glossed open mouth may be engaged in conversation with Angel, but she could just as easily bend her mouth to his fully-foregrounded nipple, ripe for the viewer's eye.

The intimate camera places the viewer close enough to see the texture of Angel's skin, the tone and shape of his nipple. We do not, however, see his wound, which exists on the right side of his body, away from the camera. Angel presents as neither Barbara Creed's monstrous male body nor the wounded warrior. As Creed says at the beginning of her essay "Dark Dreams: Male Masochism in the Horror Film," "Whenever male bodies are represented as monstrous in the horror film they assume characteristics usually associated with the female body: they experience a blood cycle, change shape, bleed, give birth, become penetrable, are castrated" (118). Although Angel bleeds and is penetrated in this scene, only Buffy sees his open wound. To the viewer, he stands an embodiment of virility, his nipple erect, his flesh pressing close to the screen and to Buffy.

Figure 2.1 Buffy dresses Angel's wound.

The back and forth nature of this intimate shot/reverse shot simultaneously enhances Angel's beauty and highlights Buffy and the audience beholding his beauty. Distance and then proximity to his body casts the spectator's look as both voyeuristic and erotic, a distinction Neale borrows from Mulvey in order to discuss modes of looking at male bodies. Where Mulvey uses *film noir* to analyze these ways of looking, Neale chooses Westerns and specifically gun-duels to corral the discussion to a primarily all-male spectacle. Voyeuristic viewing places the spectator at a distance from the spectacle, in a position of power, and a fetishistic look draws the spectator close. In gun-duels, Neale argues, "the look begins to oscillate between voyeurism and fetishism as the narrative starts to freeze and spectacle takes over" (17). Insofar as this scene between Angel and Buffy occurs post-fight, we can see the continuity between the voyeuristic spectacle of combat and the fetishistic close-up that stops the narrative "in order to recognize the pleasure of display" (Neale 17). This pleasure, however, differs from the gun-duel because it savors the virile rather than the vulnerable male body.

Angel himself acknowledges the possibility—and probability—of his body's continued vulnerability, for when, at the end of this episode, Buffy asks Angel how he is doing, he replies, "If I can go a little while without being shot or stabbed, I'll be all right." Indeed, Angel makes it through the rest of Season One without a scratch. In fact, his absence informs the rest of Season One, as Buffy does not see him again until the season finale. The closing image of the "Angel" episode, however—of Angel's raw, seared flesh branded from Buffy's cross—remains indelible and foreshadows the torment Angel will suffer midway through Season Two.

The beginning arc of Season Two overlays the carnal with the emotional, as Buffy and Angel admit and try to resist their love and desire for each other. Buffy seeks comfort in Angel's arms after dealing with the aftermath of her fight with the Master ("When She Was Bad" 2001), and Angel admits his jealousy ("Some Assembly Required" 2002, "Lie to Me" 2007). They argue ("Reptile Boy" 2005), they kiss ("Halloween" 2006), and when Buffy feels close to Angel, the camera pulls in to his beautiful face, so we, too, can behold it and be held by it. Of Angel's naked torso, however, we see no sign until he suffers, once again, while trying to protect Buffy ("What's My Line?—Part Two" 2009). The title of this episode refers overtly to a line of work, as Sunnydale High holds a career fair, and Buffy begrudges the fact her career is preordained. Other meanings, however, suggest ethical positions: crossing—or holding—a line; or having a bottom line. Angel's naked torso exposes all these possibilities.

This two-part episode introduces the hard-line vampire slayer Kendra, who—unbeknownst to Buffy and Giles—becomes a slayer when Buffy dies briefly at the end of Season One. When she sees Buffy kissing Angel's vampire face, Kendra assumes both Buffy and Angel are vampires, and therefore must be killed. She locks Angel in a storage room in the bar owned by Willy-the-Snitch and leaves Angel to incinerate. When Willy drags Angel from the room only minutes before the sun comes up, Angel's weakened state means he puts up no resistance, even when Willy dumps him into the sewer for collection by Spike. Exhausted and near death, Angel lands unceremoniously in the sewer, his open shirt revealing his nipple, a sign of his suffering vulnerability but also a reminder of his eroticism, which we first glimpsed in Season One when Buffy tends to the Christ-like gash in his side. If that episode sketches Angel as a sacrificial figure, then "What's My Line?—Part Two" turns that sketch into a spectacular tableau.

The spectacle of Angel's torture begins after Giles discovers Spike and Drusilla need to kill Angel in order to complete a ritual to restore Drusilla's health. Enraged, Buffy says to the Scooby Gang and the spectator, "You can attack me. You can send assassins after me. That's fine. But nobody messes with my boyfriend." Buffy's words segue into the next scene, which shows Drusilla "messing with" Angel, that is, literally messing up his body or figuratively "messing him up." Drusilla's hand languidly caresses the top of a box marked "Holy Water." As Drusilla opens the box, the camera pulls back to an over-the-shoulder shot that features Angel in the foreground, struggling to free himself from the ties that bind his arms to the posts at the end of Drusilla's bed, a posture not dissimilar from being tied to a cross. The camera swings to a two-shot as Drusilla pours holy water down Angel's naked chest, first in dribbles and then in a torrent that makes Angel scream. His head arches back on the bed, and the camera pulls in to a close-up of Angel's mouth open in a scream, creating an iconography that intermingles the erotic and the holy. The effects of Drusilla's torture rake down Angel's chest in lurid red, both marring his beauty and calling more attention to his fleshliness. As Drusilla points out to Spike, Angel's skin "makes pretty colours."

The erotic and holy spectacle reaches its apex when Spike binds Drusilla and Angel together and hangs them on a church altar. Drusilla's full-length long-sleeved black gown accentuates Angel's beautiful flesh and naked vulnerability. Joined at the hips, one arm from each raised high above their heads, they form a carnal crucifix, made all the more explicit when Spike plunges a dagger through their hands to intermingle their blood and Drusilla arches back in ecstasy while Angel screams in agony. Dragged by Spike's vampire henchman into the church at this moment, Buffy bears witness to Angel's torment, her horrified facial expression mirroring the spectator's gaze. Head thrown back, his neck exposed, Angel suffers, an object of the gaze yet unaware of it in his near-unconscious state. When Buffy fights and escapes from Spike's henchmen and releases Angel from his bind, he collapses onto the floor of the sanctuary. Buffy kneels down, cradles his head in her lap, and tenderly caresses his face. Angel's inert body sprawled across Buffy's lap recalls the pieta, further marking him an immortal, sacrificial Christ figure, a beautiful figure worthy of inspiring great art.

As critics note, Angel's suffering body signifies on multiple levels. McCracken, for instance, queers Angel's tortured body to make space for a range of viewing pleasures. Compellingly, she suggests,

> the joys of torturing Angel are linked to non-normative sexual practices, both male and female. But instead of 'demonizing' such practices in the conventional sense, *Buffy* and *Angel* open up a fantasy space in which they are acceptable, pleasurable, and empowering for girls and queer viewers.... any potentially threatening hypermasculinity is replaced by a male body that is not merely an object of female desire, but is continually and aggressively acted upon by teenage girls within the text: Angel is beaten, stabbed, burned, staked, and shot with arrows. What sets Angel apart is *not* simply the fact that his body is the show's primary eye candy, but more importantly, that it is the primary site of pain and trauma: Angel suffers, Angel bleeds, Angel screams so Buffy does not have to. Through Angel, a seemingly normative white male body is recoded as queer, not only through Angel's vampirism but more importantly through his function as a masochistic object of teen girls' erotic pleasure.
>
> (117–118)

I agree with McCracken's analysis of Angel's body as an object of pleasure, but I expand on it by describing the particulars of how his body draws the gaze both inside and outside the text, relating it back to Sobchak's passionate suffering, and to Scarry's notion that beauty requests protection. Buffy saves Angel from torture and death both to preserve his beauty and to act responsibly.

Edward's Sublime Beauty

As with Angel, Edward's beauty aligns initially with his face, at least in film, which personalizes Bella's attraction to Edward and emphasizes his individuality, to return to one of Nussbaum's criteria for love. Unlike in *BtVS*, in *Twilight* Bella and the viewer see Edward at the same time, or rather, the viewer sees Bella seeing Edward, and then sees what she sees: the Cullens walking slow motion into the school cafeteria. Recalling Carroll's methodology of looking to the emotions of human characters for cues about an audience's response, in this scene, the audience follows Bella's curious gaze as she watches the Cullens' entrance, and the music and film speed anticipate and prolong Edward's arrival. Cresting music announces Edward's entrance. A close-up and almost still shot features his face. To alleviate any doubt about the objective nature of Edward's beauty, when Bella sees Edward and asks her schoolmate Jessica who he is, Jessica replies, "That's Edward Cullen. He's totally gorgeous. Obviously." Edward's beauty—and Bella's preoccupation with it—has been well established. Lydia Kokkola refers to Bella's "incessant harping on about Edward's perfection, especially his body beauty" (177) and Natalie Wilson calls the Cullens "walking Greek gods who are classically beautiful as well as ageless, impossibly strong, and perfectly chiseled. They do not need to sleep or breathe or eat. In effect, they are dream bodies for the 21st century—thin, beautiful, young, and hard to kill" (35). Of the fifty occurrences of the word "beautiful" or "beauty" in the novel *Twilight*, almost half the usages describe Edward specifically and another nine refer to all or a particular member of the Cullen family. The final two instances when the word is used in the novel describe Bella at her prom.

Bella's use of the word "beautiful" links her perception of beauty to justice and to the sublime. In her defense of beauty, Scarry details how beauty is diminished in the shadow of the sublime which extends back to the eighteenth century and to Kant's *Observations on the Feeling of the Beautiful and Sublime*. The separation between the sublime and the beautiful does not surprise: the sublime is male, mountainous, Milton's Hell, tall trees, night, moving, dusk, disdain, eternity, great, simple, principled, noble, righteous; the beautiful is female, flowers, meadows, day, charming, lively, gay, cheer, small, multiple, compassionate, good-hearted (82–84). Most relevant to the context of the *Twilight* saga shapes around Scarry's next question and answer:

> Why should this bifurcation have dealt such a blow to beauty (a blow not intended by the original writers of the treatises nor by later writers on the sublime)? The sublime occasioned the demotion of the beautiful because it ensured that the meadow flowers, rather than being perceived in their *continuity* with the august silence of ancient groves (as they had when the two coinhabited the inclusive realm of beauty), were now seen instead as a *counterpoint* to the grove. Formerly capable of charming or astonishing, now beauty was the not-astonishing; as it was also the not-male, the not-mountainous, the not-righteous, the not-night. Each attribute or illustration of the beautiful became one member of an oppositional pair, and because it was almost always the diminutive member, it was also the dismissible member.
>
> (84)

The *Twilight* saga draws upon and destabilizes this opposition between the sublime and the beautiful. It sets up this distinction initially by aligning Edward with the sublime and Bella with the beautiful, if only through her name in the first instance. This separation between the beautiful and the sublime trembles, however, when aspects of Bella and Edward's relationship embody both elements.

In the novel *Twilight*, Bella's profusive use of the word "beautiful" to describe Edward gains more potency beside the instances in which she employs the word sparingly, at two key structural moments: the first time she uses it in the saga she describes not Edward but Forks (7); the second time she refers to a landscape as beautiful perches almost exactly midway through the novel (232). By looking closely at Bella's descriptions of Forks and Arizona—her two homes—we see how beauty and the sublime radically decenters Bella.

The novel begins with Bella describing her trepidation about moving from Phoenix, Arizona to Forks, Washington. She outlines the heat and clarity of Phoenix and the rain and gloominess of Forks (3). As Charlie drives her from the airport to their home, she stares out the window and thinks,

> It was beautiful, of course; I couldn't deny that. Everything was green: the trees, their trunks covered with moss, their branches hanging with the canopy of it, the ground covered with ferns. Even the air filtered down greenly through the leaves.
>
> It was too green—an alien planet.
>
> (7)

Bella describes the beauty of the forest as excessive and alien, and this initial description foreshadows the formative moment in the forest when Edward reveals himself to Bella in the sunlight. In this scene, Edward reifies his connection with the forest when he uses similar terminology to describe himself: "Most humans instinctively shy away from us, are repelled by our alienness..." (274). By hooking these two moments through the root "alien"—the only times when this word appears throughout the novel—Bella reveals her pull to the beautiful excess of alien otherness.

Edward, too, desires knowledge of the unfamiliar and in his urge to learn more about Bella and her home, he asks her to describe "anything he wasn't familiar with":

> I tried to describe impossible things like the scent of creosote—bitter, slightly resinous, but still pleasant—the high, keening sound of the cicadas in July, the feathery barrenness of the trees, the very size of the sky, extending white-blue from horizon to horizon, barely interrupted by the low mountains covered with purple volcanic rock. The hardest thing to explain was why it was so beautiful to me—to justify a beauty that didn't depend on the sparse, spiny vegetation that often looked half dead, a beauty that had more to do with the exposed shape of land, with the shallow bowls of the valleys between the craggy hills, and the way they held on to the sun. I found myself using my hands as I tried to describe it to him.
>
> (203)

In this description, Bella places the bitter next to the pleasant, noise next to silence, presence next to absence, space next to rock, death next to beauty. She aligns opposites and names them beautiful and when words fail her, she uses her body to bring beauty to Edward.

The first film, too, aligns landscape with the sublime, although moreso the forest and rugged wilderness of Forks, than the spiny, sparse desert Bella tries to describe in the above-cited paragraph. The film relies upon sweeping panoramas of rocky forests to establish Bella's arrival into Forks. This attention to landscape features more significantly, however, in the scene in which Bella confronts Edward about being a vampire, and Edward reveals his brilliant skin to her. I describe this moment in some detail in the next chapter as a prelude to their first kiss, but here I pay more attention to the sublime as a backdrop to and metaphor of their relationship.

Bella leads Edward into Kant's sublime—male, mountainous, tall trees, moving, dusk, disdain, eternity, great, simple, principled, noble, righteous—when she guides him from the school grounds and up into the fog-filled forest. Bella's questions, Edward's admission of his immortality, and then his insistence Bella needs to see him "up the mountain, out of the cloudbank" and into the sunlight expands the sublime setting into a description of their relationship itself as sublime. As Edward speeds with Bella on his back up the mountain, the camera shifts from a close-up of their profiles to an overhead establishing sweep of the pointy pines, and finally to a ground shot up into the silhouetted trees, which stand noble and tall, highlighted by divine streaks of sunlight.

In this sublime setting, Edward demonstrates his own sublime elements when he challenges Bella to see his monstrosity—a principled, noble, righteous act. As a third-party sutured to this scene, the spectator stands behind Bella and watches as Edward moves into the streaming patch of sunlight. A shot/reverse shot slows the scene down and builds suspense and anticipation as the shot shifts between Bella's wide-eyed gaze and Edward's back. As he turns and reveals his shimmering skin to her, Bella's heavy breaths pulse through the landscape in wonder and awe. For the first time, Edward unbuttons his shirt to reveal his naked torso, and the camera closes in on the smooth skin of his belly and chest. Bella exhales, "It's like diamonds.... You're beautiful." Bella's description interpellates Edward into an embodiment of the sublime and the beautiful, the masculine and the feminine. Edward tries to recast himself as a monster by grimacing, "Beautiful? This is the skin of a killer, Bella" and by moving out of the sunlight where he dazzles no longer. Regardless, Bella sees Edward here as radiant and wonderful, a glimmer of her leaning toward loving him.

The scene almost ends with the now-famous exchange, which I return to in Chapter 3, where Edward and Bella admit their love for each other borrowing the biblical reference to the lion lying down with or falling in love with the lamb. I say "almost ends" because this seeming closure blurs into continuity, as the sublime nature of this scene swirls into the meadow moment, which, according to Stephenie Meyer's website, inspired Bella and Edward's story. The strings and piano of Bella's lullaby—the musical backdrop to their conversation and the meadow's only sound—harmonizes the sublime with the beautiful as the camera moves up from their almost-kiss, travels over moss-covered boulders, through the tall tree tops, and finally skims over the surface of a flower-filled meadow to where Bella and Edward sit. As guitar and piano play softly together, Bella and Edward lie down together upon the meadow floor—a visual metaphor for their verbal declaration of love. The camera moves from face to face, we see Edward's chest rise and fall, and then the camera moves away from an intimate gaze to an overhead shot that establishes Edward and Bella as part of the landscape, their clothing the same hues as the meadow flowers. The camera circles overhead, like a bird, and the beloveds turn their heads away from each other to look above them, as the sun reaches down. Edward's face shines like the sun, and as the camera pulls back, we see the meadow framed by the moss-covered branches of tall trees. No longer does the sublime demote the beautiful, for in this scene, the meadow flowers are continuous with the "august silence of the ancient groves"—to return to Scarry's characterization. Meadow flowers and forest, Bella and Edward, the sublime and the beautiful "coinhabit[] the inclusive realm of beauty" and emerge as a metaphor for their relationship.

New Moon reuses this meadow-and-forest metaphor in the opening scene of the film, in which Bella dreams her older self in the meadow with Edward, and again midway through the film when Bella returns to the meadow hoping her visions of Edward will reappear in the place that symbolizes the beginning of their relationship. Instead of the beautiful green meadow dotted with flowers, she finds the grass brown and dead, like her relationship with Edward. Laurent not Edward now stands waiting for her. The meadow becomes a site of her near death, as Laurent strokes her face, an intimate, deadly caress. She closes her eyes and waits for death, but the wolves appear and attack Laurent, which gives Bella time to run away. The presence of the wolves, and especially Jacob, in this meadow brings uninhibited male beauty into Bella's world, a naked beauty unlike Edward's sublime—tactile and inviting rather than hard and cold.

Like Angel's tortured torso, Jacob's shirtless body draws both a voyeuristic and fetishistic gaze, a convention the films exploit both humorously and deliciously. The first time Jacob removes his shirt in the saga occurs when Bella crashes her motorbike, and Jacob lifts his t-shirt over his head to dab blood away from Bella's forehead. The spectator's gaze aligns with Bella's in an over-the-shoulder shot that shapes Jacob's body into a spectacle of ripped abs and toned biceps, a moment that caused the movie theatre audience of which I was a part to gasp and then giggle. Jacob squats down in front of Bella, and the scene now takes place over Jacob's shoulder so we see Bella looking at Jacob. Her eyes move up and down his face, and when Jacob asks, "What are you staring at?" Bella answers, "You're sorta beautiful." Jacob diffuses the potential romantic tension in the situation with humor, and the next film, *Eclipse*, similarly uses humor in the self-referential moment from which this chapter takes its title.

In this scene, Edward drives Bella to a pre-arranged meeting with Jacob, who has agreed to protect Bella while Edward hunts on the eve of their battle against Victoria's army of newborn vampires, a scene I analyze in Chapter 6. Jacob waits for Bella, leaning against the trunk of his car, wearing only a pair of cut-off shorts. As Edward and Bella emerge from their truck, the camera pans to Jacob and freezes the shot to allow for a lingering look at Jacob's muscular chest, bulging arms, and provocative hipbones. This centerfold freeze then cuts to a head shot of Edward looking off screen and asking Bella, "Doesn't he own a shirt?" In a scene characterized by voyeurism, Edward asserts his own sexuality by kissing Bella deeply in front of Jacob. The kiss is filmed in an over-the-shoulder shot in which we watch Jacob watching Bella and Edward kiss. The kiss ends and Bella walks over to Jacob, who embraces her against his naked chest. Her hands touch his skin in her own tentative hug as Edward looks on, the jacketed bodies of Bella and Edward accentuating Jacob's tactile nakedness (Figure 2.2).

Figure 2.2 Doesn't he own a shirt?

Jacob's toned and muscular body provides a startling contrast to Edward's nearly-emaciated torso, which he reveals near the end of *New Moon* when he believes Bella to be dead and decides he does not want to live without her. He goes to the Volturi to goad them into killing him by breaking one of the only vampire rules: not to make a spectacle of oneself. Alice foresees his plan to reveal himself at noon to the people in the town square who gather there for the yearly Saint Marcus Day festival, so she and Bella speed to Volterra to stop Edward from exposing himself. As Buffy saves Angel from death on the church's altar, so Bella protects Edward's beauty: first by moving him out of the sunlight; and then by offering herself as a sacrifice in place of Edward.

Sharing some of the religious iconography that occurs in "What's My Line?—Part Two" of *Buffy*, Edward embodies the emaciated eroticism of a martyr. Church bells chime noon, as Edward walks down an arched corridor moving forward toward the spectator in the center of the frame. He unbuttons his long-sleeved shirt and slides it off his shoulders to reveal his pale gaunt torso, his hipbones knifing into a sharp V, an arrow to his crotch. His eyes downcast, he presents his body as spectacle to the audience in Volterra and beyond the screen. The scene intercuts the simplicity of his exposure with the frantic chaos of Bella running through the crowd trying to reach Edward, editing the scene between beholder and beheld. As Edward crosses the threshold into the sunlight, his eyes resolutely closed, Bella launches her body at him, wraps her arms around him, and entreats him to move inside, out of the sunlight.

Edward's body remains religiously marked when two members of the Volturi arrive to take Edward and Bella to see Aro, leader of the Volturi. They provide Edward with a long red hooded monastic robe that belts in the front and leaves his chest exposed, thus enhancing both his eroticism and his asceticism. This visual metaphor becomes even more overt when

Edward tries to protect Bella during their conversation with Aro in the next scene. When Aro learns Edward cannot read Bella's thoughts and then discovers he himself cannot see her thoughts, he decides to test if Bella is immune to all vampire power. Aro turns to Jane, and Edward intercedes trying to shield Bella from Jane's painful mind power. Jane turns her power on Edward instead and tortures him with her mind. His body writhes in excruciating pain—his head jerks back, the veins on his neck bulge. As the camera pulls back to a full-length shot, Edward's arms outstretch, and his body assumes the shape of a crucifix as he bends to his knees in seeming supplication.

Bella's intervention to protect Edward is more successful than his attempts to deflect pain from her. She pleads with Aro to stop and he listens, and when Jane tries to inflict pain on Bella, she fails. Regardless, Aro decides Bella knows too much about vampires and therefore needs to be killed. Once again, Edward intervenes and, once again, he fails and Bella succeeds. Although critics such as Wilson foreground the impermeability of Edward's body, in this scene, the cracks show—literally. Felix bodyslams Edward to the ground, and Edward's face cracks like the marble floor upon which he lands. Although the crack in his face closes, the violent ferocity with which Edward and Felix fight—and a previous flashback that shows Felix ripping the head off another vampire—does little to alleviate Bella's, and the spectator's, fears for Edward's life. Bella, therefore, pleads again with Aro to stop hurting Edward, and offers her life in exchange for Edward's. Aro gestures to Felix to stop, impressed Bella would give her life to save a vampire. Although it is Alice's affirmation that Bella will become a vampire and not Bella's sacrificial offering that saves Bella and Edward's lives, the main point here is Bella does all she can to protect the beauty of her beloved, her beautiful beloved.

Hidden Stefan and Exposed Damon

The Vampire Diaries provides a cornucopia of beautiful vampire torsos for the eye to feast upon. Where Angel's unclothed body appears sporadically and wounded, and Edward withholds his naked flesh as much as he resists the temptations of it, Stefan and Damon's shirtless torsos feature regularly, at least for the first half of the first season. Eight episodes out of the first ten provide a taster of vampire torso, a tempting treat for the television spectator, who waits with anticipation for the next mouthwatering morsel. After Stefan and Elena have sex for the first time in episode ten, however, aptly titled "The Turning Point," only five out of twelve episodes include a flash of flesh. The first half of the season establishes the pull of Stefan and Damon's beauty, while the second half focuses on the protection of it.

As with Angel and Edward's beauty, so the public first establishes Stefan's attractiveness. In the first episode ("Pilot" 1001), Stefan walks up the sidewalk and down the corridors of Mystic Falls High School and appreciative eyes track his movements. His face remains hidden from the camera, however, until Elena finally talks to him. In other words, his "hot" factor, to use Bonnie's term, appears to Elena and the television spectator at the same time, thus initially aligning the spectator's gaze with Elena's. Halfway through the first episode, however, the spectator alone sees Stefan's naked beauty when a conversation between Stefan and his so-called uncle Zach opens with a shot of Stefan's unclothed torso just before he pulls a t-shirt over his head. In a now-familiar beautiful vampire semantic, such as I discussed in relation to Angel, Stefan faces the camera so his body fills the frame for the viewer's pleasure. Although Stefan is getting dressed, the camera undresses him as it travels from the top of his jeans, over his flat stomach, protruding hipbones, and muscled chest.

Damon, on the other hand, makes his entrance as foreboding brother rather than tantalizing beauty, although the *way* in which he appears does not diminish the effect of his appearance. To return to Bonnie's characterization of the brothers, if Stefan is the "hot" brother, then Damon is "older, sexy, danger guy" ("Family Ties" 1004). The entirety of Season One comprises of Damon controlling the gaze by appearing and disappearing suddenly, and he employs similar tactics of control against Stefan, Elena, and later Caroline. For instance, he announces his return to Stefan in the same way he prefaces his presence with Elena: a crow screeches into the room to distract from Damon's entrance. Through this tactic, Damon controls his initial meetings with both Stefan and Elena and manipulates their gaze by avoiding it until he wants to be seen. When making a sudden appearance he often uses proximity as a strategy of intimidation, leaving little space between his body and the body of his prey. From a distance, however, he stands equally compelling, for he strikes a commanding presence, posing as bait to lure his victims closer, but more often than not, he disappears before they reach him. He draws the gaze to feed desire, and then he withdraws until he stands close enough to control.

Whereas Damon flaunts his beautiful body within the narrative, Stefan keeps his body hidden, a dynamic that sets up the characteristics of their personalities without denying television audiences voyeuristic pleasure. Although the gaze of Elena and the television spectator align when beholding Stefan's face and clothed body, the viewer has access to Stefan's bedroom and his naked body—at least its upper half—long before Elena. The spectator occupies a space in Stefan's bedroom and watches as he goes about his private habits of preparing for his day: putting on a shirt while sitting on his bed; getting out of bed; looking out the window. Repeatedly, Stefan's actions are interrupted by a third-party, so his disclosure of his body to other characters is unintentional, even as the television audience watches voyeuristically: Uncle Zach walks in while Stefan pulls a t-shirt over his head ("Pilot" 1001); Damon talks to Stefan while he puts his shirt back on ("Friday Night Bites" 1003);

Lexi storms in while Stefan dresses for his birthday party ("162 Candles" 1008); and Damon wakes Stefan and watches while Stefan gets dressed ("History Repeating" 1009).

We glimpse Stefan's body in the process of being dressed, but Damon presents his body to us explicitly as an erotic site. In other words, Stefan covers up and Damon uncovers, which characterizes the sensibility of their personas. Whereas Stefan leans towards secrecy, Damon bares all and dares others to look away. His direct gaze, however, challenges and confronts, which creates a dangerous eroticism that becomes explicit the first time we see his naked body sprawled across the sheets of Caroline's bed ("Friday Night Bites" 1003). The sun comes up on this episode as the establishing shot, and then fades into a bedroom and follows the line of a woman's prone body: an elbow; hands resting across the belly of a soft blue negligee; the smooth skin of a woman's chest; a vicious raw gash in the side of her neck. Caroline's eyes flutter open, she gasps, sits up in bed, and looks into a mirror at the end of the bed, directly into the viewer's eyes. Beside her now-alert body lies another body, an arm flung outside the covers, the face in the shadows. The camera swings overhead, as Caroline touches her neck and looks beside her and then follows her gaze, so we see Damon asleep. He looks peaceful, vulnerable, his chest and belly exposed, his head turned sideways, so the normal challenge of his eyes does not threaten. Regardless, the foreboding music and Caroline's tentative movements as she tiptoes across the floor composes the bedroom as a site of terror. Her hand reaches slowly for the doorknob. She turns her head to look back at the now-empty bed. A cheery "good morning" terrifies, as Caroline swings around and comes face-to-face with Damon. Although Damon's compulsion of Caroline defuses the scene so she no longer feels fear, the possibility of his dangerous eroticism remains.

Damon's eroticism overlays Stefan's restraint, which appears through the gesture of Stefan repeatedly putting on his shirt whereas Damon takes off his shirt, or leaves it unbuttoned all the way, so it hangs from his body and highlights rather than hides his sexiness. One of the most overt instances of this distinction takes place in the same episode ("Friday Night Bites" 1003) I describe in the previous paragraph and occurs in a dream that foreshadows and suggests Elena's attraction to both brothers. Although Damon seemingly manufactures the dream, rather than it stemming from Elena's own unconscious, it nevertheless leaves her screaming and breathless. The dream takes place shortly after a dinner party Elena holds so Stefan and Bonnie might become better acquainted. Damon compels Caroline to attend the dinner, so he can be invited into Elena's house. I discuss this episode more fully in Chapter 3 because it reveals Damon's tenderness, but in this instance, it also features Damon's power of control.

The scene follows seamlessly from the end of the dinner party, so the viewer has no sense it is a dream until Elena awakens from it. It, therefore, erases the separation between dreams and waking life, between desire and action. The dream opens with Stefan and Elena sitting on her bed, talking about the evening. Elena admits to Stefan she had fun and says Damon "isn't as bad as you make him out to be." Stefan puts a finger to Elena's mouth to stop her from talking and then leans in to kiss her. As the kissing becomes more intense, Elena pushes Stefan back on the bed, kneels above him, and pulls her shirt over her head. She leans down to kiss him and then sits up to watch him take off his shirt. As he pulls the shirt above his face, Elena—and the spectator—see not Stefan's face but Damon's, smiling smugly up at her. She screams, jumps off his now-naked chest, and awakens. This visual metaphor shows Elena straddling the two brothers, one reserved and silencing, the other cocky and shocking—but both beautiful.

Following the syntax set forth in *Buffy* and the *Twilight* saga, now the human girl—in this case Elena—has established and beheld the beautiful, impermeable vampire body, it reveals itself as more vulnerable and penetrable. For instance, although Stefan breaks a finger and suffers a cut to his hand in "Friday Night Bites," these wounds do not mar his beauty or threaten his existence. Rather, the torso—the site of the heart—signifies beauty, love, and weakness, since a wooden stake through the heart functions as one of the easiest ways to kill a vampire. One of the most explicit examples of the penetrability of the beautiful vampire body occurs early in Season One of *The Vampire Diaries* in a complicated scene of violence, anger, power, and eroticism, in which the Salvatore brothers penetrate each other and therein expose their mutual yet variable vulnerability ("Family Ties" 1004). Damon's practice of drinking human blood makes him stronger and less physically at risk than Stefan, and this episode edifies this distinction between the brothers.

The episode begins with Damon showing off his mental strength through his ability to give Stefan a nightmare in which Damon terrorizes Elena. Stefan awakens from his dream, sits up in bed, and finds Damon seated casually at a desk in Stefan's bedroom. Damon goads Stefan with how easy it is to get into his head, so Stefan speeds out of bed, picks up a letter opener, and throws it across the room into Damon's chest, just below his heart. Damon slowly stands up, pulls the letter opener out of his chest easily, and says, "All right. I deserved that." As their conversation continues in a shot/reverse shot sequence, Damon moves slowly towards Stefan, who reminds Damon that Elena wears a Vervain necklace, which keeps Damon out of her head. Coming ever closer to Stefan, Damon seductively and tauntingly replies, "maybe that's not my target. Believe it or not, Stefan, some girls don't need my persuasion. Some girls just can't resist my good looks, my style and my charm. And my unflinching ability to listen to Taylor Swift." Damon finishes speaking, and then he swiftly plunges the letter opener into Stefan's side. As Stefan crumples to his knees in agony, Damon looks at the cut in his t-shirt and quips, "This is John Varvatos, dude. Dick move," before he walks out of the room. Stefan groans, pulls the letter opener out slowly, and then lifts up his shirt to look at the wound. Filmed as a full frontal medium shot level with Stefan's torso, the sequence invites the eye and the hand in its familiarity with the scene in which Buffy tends to Angel's wound. Here, however, the bleeding cut may as well be the vertical line that defines Stefan's six-pack until the camera moves in to an extreme close-up of abs, cut, dripping blood, and finally the fast-healing flesh that seals itself, not unlike the way the crack in Edward's cheek closes. The t-shirt comes back down, Stefan exhales, looks towards Damon's exit, and the credits roll. In this opening sequence, Damon and Stefan penetrate and are penetrated by each other, and Damon's comment to Stefan about making a "dick move" heightens the homo/eroticism of the scene. Damon's control of the situation, his refusal to show his wound, and his witty one-liner in which he riffs about his attractiveness to women casts him as more hegemonically masculine, but Stefan's exposed and wounded flesh draws the spectator close (Figure 2.3).

The characteristics that define the brothers—of Stefan as good and modest and Damon as evil and annoying—come to a turning point in the same appropriately-titled episode in which Damon's vulnerability and Stefan's eroticism emerge and change the dynamics of the series and an understanding about the unfixed nature of good and evil ("The Turning Point" 1010). In this episode, Stefan and Damon must work together to protect Elena and Mystic Falls from Logan Fell, a new rogue vampire on a killing spree. As the episode progresses, it becomes clear Stefan no longer stands firmly as the virtuous good brother and Damon as the immoral bad boy, and Damon's visibly wounded body

Figure 2.3 Damon stabs Stefan with a letter opener.

and Stefan's sensual body mark this shift. Damon's body, riddled with bullets, demonstrates he can be hurt, and Stefan's willingness finally to remove his shirt shows his erotic side. The change also links to just action as Damon works with Sherriff Forbes to protect the citizens of Mystic Falls, and Stefan changes his mind about leaving town so he can protect Elena from Logan.

Damon and Stefan divide the protection duty between them with Damon tracking Logan and Stefan protecting Elena. Damon finds Logan in a storage unit where Logan disposes of the bodies of his victims. Angry at Damon for being the one who killed him initially, Logan shoots Damon with wooden bullets in his arms, chest, and legs, which incapacitates but does not kill him, and then leaves Damon writhing in pain, so Logan can make his escape. The next time Damon appears, he is back at home, talking to Stefan on the phone, telling him about being ambushed by Logan. As he talks, he stands in front a mirror angrily shrugging out of his shirt, exposing his torso in the mirror and his back to the camera. Here, for the first time, the spectator sees that Damon, too, can be wounded, for his side, chest, and shoulder bear streaks of blood, although his beautifully-muscled back remains flawless.

In this episode, the exposure of Damon's physical pain parallels the visibility of Stefan's emotional pain. Although I discuss in Chapter 4 the scene in which Elena convinces Stefan not to leave her, a scene that leads to the first time they have sex, this scene also resonates here, for as Stefan opens himself to Elena's love, Plumb's song "Cut" articulates that tears "drip sore" and love cuts. When Stefan finally—finally!—takes off his shirt, the moment oozes sensuality as Elena places her hands on either side of his naked torso and gazes at its beauty. The scene accelerates into a series of cut shots: her hands grasp his sides, his hands brush her face, lips taste lips, her cheek presses to his chest. This moment of their intimacy pulls the viewer into tactile proximity, while the musical ecstasy proclaims over and over, "I am cut."

The syntax that occurs in *Buffy* and the *Twilight* saga in which the human girl beholds the beauty of the vampire boy and then takes action to protect his beauty continues in *The Vampire Diaries*. Elena's discovery that she looks like Katherine cuts short the bliss of Elena and Stefan's love-making, opens a space in Elena's heart for Damon, and initiates the possibility she finds both brothers beautiful and worthy of, and in need of, protection. Over the next seven episodes, Elena saves Damon's life ("Bloodlines" 1011); Elena, Stefan, and Damon occupy the same bed ("Children of the Damned" 1013); and Elena's pull towards Damon becomes apparent through a gesture in which she buttons up Damon's shirt for him as Stefan walks into the room ("A Few Good Men" 1015). Taken together, these episodes more than suggest an erotic threesome, and as Damon teases, "You know, I really like this whole ménage-a-threesome team thing. It's got a bit of a kink to it. Don't screw it up" ("Children of the Damned" 1013). The "kink" and "screw" of the dynamic between the three of them implies an alternative eroticism, but when Pearl—a 500-year old vampire released from the tomb—thrusts her fingers into Damon's eye sockets ("There Goes the Neighbourhood" 1016), she reminds Damon that penetration can be unpleasantly violent, too.

Stefan's physical weakness and Elena's commitment to protecting him from bodily harm occurs for the first time near the end of Season One and initiates a narrative arc about saving—or protecting—a beloved that repeats throughout the series. The arc begins when a group of vampires kidnap Stefan because they blame Stefan and Damon for their imprisonment in a tomb. They seek revenge through torturing Stefan: they stab him in the side, use Vervain-soaked ropes to hang him by his arms from the ceiling, and then slice open his skin in a line from above his heart to the other side of his chest, therein marring his body ("Let the Right One In" 2017). Stefan's strung-up body resembles Angel's hanging body in the ritual to save Drusilla, and Edward's suspended and tortured body under the power of Jane. In all three cases, the human beloveds—with the help of their friends—break the bonds that torment their beautiful vampires, literally, in this instance, as Elena releases the Vervain ropes, while Damon and Alaric fight the other vampires to distract from Elena and Stefan's escape.

Although Damon's body sustains wounds from bullets, a letter opener, fists, and fingers, his greatest pain occurs not physically but emotionally. Season One sets up the premise that Damon returns to Mystic Falls in order to free his great love Katherine from the tomb in which she has been imprisoned for the past 145 years. After he discovers she was never in the tomb ("Fool Me Once" 2014), he shifts his attention from saving Katherine to saving Stefan, who succumbs to his addiction to human blood. Damon and Elena grow closer, as they work together to help Stefan. When Damon seemingly kisses Elena in the final episode but then learns he actually kissed Katherine, his old wound for her reopens. I analyze this scene more fully in Chapter 3, but I close this current chapter with a brief discussion about how Damon's physical body reveals his emotional pain.

This chapter puts flesh on the bones of an argument that the beautiful, physically penetrable bodies of the vampire beloveds reveal their emotional vulnerability, a necessity for opening oneself to a lover. Damon appears to be the most emotionally impenetrable beloved because he repeatedly refuses to declare his ability or willingness to love. Elena, however, introduces—and Damon confirms—his emotional vulnerability in the first episode in Season Two ("The Return" 2001) when he discovers he kissed Katherine and not Elena. Elena approaches him at Mayor Lockwood's funeral and asks him how he is doing in relation to Katherine's return, and the following conversation takes place:

DAMON: I kissed you. I thought you kissed me back. Doppelgänger hijinks ensued. How do you think I'm doing?

ELENA: I think that you're hurt.

DAMON: Mmmm, no, I don't get hurt, Elena.

ELENA: No, you don't *admit* that you get hurt. You get angry and cover it up and then you do something stupid.

DAMON: You're scared. You think Katherine's going to send me off the deep end, don't you? I don't need her for that. You know what? Why is it such a surprise that I would kiss you?

ELENA: That's not a surprise. I'm surprised you that thought I'd kiss you back.

DAMON: Now I'm hurt.

Although Elena does not speak cruelly, her words cut and the pain registers on Damon's face, as his smile drops away and he swallows deeply before responding. In one of the many interruptions that break the intimacy between Damon and Elena, Bonnie arrives, and the conversation ends.

Damon reveals his naked vulnerability in matters of the heart even more emphatically later in the same episode. After the funeral, Damon returns home to find Katherine waiting for him, so she can say goodbye. When she asks Damon for a goodbye kiss, he says, "Why don't I kill you instead?" She scoffs, "Kiss me. Or kill me. Which will it be, Damon? We both know that you're only capable of one." The ensuing kiss begins with his hand on her throat—the kill that turns into a kiss—and eventually builds until Katherine rips open his shirt and he pauses,

> Ok, wait wait. I have a question: answer it and it's back to the fireworks and rockets' red glare. Answer it right, and I'll forget the last hundred and forty-five years I've spent missing you. I'll forget how much I loved you. I'll forget everything, and we can start over. This can be our defining moment because when we have the time... that's the beauty of eternity. I just need the truth. Just once.

As he speaks—his open shirt exposing his naked chest, his vulnerable heart—he moves closer and closer to her until he caresses her face and brushes her hair back from her cheek in the intimate tender gesture with which he touches Elena while she sleeps, which I discuss in the next chapter. Katherine stops him saying she knows his question and she knows its answer: "The truth is: I've never loved you. It was always Stefan." She removes his hands from her face and walks away, and the swelling string music cannot cover the sound of Damon's tormented gasp. His vulnerability and his willingness to expose himself for love mark Damon from this point forward.

This chapter establishes the male body as a site of pleasure and pain, impermeability and vulnerability, beauty to be beheld and protected.

Each series establishes beauty to be protected and equates such protection to right action, but the beholders inside and outside the narratives also take pleasure in observing such beauty. Drawing upon Kant's observation about the inexhaustibility of our desire for beauty, Scarry observes, "No matter how long beautiful things endure, they cannot out-endure our longing for them.... Efforts may even be made to prolong our access to its beauty beyond its death..." (50). The beauty of immortals such as Angel, Edward, Damon, and Stefan endures *even though* they are dead, and for their beloveds the longing continues because their beauty never fades. The same might be said about the pleasure of viewers for whom access to these beautiful immortals continues as long as DVDs, reruns, Netflix, iTunes, and their next incarnations exist.

Works Cited

"162 Candles." *The Vampire Diaries.* Writ. Kevin Williamson and Julie Plec. Dir. Rick Bota. CWTV. 5 November 2009. Television.

Abbott, Stacey. *Celluloid Vampires: Life after Death in the Modern World.* Austin: U of Texas P, 2007. Print.

"A Few Good Men." *The Vampire Diaries.* Writ. Kevin Williamson and Julie Plec. Dir. Joshua Butler. CWTV. 25 March 2010. Television.

"Angel." *Buffy the Vampire Slayer: The Complete First Season on DVD.* Writ. David Greenwalt. Dir. Scott Brazil. Twentieth Century Fox, 2001. DVD.

"Becoming, Part One." *Buffy the Vampire Slayer: The Complete Second Season on DVD.* Writ. and Dir. Joss Whedon. Twentieth Century Fox, 2002. DVD.

Berger, John. *Ways of Seeing.* New York: Viking P, 1973. Print.

"Bloodlines." *The Vampire Diaries.* Writ. Kevin Williamson and Julie Plec. Dir. David Barrett. CWTV. 21 January 2010. Television.

"Children of the Damned." *The Vampire Diaries.* Writ. Kevin Williamson and Julie Plec. Dir. Marcos Siega. CWTV. 4 February 2010. Television.

Creed, Barbara. "Dark Desires: Male Masochism in the Horror Film." *Screening the Male: Exploring Masculinities in the Hollywood Cinema.* Eds. Steven Cohan and Ina M. Hark. London: Routledge, 1993. 118–133. Print.

Diamond, Fleur. "Beauty and the Beautiful Beast: Stephenie Meyer's *Twilight* Saga and the Quest for a Transgressive Female Desire." *Australian Feminist Studies* 26.67 (2011): 41–55. Print.

Edwards, Kim. "Good Looks and Sex Symbols: The Power of the Gaze and the Displacement of the Erotic in *Twilight*." *Screen Education* 53 (2009): 26–32. Electronic.

"Family Ties." *The Vampire Diaries.* Writ. Kevin Williamson and Julie Plec. Dir. David Barrett. CWTV. 21 January 2010. Television.

"Fool Me Once." *The Vampire Diaries.* Writ. Brett Conrad. Dir. Marcos Siega. CWTV. 11 February 2010. Television.

"Friday Night Bites." *The Vampire Diaries.* Writ. Barbie Kligman and Bryan M. Holden. Dir. John Dahl. CWTV. 1 October 2009. Television.

"Halloween." *Buffy the Vampire Slayer: The Complete Second Season on DVD.* Writ. Carl Ellsworth. Dir. Bruce Seth Green. Twentieth Century Fox, 2002. DVD.

"The Harvest." *Buffy the Vampire Slayer: The Complete First Season on DVD.* Writ. Joss Whedon. Dir. John T. Kretchmer. Twentieth Century Fox, 2001. DVD.

"History Repeating." *The Vampire Diaries.* Writ. Bryan M. Holdman and Brian Young. Dir. Marcos Siega. CWTV. 12 November 2009. Television.

Interview with the Vampire. Writ. Anne Rice. Dir. Neil Jordan, 1994. DVD.

Kokkola, Lydia. "Virtuous Vampires and Voluptuous Vamps: Romance Conventions Reconsidered in Stephenie Meyer's *Twilight.*" *Children's Literature in Education* 42 (2011): 165–179. Print.

"Let the Right One In." *The Vampire Diaries.* Writ. Kevin Williamson and Julie Plec. Dir. Dennis Smith. CWTV. 8 April 2010. Television.

"Lie to Me." *Buffy the Vampire Slayer: The Complete Second Season on DVD.* Writ. Joss Whedon. Dir. Joss Whedon. Twentieth Century Fox, 2002. DVD.

The Lost Boys. Writ. Janice Fischer and James Jeremias. Dir. Joel Shumacher, 1987. DVD.

McCracken, Allison. "At Stake: Angel's Body, Fantasy Masculinity, and Queer Desire in Teen Television." *Undead TV: Essays on Buffy the Vampire Slayer.* Eds, Elana Levine and Lisa Parks. London: Duke UP, 2007. 116–144. Print.

Meyer, Stephenie. *Breaking Dawn.* New York: Little Brown, 2008. Print.

———. *Eclipse.* New York: Little Brown, 2007. Print.

———. *New Moon.* New York: Little Brown, 2006. Print.

———. *Twilight.* New York: Little Brown, 2005. Print.

Mulvey, Laura. *Visual and Other Pleasures.* Bloomington: Indiana UP, 1989. Print.

Murdoch, Iris. *The Sovereignty of Good.* 1970. New York: Routledge, 2013. Print.

Neale, Steve. "Masculinity as Spectacle: Reflections on Men and Mainstream Cinema." *Screening the Male: Exploring Masculinities in the Hollywood Cinema.* Eds. Steven Cohan and Ina M. Hark. London: Routledge, 1993. 9–20. Print.

"Never Kill a Boy on the First Date." *Buffy the Vampire Slayer: The Complete First Season on DVD.* Writ. Rob Des Hotel and Dean Batali. Dir. David Semel. Twentieth Century Fox, 2001. DVD.

"The Pack." *Buffy the Vampire Slayer: The Complete First Season on DVD.* Writ. Matt Kiene and Joe Reinkemeyer. Dir. Bruce Seth Green. Twentieth Century Fox, 2001. DVD.

"Pilot." *The Vampire Diaries.* Writ. Kevin Williamson and Julie Plec. Dir. Marcos Siega. CWTV. 10 September 2009. Television.

Plumb. "Cut." *Chaotic Resolve*, Curb, 2006. Song.

"Reptile Boy." *Buffy the Vampire Slayer: The Complete Second Season on DVD.* Writ. and Dir. David Greenwalt. Twentieth Century Fox, 2002. DVD.

"The Return." *The Vampire Diaries.* Writ. Kevin Williamson and Julie Plec. Dir. J. Miller Tobin. CWTV. 9 September 2010. Television.

Scarry, Elaine. *On Beauty and Being Just.* Princeton: Princeton UP, 1999. Print.

Sobchack, Vivian. *Carnal Thoughts: Embodiment and Moving Image Culture.* Berkeley: U of California P, 2004. Print.

"Some Assembly Required." *Buffy the Vampire Slayer: The Complete Second Season on DVD.* Writ. Ty King. Dir. Bruce Seth Green. Twentieth Century Fox, 2002. DVD.

Spooner, Catherine. "*Gothic Charm School*; or, How Vampires Learned to Sparkle." *Open Graves, Open Minds: Representations of Vampires and the Undead from the Enlightenment to the Present Day.* Eds. S. George and B. Hughes. Manchester: Manchester UP, 2013. 146–164. Print.

Taylor, Jessica. "Romance and the Female Gaze: Obscuring Gendered Violence in *The Twilight Saga.*" *Feminist Media Studies* 14.3 (2014): 388–402. Print.

"Teacher's Pet." *Buffy the Vampire Slayer: The Complete First Season on DVD.* Writ. David Greenwalt. Dir. Bruce Seth Green. Twentieth Century Fox, 2001. DVD.

"There Goes The Neighbourhood." *The Vampire Diaries.* Writ. Bryan Oh and Andrew Chambliss. Dir. Kevin Bray. CWTV. 1 April 2010. Television.

"The Turning Point." *The Vampire Diaries.* Teleplay Kevin Williamson and Julie Plec. Story Barbie Kligman. Dir. J. Miller Tobin. CWTV. 19 November 2009. Television.

Twilight. Writ. Melissa Rosenberg. Dir. Catherine Hardwicke, 2008. DVD.

The Twilight Saga: New Moon. Writ. Melissa Rosenberg. Dir. Chris Weitz, 2009. DVD.

Wasson, Sara and Sarah Artt. "The Twilight Saga and the Pleasures of Spectatorship: The Broken Body and the Shining Body." *Open Graves, Open Minds: Representations of Vampires and the Undead from the Enlightenment to the Present Day.* Eds. S. George and B. Hughes. Manchester: Manchester UP, 2013. 181–191. Print.

"Welcome to the Hellmouth." *Buffy the Vampire Slayer: The Complete First Season on DVD.* Writ. Joss Whedon. Dir. Charles Martin Smith. Twentieth Century Fox, 2001. DVD.

"What's My Line?—Part One." *Buffy the Vampire Slayer: The Complete Second Season on DVD.* Writ. Howard Gordon and Marti Noxon. Dir. David Solomon. Twentieth Century Fox, 2002. DVD.

"What's My Line?—Part Two." *Buffy the Vampire Slayer: The Complete Second Season on DVD.* Writ. Marti Noxon. Dir. David Semel. Twentieth Century Fox, 2002. DVD.

"When She Was Bad." *Buffy the Vampire Slayer: The Complete Second Season on DVD.* Writ. and Dir. Joss Whedon. Twentieth Century Fox, 2002. DVD.

Wilson, Natalie. *Seduced by Twilight: The Allure and Contradictory Messages of the Popular Saga.* Jefferson, NC: McFarland & Co, 2011. Print.

3 "I Could See Your Heart"
Looking Leads to Kissing

> Did you think she'd understand? That she would look at your face—your true face—and give you a kiss?
>
> —("Angel" 1007)

Really looking—open eyes—leads to open mouths, a dangerous proposition when one kisses a vampire. In his article, "Love as a Moral Emotion," J. David Velleman engages with Iris Murdoch's theory that "love is an exercise in 'really looking'" and suggests this process of loving "arrests our tendencies toward emotional self-protection from another person, tendencies to draw ourselves in and close ourselves off from being affected by him. Love disarms our emotional defences; it makes us vulnerable to the other" (361). This chapter maps how looking—and sometimes lurking—begins this process of disarming defences and how kissing brings the gaze even closer. It charts the development of love between Angel and Buffy; Edward and Bella; Stefan and Elena; and Damon and Elena from moments of "really looking" through their first kisses, which establish their love, openness, and vulnerability.

By following Angel, Buffy, Edward, Bella, Damon, Elena, and Stefan through years and stages of their love, we attend to the details of their relationships, and we learn about what it might mean to love. Nussbaum reminds us, "love ... cannot be well understood unless we examine it as part of the complex fabric of a story that extends over time" (*Upheavals* 473), and she argues, "a certain sort of story shows or represents emotion but also that emotion itself is the acceptance of, the assent to live according to, a certain sort of story. Stories, in short, contain and teach forms of feeling, forms of life" (*Love's Knowledge* 287). These vampire-human love stories situate emotions and especially love at the heart of what it means to live ethically, even when it means allowing oneself to be vulnerable.

Looking, Lurking, and Loving

Before Buffy knows Angel exists, Angel watches her and sees how she struggles alone, and in watching he begins to love her. Bella and Edward watch each other across cafeterias, down corridors, and around cars before their looking turns into loving. Finally, Damon's moments of looking open him to Elena far more than Stefan's innocuous presence. Each of the three series links looking to loving: *BtVS* establishes Angel's connection to Buffy over several episodes and seasons; *Twilight* relies upon close-ups and lingering looks; and *The Vampire Diaries* constructs a tension between Stefan and Elena's epic fated love and Damon's volatile challenges to their love. In this section, I analyze the establishment of love through looking and suggest, following Murdoch, such attention to the beloved takes place over time and attaches to the growth of virtue:

> Where virtue is concerned we often apprehend more than we clearly understand and *grow by looking*. ... if we consider what the work of attention is like, how continuously it goes on, and how imperceptibly it builds up structures of value round about us, we shall not be surprised that at crucial moments of choice most of the business of choosing is already over. ... The moral life, on this view, is something that goes on continually, not something that is switched off in between the occurrence of explicit moral choices. What happens in between such choices is indeed what is crucial.
>
> (30, 36)

Moments of looking, of being attentive to the beloved over time, nourishes the moral fiber of the vampire lover. As he watches her and grows to love her, he considers his morals and these considerations inform his later public actions, which I discuss in the next chapter.

For the first six episodes of *BtVS*, Angel lurks around corners, makes quiet comments about Buffy's actions, and materializes in unexpected places. These appearances indicate he watches her closely, without her knowledge. For instance, after Buffy kills the vampire Luke and ends the Harvest, which stops the Master from rising and bringing about an apocalypse, the scene concludes with a shot of Angel standing in the darkness as Buffy and her friends leave the Bronze, the bar in which the Harvest takes place. He whispers to himself, "She did it. I'll be damned" ("The Harvest" 1002), and a poster behind Angel cautions, "Watch your step." Angel's humorous aside and the poster point to the obvious—Angel is indeed damned and one needs be careful—and to Angel's commitment to ensuring both Buffy and the world's continuation.

Angel's presence and his verbal asides demonstrate his dedication to an ethical life, but his initial interactions with Buffy cloak these intentions from her, which place the viewer in a more knowing position than Buffy herself, and is a strategy *TVD* also employs. In the first episode of *BtVS*, Angel follows Buffy down dark streets and back alleys, and when she finally confronts him, he says to her, "Truth is, I'd thought you'd be taller. Or bigger muscles and all that. You're pretty spry, though"

("Welcome to the Hellmouth" 1001). His words indicate her reputation precedes her, but he has never seen her before. Fast forward 2 years to Buffy's eighteenth birthday, and Buffy discovers Angel watched her long before she first met him.

In this birthday episode "Helpless" (3012), the Watcher's Council orders Giles to rid Buffy of her Slayer powers temporarily—without her knowledge—because the Council wants to test her ability to function as a normal human in a ritual to which the Council subjects every Slayer on her eighteenth birthday. Before the test takes place, Buffy goes to Angel's mansion to celebrate her birthday with him. Nestled in front of the fire, Angel gives Buffy a copy of Elizabeth Barrett Browning's *Sonnets from the Portuguese.* Buffy opens the book and sees the inscription, "Always." She then turns the page to the Table of Contents, which lists the first lines of fourteen of the poems, the table itself thus forming a sonnet, which ends with the first lines of Sonnets 43 and 44: "How do I love thee? Let me count the ways / Beloved, thou has brought me many flowers." These opening lines and Angel's inscription confirm Angel's passionate love for Buffy, which makes their break-up eight episodes later all the more devastating.

Furthermore, if we look more closely at Sonnet 43, we see the poem provides an emotional and ethical depth to Angel's love for Buffy, and it also connects their love and emotions to a genealogy of lovers:

How do I love thee? Let me count the ways.
I love thee to the depth and breadth and height
My soul can reach, when feeling out of sight
For the ends of being and ideal grace.
I love thee to the level of every day's
Most quiet need, by sun and candle-light.
I love thee freely, as men strive for right;
I love thee purely, as they turn from praise.
I love thee with the passion put to use
In my old griefs, and with my childhood's faith.
I love thee with a love I seemed to lose
With my lost saints. I love thee with the breath,
Smiles, tears, of all my life; and, if God choose,
I shall but love thee better after death.

The first quatrain addresses a rather standard expansiveness of love, but if we hear this "I" in Angel's voice, then the word "soul" speaks of a unique love between the only vampire with a soul and his human beloved. This soulfulness then infuses the rest of the poem as a promise to love well and to act virtuously because of this love. To "love thee freely, as men strive for right" could be Nussbaum's words describing love and striving as fundamental to moral action. The melancholic tone that underpins this poem attaches to Angel's comparison of his love to the actions of men, an admission he is not a man. Even the reference to "old griefs" may be read as Angel's endeavors to make reparations for his past evil actions. Finally, in an ironic inversion, the last line and its closest rhyme unite breath and death. The poem's speaker puts emphasis on loving with all her breath, but given the undead vampire does not breathe, the final line, from Angel's perspective implies he loves her better now than he could have as a human, in part because his love exhales beyond breath and into infinity.

The gift and the poem also lend more gravity to Angel's confession he watched her and loved her before they met. In a humorously serious classic *BtVS* moment, Buffy reveals to Angel her fears about losing her Slayer powers:

BUFFY: Before I was the Slayer, I was … well, I don't want to say shallow, but … Let's just say that a certain person who will remain nameless, we'll just call her Spordelia, looked like a classical philosopher next to me. Angel, if I'm not the Slayer, what do I do? What do I have to offer? Why would you like me?
ANGEL: I saw you before you became the Slayer.
BUFFY: What?
ANGEL: I watched you, and I saw you called. It was a bright afternoon out in front of your school. You walked down the steps … and … and I loved you.
BUFFY: Why?
ANGEL: 'Cause I could see your heart. You held it before you for everyone to see. And I worried that it would be bruised or torn, and more than anything in my life I wanted to keep it safe … to warm it with my own.
BUFFY: That's beautiful. Or taken literally, incredibly gross.
ANGEL: I was just thinking that, too.

Now, Angel's "Always" inscription extends back to the moment he first saw Buffy and forward into an unbounded future. At this stage, the story gives no sense of how long Angel watched Buffy before he saw her called, but, regardless, his emphasis on seeing her before she became a Slayer comingles love and looking. When Buffy rightly asks why watching leads to loving, suspicious that watching is not enough, wary he seeks to comfort her rather than speak the truth, Angel responds with a metaphor that encapsulates how Buffy's expansive love awakens Angel's love. Significantly, both Buffy's openness and Angel's protective response project love outward to an other and initiates moral action. He seeks to protect and warm her, and together those impulses become gestures of justice that stitch together the rest of her series and his.

Looking initiates love in the *Twilight* saga more mutually than in *BtVS*. Buffy and Angel's love begins with Angel's watching and Buffy's response to his loving looks and actions, but Bella and Edward's relationship builds as they watch each other. In her article "Good Looks and Sex Symbols: the Power of the Gaze and the Displacement of the Erotic in *Twilight*," Kim Edwards argues, *Twilight* "explores the influence of 'the look' in constructing teen identity, high school culture and sexual awakening: that we can look to learn, control, attack and sexualize" (28). I agree the look forms part of these actions, and we see the look controlling or compelling explicitly in *The Vampire Diaries*. The look also can be reciprocal, however, and in that shared look beholder and beheld meld together and contain the potential to mold into love.

Bella and Edward establish their relationship by first gazing upon each other. Bella spies Edward on her first day of school, as she sits with her new classmates in the cafeteria. Not expecting anyone to catch her eye, Bella is drawn towards Edward and the other younger members of the Cullen clan—Alice, Jasper, Rosalie, and Emmett—as soon as they waft into her line of sight. In the novel, Bella "stares" at the Cullens, who "caught, and held, [her] attention" (*Twilight* 17). As the scene progresses, she continues to stare and can't "look away" (18). When Bella and Edward meet each other's eyes for the first time, their initial dynamic—her insecurity and his boldness—appears:

> As I examined them, the youngest ... looked up and met my gaze, this time with evident curiosity in his expression. As I looked swiftly away, it seemed to me that his glance held some kind of unmet expectation.
>
> "Which one is the boy with the reddish brown hair ?" I asked. I peeked at him from the corner of my eye, and he was still staring at me, but not gawking like the other students had today—he had a slightly frustrated expression. I looked down again.
>
> (22)

Edward's "staring" contrasts with the other students' "gawking," which distinguishes between different types of looking and suggests Edward's gaze contains a depth and particularity that pertains to Bella's uniqueness and not to her position as the new girl in school.

The film translates the novel's verbs and mood into a series of slow-motion shots and close-ups on Edward and Bella's eyes. As Edwards astutely notes,

> in *Twilight* the obsession with the gaze in the novel translates onto the screen with new intensity. We are looking through the camera that is looking at the characters who are looking at each other. Viewers not only gaze with desire at the enviable young breed of performers who

> exemplify teen fantasy perfection, but are able to use the viewing experience to directly empathise with the characters' own fascination with the act of looking and thus identify with and map themselves onto the visual narrative. The shifting and interrelated meaning between the novel's nouns and verbs of seeing ... are developed in the film with the interplay of 'good-looking' and 'good looking' as the double attraction of scopophilia.
>
> (28)

In this passage, Edwards links beauty or "good-looking" to close attention or what she calls "good looking." This good looking attaches to ethics, and while Edwards cites empathy here, I extend this ethical pull to other forms of right action, which I develop throughout this book.

Stylistically, *Twilight* employs conventions of vampire films, especially in its focus on a vampire's eyes, and their power to compel. With the dual attention on Bella and Edward's eyes, the film establishes their mutual looking and foreshadows their love and Bella's eventual transformation into a vampire. In this introductory scene, the attention on looking begins when Angela, one of Bella's classmates, points the large lens of a camera at Bella's face and says, "Smile." Bella nervously looks down, as Angela explains she intends to write a feature story about Bella.

This unwanted attention—or not "good looking" to use Edwards' terminology—contrasts to Bella's own sustained looking when she sees the Cullens approach. Guitar music underpins and softens the chaos of the school lunchroom, as Bella sees the Cullens walking past the window, their bodies slivered by horizontal louvered blinds, thus impeding her initial view. In pairs—Rosalie and Emmett, Alice and Jasper—the Cullen family sweeps into the cafeteria in slow motion, as the music crescendos in the background. Edward enters last and alone, metaphorically leaving a space for Bella to fill. The rest of the scene continues to pair Bella and Edward through a series of medium shots that switch between the Cullens' table and the table across the room where Bella sits. In a wordless scene, the camera alternates between Bella looking openly over her shoulder at Edward and him staring forward at her, a frown creasing his brow.

Told from Bella's first-person perspective in the novel and through her voiceover in the film, the story focuses on her perception of Edward and her reading and misreading of his gaze and actions. After their lunchroom encounter, Bella and Edward meet later the same day in Biology class, where Bella perches on a stool next to Edward. Bella peppers her version of the hour-long class with descriptions of his hostile actions. His initial "antagonistic stare" leads her to peek at him occasionally from behind her hair. Near the end of class she looks at him one more time: "He was glaring down at me again, his black eyes full of revulsion. As I flinched away from him, shrinking against my chair, the phrase *if looks could kill* suddenly ran through my mind" (24). The ironic yoking of looking and killing portends the immediate future of their relationship as Edward struggles with his raging desire to kill her by feeding on—not looking at—her. This connection between looking and feeding, however, is made explicit by her classmate Mike later in the narrative after Bella and Edward begin dating. Mike says to her, "You and Cullen, huh? ... I don't like it ... He looks at you like ... like you're something to eat" (*Twilight* 221).

Regardless of Mike's humorous and accurate assessment of this undercurrent in Bella and Edward's budding relationship, the early sections of the novel and the film emphasize Bella and Edward's mutual consideration, although Bella watches more with fascination and Edward with seeming consternation. Bella interprets Edward's apparent aversion to her as hatred, but it eventually emerges he suffers from the twin pains of the unbearable urge to feed on her and the frustration he cannot hear her thoughts. Edward recognizes Bella's particularity, and it drives him to attend to her needs more closely, in part because he cannot hear her thoughts from afar.

Sometimes the act of watching, of really looking, slips from an act of love to a gesture of menace and back again. *Twilight* repeatedly transforms scenes of danger into moments of intimacy, and one of the most disturbing interactions early in the saga occurs when Edward admits to Bella he enters her house secretly. Bella responds, "You spied on me?" But somehow I couldn't infuse my voice with the proper outrage. I was flattered" (292). In the novel, this interaction reads as relatively harmless, especially given Bella's response. She knows the "proper" response should be outrage, but she feels flattered rather than angry or afraid, and her horror stems from the fact he listens to her as she talks in her sleep rather than from the possibility of her demise.

In film, however, the semantics of a vampire entering a woman's bedroom while she sleeps rarely ends well. From the earliest vampire films including Tod Browning's *Dracula*, a woman's bedroom becomes a site of seduction, infused with sexuality and vulnerability. Gaining unwanted entry through a window, the vampire approaches the woman's bed, leans over, and bites her, beginning her transformation into death. *BtVS* draws upon the power of this moment at the beginning of one of its most devastating episodes, "Passion" (2017).

"Passion" takes place three episodes after Angel becomes Angelus, who torments Buffy and her friends. Unable to admit Angel no longer exists in Angelus, Buffy resists killing him. Angelus, in turn, increases the intensity of his torment. The episode begins with Angelus's voiceover defining passion's power: "Passion. It is born, and though uninvited, unwelcome, unwanted, like a cancer, it takes root. It festers. It bleeds. It scabs, only to rupture and bleed anew. It grows, it thrives, until it consumes. It lives, so it must die, in time." The accompanying visuals show Buffy and her friends leaving the Bronze, as Angelus bites a girl in the background. The setting shifts, and we watch Buffy through her bedroom window, beginning to remove her dress. An overlapping dissolve shot transitions to the interior of Buffy's bedroom, where Buffy crawls into bed and turns off her light. Angelus, silhouetted by the moonlight, stands at her window. Another dissolve reveals Buffy sleeping. The camera edges in to Buffy's face, where a single lock of hair tumbles down her cheek. A hand enters the frame and gently lifts the hair from her face. The camera withdraws with the hand and reveals Angelus sitting on Buffy's bed. When Buffy awakens the next morning, she finds next to her pillow a sketch of herself sleeping and realizes Angelus watched her sleep.

As I discuss later in this chapter, *The Vampire Diaries* uses a very similar moment to conclude a pivotal episode for an opposite effect. In "Passion," however, the tenderness of the gesture to brush a lock of hair off Buffy's face jars against the ruthlessness with which Angelus casts aside his victim outside the Bronze and the glee with which he breaks the neck of Jenny Calendar later in the episode. In his opening voiceover, Angelus suggests the line between passion and love narrows to a moment of true happiness. In other words, Angel/Angelus becomes a metaphor for love/passion, both of which materialize unbidden. Angelus makes the link between pain and love three episodes earlier when he says to Spike, "She's stronger than any Slayer you've ever faced. Force won't get it done. You gotta work from the inside. To kill this girl, you have to love her" ("Innocence" 2014). Angelus moves literally inside Buffy's bedroom to work metaphorically from the inside. His sketch of her, which the shooting script describes as "lovingly rendered," portrays his closeness to her and the depth of his knowledge of her. He really looks at her, and in this looking he loves her enough to know how to kill her.

Given these precarious lines between love and death, tenderness and cruelty, "Passion" establishes, it is no wonder the moment in the *Twilight* film when Edward stands at the foot of Bella's bed unsettles. This scene follows on from an argument between Bella and Edward when she confronts him in the hospital where she has been taken after Edward first displays his superhuman speed and strength when he saves Bella from being killed by a truck in the school parking lot, a scene that establishes their mutual looking, as they stare across the parking lot at each other. Edward denies Bella's assertions she saw him standing on the other side of the parking lot and not next to her, as he claims. In other words, Bella trusts what she sees, even as Edward tries to convince her she is mistaken.

This bedroom scene transitions from the bright hospital hallway to a medium shot of the full moon. The overlap edit turns the moon into the circumference of Edward's iris in a close up of his eyes and nose, visual metaphors for the two senses that draw Edward to Bella. The camera cuts to a medium shot of Bella asleep in her bedroom. The sound of a piano—what we later learn is the lullaby Edward has written for Bella—and the soft lighting creates a sensuous atmosphere. Bella's face turns toward the camera, and her gentle writhing indicates her pleasurably agitated dreaming. Suddenly she startles and looks towards the foot of her bed. The camera keeps time with her line of sight, so we share Bella's vision of Edward standing in her bedroom, staring intently at her bed. Edward's expression is intense, but his arms hang by his side, so his body language does not appear threatening, even as his shadow looms large on the bedroom wall behind him. Bella looks at him but does not panic. She turns to flick on the bedside light, and when she looks back to where he stands, the room appears empty. Bella runs her fingers through her hair, shakes her head, and laughs, as if mocking herself for conjuring Edward in her bedroom. Her voiceover reflects, "And that was the first night I dreamt of Edward Cullen." Having shared this moment with her, knowing the implied threat of a man—and/or a vampire—in a woman's bedroom, we fear for Bella's safety, but as Wilson argues, *Twilight* takes "the controlling male gaze and render[s] it both protective and erotic" (*Seduced by Twilight* 120). And as Carroll reminds us about horror films, viewers take their cues from the main character, so Bella's unflappable response to Edward's presence is meant to soothe rather than startle (Figure 3.1).

Edward's habit of watching Bella sleep reworks the vampire bedroom scene and posits a syntactic redetermination—to return to Altman's phrasing—of the bedroom as a site of danger. As I shall discuss shortly, however, the bedroom remains coded as a place of revelation and risk in its staging of the kiss that no longer kills, but still contains the possibility of pain. Before moving on to a discussion of the kiss, however, let me turn to *The Vampire Diaries* to discuss how really looking manifests differently in the relationships between Elena and Stefan and Elena and Damon. Although Stefan and Elena are cast as fated lovers, destined to be together, Damon and Elena offer an alternative to this version

Figure 3.1 Edward watches Bella sleep.

of romantic love. Their relationship challenges fate and creates its own powerful and unique love based on mobility and volatility that connects to Damon's growth as a moral being.

I draw this distinction from Nussbaum's work in *Love's Knowledge*, which privileges "passional response" over "detached thinking" as a way of cultivating morality and "practical insight" (78). I argue Damon's passionate responses arise out of his love for Elena and lead him towards morality. Nussbaum states, "Morality, at its most generous and best, is something mobile and even volatile, something actively caring and sustaining. Its gestures will be nothing more than gestures of death, if it does not retain its capability to move beyond itself into love" (363). Damon moves from gestures of death to acts of love as he strives towards morality, and his volatility staccatos against Stefan's measured solidity. When Elena finally professes her love to Damon in the last episode of Season Four, the crackling fire in the background suits their passion, while Stefan sits unmoving as he eavesdrops from another room on their conversation.

As with the *Twilight* saga, *TVD* continues vampire film conventions through its use of extreme close-up shots on eyes. Whereas the close-ups of Bella and Edward's eyes signify the romantic intimacy of their bond, the zoom shot of a vampire's eyes in *TVD* indicates a moment of compulsion. *TVD* thus recuperates one of the semantic elements of vampire films both *BtVS* and the *Twilight* saga mostly ignore.[1] The series uses the power to compel primarily for three reasons: 1) to force another being to perform particular actions; 2) to erase someone's memory; and 3) to incapacitate a vampire. Where garlic and crosses serve as icons of protection in early vampire films—and in *BtVS* to some extent—*TVD* introduces Vervain—a small purple flower—as a source of protection. Vervain functions semantically as a mixture between garlic and holy water; if a human wears Vervain on her or his body—such as in a necklace or a bracelet—or consumes it in a drink, then that person cannot be compelled by a vampire. If a vampire touches vervain, it acts similarly to acid, or holy water. Most commonly, humans use Vervain to spike a drink and therein perform a test to determine if someone is a vampire. Finally, some vampires—such as Katherine—drink a very very small amount of Vervain, so they become immune to its power. In episode three of the first season, which I shall discuss in more detail shortly, Damon tries to compel Elena, but he quickly discovers—when Elena slaps him in the face for trying to kiss her—Stefan has given Elena a locket that contains Vervain, which makes her immune to his efforts to compel her. When Elena temporarily loses her necklace in a very moving episode I analyze in the next chapter, Damon takes the opportunity to tell her he loves her and then erases her memory of this moment ("Rose" 2008).

If close-up shots of eyes represent proximity and vulnerability as well as control, then Stefan hides himself as early as the opening scenes of the first episode. Stefan arrives at high school wearing sunglasses, already metaphorically shielding himself and his eyes from others. The camera follows him from behind, and when Bonnie and Elena first see him, he stands in the office, his back to the camera. Bonnie stops Elena and asks, "Who's this?" and Elena quips, "All I see is back." The camera swings to a profile close-up of Stefan's eyes, but unlike in *Twilight* where the extreme close-up establishes an intimacy between Bella and Edward, Stefan's sunglasses shield his eyes, until he removes them so he can compel the school secretary to ignore the fact his transcripts are missing. The first words Stefan speaks are to the secretary, when he asks her to "please look again." His first moments of looking, in other words, are not love-based but practical and based on compulsion for his own gain.

Elena, unlike Bonnie, seems uninterested in Stefan. Bonnie continues to gaze at Stefan, but Elena sees her brother Jeremy over Bonnie's shoulder and goes to follow him into the men's washroom. The camera closes in on Jeremy's face as he tips drops into his drug-affected eyes. Elena marches up to him, grabs his face, looks deep into his eyes, and sees he is stoned. She warns him she will be watching him, looking out for him, even if it means "ruining his buzz every time." Elena's love and concern for her brother holds her attention more deeply than a potential love for Stefan, and this consideration repeatedly asserts itself throughout the series as she chooses to protect and care for her family and friends rather than to attend to her own longings.

These gestures of sibling love, however, bump against her future romantic love, literally in this case, when Elena crashes into Stefan as she emerges from the men's bathroom. This scene begins with a transition edit back to the school office where Bonnie continues to watch Stefan. In an over-the-shoulder shot, Bonnie stares intently at Stefan, but Stefan's face remains hidden from the viewer. The camera then tracks Stefan as he walks down the hallway, attracting the stares of Bonnie and Caroline. The shot cuts to Elena in the bathroom, fuming, and as she emerges from the bathroom looking away from the camera, she turns and bumps into Stefan. The camera continues to focus on Elena's face as she stands, speechless, gazing at Stefan. Finally, the camera switches to Stefan, and the viewer sees his face for the first time. The rest of scene plays out in a series of reverse two-shots as the camera switches between Elena and Stefan's faces as they try to move past each other. Stefan finally steps out of the way to allow Elena to pass, and then he turns around to watch her walk away. Elena, too, casts one more look at him over her shoulder, but her face looks more inquisitive than enthralled.

For the first two episodes, the bond between Stefan and Elena grows, as they exchange looks in class—"HAWT-E. STARING @ U," texts Bonnie to Elena—converse at school, and write their thoughts and yearnings in their private journals, which become conversations with each other through their voiceovers. The first lengthy conversation they share takes place on the edge of a cemetery, where Elena has been visiting the grave of her parents and writing in her journal. When Stefan introduces himself to Elena, she says, "I know. We have History together," and the double meaning diminishes when Stefan responds, "And English and French." While Elena means they are in the same History class together, her words also imply they share a history, which is true on multiple levels: Stefan eventually tells Elena he rescued her from drowning in the car crash that killed her parents and then watched her for months afterwards to ensure she was not Katherine ("Bloodlines" 1011); and their many doppelgängers link their fates through centuries.

Elena and Stefan's initial meeting and continued conversations establish their mutual looking and interest and seem to be a solid core for their love. Nussbaum argues for the evolution of love over time and through reciprocity, and it appears as though Elena and Stefan satisfy these criteria: "love cannot exist in a single instant, but requires a pattern of exchange and mutuality, of mutual attention evolving over time ... love is fundamentally a relation, not something in a single person at all—a relation that involves the give and take, over time, of feeling, thought, benefits, conversations" (*Love's Knowledge*, Nussbaum 344). While Stefan and Elena's love does deepen over time, I wonder about its evolution. The relative speed with which Stefan and Elena come together—and Stefan's measured responses and avoided questions—lack relationality. Damon, on the other hand, seemingly refuses to rein in his nature, which results in more reciprocity than Stefan's secrecy.

Damon's hovering presence irritates and worries Stefan, and Damon himself thrives on Stefan's responses. Damon takes great pleasure in watching over and insinuating himself into Stefan's life and playing the part of the bad, unpredictable brother, who potentially threatens Elena's safety. He gleefully and overtly slips into the role of an evil and stereotypical vampire, who stares intently and wafts dramatically into a space in a cloud of fog or screeches into a room in the shape of a crow. He exudes seductive vampiric charm with the quirk of an eyebrow as much as he celebrates his power and nature to kill. When he first meets Elena, he borrrows a classic vampire entrance: a crow streaks into the living room and when Elena turns around, Damon stands dangerously close to her, staring intently at her. He introduces himself to her and flatters her, but then baits her with information he knows will introduce a rift between her and Stefan: he tells her he can see why Stefan is so smitten with her, and then he proceeds to tell her he worries about Stefan because his last girlfriend nearly destroyed him ("The Night of the Comet" 1002). In these initial meetings, Damon seems too simplistically evil, with his vampire tricks, one-liner quips, and piercing blue eyes that seem to be all-seeing.

Midway through episode three, "Friday Night Bites," however, Damon's tightly-bound persona begins to unravel. The title intertextually references the popular film and subsequent television drama, *Friday Night Lights*, which focuses on a small-town high school football team and their loves and losses. In this pivotal episode, Stefan tries out for the football team in an attempt to fit into high school culture and to shun his "mysterious loner guy" reputation. Meanwhile, Damon continues to torment Stefan and to weave himself into Stefan and Elena's lives. At the end of the previous episode, Damon bites Elena's friend Caroline, and in this episode he begins to build a sexual relationship with her, so he can use their intimacy to compel her to act on his behalf. In episode three, he and Caroline arrive uninvited to a dinner party Elena hosts in an attempt to build a friendship between Bonnie and Stefan. Throughout the evening, Damon engages in conversation, but his seemingly compassionate speech acts repeatedly contain his usual double meanings. For instance, when Caroline makes reference to Elena's mistakes in cheerleading practice and blames it on the death of her parents, Damon breaks the awkward silence saying, "I'm sorry, Elena, I know what it's like to lose both your parents. In fact, Stefan and I have watched almost every single person we ever cared about die." On the surface, this admission sounds empathetic, but the underlying implication is because they are vampires and immortal, they watch humans die as they continue to live.

Later in this episode, however, Damon and Elena hold a conversation in the kitchen that initiates a compassionate, reciprocal, and individual relationship between them, which relies upon and reveals their mutual viewing of each other. This two-shot scene pans back and forth between Damon and Elena as they share simple normal domestic tasks, such as doing the dishes and folding linen. Although Elena needs no assistance, Damon reaches for a plate and Elena hands one to him, as though serving his own smugness to him on a platter. As dishes pass between them, so do looks and words, which Damon in past episodes uses to compel and influence. Whereas Stefan repeatedly avoids answering Elena's questions and writes in his diary as a means of expression, Damon does not shy away from Elena and her queries, which makes their relationship satisfy Nussbaum's condition of exchange and mutuality more fully than Stefan's impulse to secrecy.

Damon usually uses words to wound and to woo, but in this moment, he speaks sincerely and with attention to details about Elena's emotional state. The conversation begins when Elena picks up the earlier discussion about the death of his and Stefan's loved ones. When Elena asks what Katherine was like, Damon pauses, and then reflects, "She was beautiful. A lot like you in that department. She was also very complicated. And selfish. And at times not very kind but very sexy and seductive." Elena looks at Damon, picks up a plate, passes it to him, and asks, "So, which one of you dated her first?" Damon takes the plate, chuckles, and comments, "Nicely deduced." Elena notes the nuances that suggest a larger truth beneath what Damon says and, in turn, Damon lets Elena know he sees her sadness when he tells her, "I'd quit cheerleading if I were you. … I saw you at practice. You were miserable." Elena says, "You saw that?" and Damon asks, "Am I wrong?" Although this conversation may seem innocuous and trite, Damon's assessment of Elena's unhappiness portrays a depth of attention to her emotions and her everyday life, and Elena recognizes it as such. His attention to her leads her to look at him and say, "I'm sorry." Damon's brow furrows in confusion, and Elena continues, "About Katherine. You lost her too." Damon stares at Elena, taken aback. His mouth opens and closes, and in his silence, a bond begins to form as their hearts respond to each other in the reciprocal way they attend to each other emotions. The camera frames and follows them in this intimate scene of domesticity, the non-diegetic piano music creates a sweet atmosphere, and the position of the scene at exactly half way through the episode signals its importance as a hinge between the two halves of the episode.

The closing sequences of "Friday Night Bites" encapsulate the tension that infuses the rest of the series by showing Damon to be both a heartless killer and potentially a tender, attentive lover. Stefan confronts Damon about how Damon's love for Katherine—and, by implication, Elena—proves his humanity and then Damon attempts to perform his lack of humanity by mauling the high school football coach to death. Ironically, the coach also teaches History, so Damon metaphorically kills history: the History Stefan and Elena share and the history which has not been kind to Damon in his affairs of the heart. The closing two minutes of the episode, however, undermines Damon's performance as a killer beyond redemption and reveals Stefan's own ability to pretend to be other than what he seems. When Stefan lies to Elena after she confronts him about a cut on his hand that miraculously heals, his lies seem more measured and intentional, more designed to deceive, than Damon's lies to Stefan. Damon resists admitting to his humanity, and Stefan refuses his monstrosity, but Stefan's words mislead others while Damon fools himself.

In a similar closure to the first two episodes, the ending of this one also begins with Stefan's diary voiceover. Instead of harmonizing with Elena's voice, however, Stefan's words become a counterpoint to Damon's actions. Stefan voices the words he writes in his diary and the camera pans from an exterior shot of his house to an interior view of Stefan writing at his desk: "I thought there was hope. That somewhere deep inside, something in Damon was still human. Normal." Stefan's face fades into the blankets on Elena's bed in an edit cut to Elena's bedroom, but this time instead of writing in her own diary as she does in the first two episodes, she lies sleeping in her bed, her diary on top of the bed sheets rather than in her hand. The camera slowly pans over the covers at the bottom of her bed, to the diary, and then to Elena's sleeping form. Stefan's voice continues, "But I was wrong. There's nothing human left in Damon. No good. No kindness. No love." This bedroom scene recalls Angelus's presence in Buffy's bedroom, Edward standing at the foot of Bella's bed, and numerous other vampire movies that draw on a complex combination of fear and yearning a bedroom implies. It borrows these semantics and reapplies them to the specificity of this situation, for as Stefan asserts Damon has no love, he appears in a moment of loving tenderness, gazing down at Elena while she sleeps. The soft glow of Elena's bedside light throws the profile of Damon's face into darkness, and in a similar gesture to Angelus's, the camera travels down Damon's arm until we see his fingers moving ever-so-gently down the hair that frames Elena's face and then softly stroking her cheek with the back of his index finger. The camera pulls back to Damon's face, and now the light illuminates half his face, so he appears as a figure of light and dark simultaneously. This visual metaphor of Damon's embodiment of good and evil jars against Stefan's words that damn Damon as a creature of absolute evil, "a monster who must be stopped."

Even more than the lighting, the music suffuses this scene and Damon's character with a loving tone. The song, Moby's version of New Order's "Temptation," elaborates on the emotional nuances of a scene, and the lyrics and the melody unclothe Damon to reveal his naked yearning, or as Brian Sumner of "New Order" says about the song, "He [Moby] slowed the track down and stripped it to its basic elements ... It displays the words and the melody in all their wonderful nakedness." If we can set aside the now-common creepy-but-at-times-intimate vampire-watching-his-beloved-sleep-without-her knowing moment, we see Damon in an emotionally wonderful nakedness, stripped of his words, which are replaced by Laura Dawn's haunting voice and Moby's lyrics: "Up, down, turn around, please don't let me hit the ground. Tonight I think I'll walk alone, find my soul as I go home. Oh, it's the last time. Oh, it's the last time. ..." If you listen to this song through headphones, the lyrics "up, down, turn around, please don't let me hit the ground" move from one ear to the other—an intimate whisper—while the slow drawn out pulse of the breathy admission, "Never met anyone quite like you before" grounds the music like a heartbeat. Perhaps, in this haunting music, we hear Damon's heartbeat, his solitary footsteps, his search for his soul, and because we, too, respond to another's heart, we enter into the story, pulled by our own heartstrings, against our better judgment.

When Elena awakens to an empty room and turns off her light, the music continues until the final credits roll, and the lyrics take on a slightly different meaning. Now the two layers of the song, "Up, down, turn around, please don't let me hit the ground. Tonight I think I'll walk alone, find my soul as I go home" and "Never met anyone quite like you before" harmonize to become Damon's solitary search for his soul and Elena's admission of Damon's uniqueness. In her article, "Serial Monogamy: Extended Fictions and the Television Revolution," Margaret

Mackey analyzes "thoughtful and provocative juxtapositions of story and music" (159) in the television series *Felicity* and her comments about the songs that end certain episodes also can be applied to *TVD*:

> The placing of many of these fragments of song at episode boundaries ... enables the song to linger in the void created by the ending of the story. In the television experience, this lingering afterlife adds plurality and sometimes depth to the emotional resonance of a given episode. ... what struck me very forcibly when I began to consider the role of the concluding song, was the sheer pleasure for viewers of adding complexity to the interpretative experience, the surprise and delight of registering another semiotic channel. I suspect this pleasure is heightened for those in a better position to recognize the songs and to take a more detailed pleasure in their evocations.
> (159–160)

I agree with Mackey about the pleasurable surprise and delight in engaging with the multiple levels of meaning the music invokes and the joy I experience when I recognize a favorite or familiar song, such as the moment when I heard "Terrible Love" by The National during a time period when *High Violet* and *Trouble Will Find Me* played on a repeat loop on my iPod. I delight in the musical clues Music Director Chris Mollere drops throughout *TVD* and its spin-off show, *The Originals*. For instance, he first uses "Terrible Love" in an episode of *TVD* titled "The Originals," and then he replicates the entire song list in the pilot episode of *The Originals*, which creates an atmospheric overlay between the two shows.

More than this pleasure of recognition, however, I revel and writhe in the emotional pain certain songs evoke, despite my initial intentions to maintain my intellectual composure, which, in reflection, seems against the spirit of this project. I sigh and hand myself over to the piano keys that beat against my heart and kick-start my tear ducts. As Nussbaum asserts, "Music can bypass habit, use, and intellectualizing, in such a way that its symbolic structures seem to pierce like a painful ray of light directly into the most vulnerable parts of the personality. ... music seems to elude our self-protective devices, our techniques of manipulation and control, in such a way that it seems to write directly into our blood" (*Upheavals* 269). Here, Nussbaum points to a synchronicity between music, pain, vulnerability, and the body, and *TVD* creates emotional moments and responses by crafting such symbolic structures. I still cannot watch Elena and Damon's motel balcony kiss—which I discuss in the next section—without getting goosebumps and scrambling for the closest box of tissues.

Mollere molds the most devastatingly heartbreaking moments around the sounds of the piano, which functions as a type of dramatic irony, connecting the viewer to the emotional intensity of a scene while the characters most affected often remain isolated in their suffering. Songs relate to the characters and the situation on screen, but also refuse this connection because they are extra-diegetic, separate from them. In this separateness, the music transfers to a general experience and to a specific moment of the implied viewer/listener:

> The spectator's emotions are, then, real emotions, of a complex sort. They include emotions such as fear and pity and grief assumed through empathy with a perspective or perspectives embodied in the work; sympathetic emotions responding to the presence of those structures in the work; closely connected emotions about human life in general and about her own possibilities; and, finally, emotions of wonder and delight that take the artwork itself as their object.
>
> (*Upheavals*, Nussbaum 278)

As I summarize in the Introduction, Carroll argues a similar position to Nussbaum, but in relation to fear and horror specifically. Nussbaum extends these contentions about the relationship between spectators and characters—and the ethical implications of these connections—by adding pity and grief, love-based emotions, to the feelings a spectator might experience. To relate these ideas back to the scene between Damon and Elena that ends "Friday Night Bites," we see how fear, pity, and grief combine to create an empathy with Damon. I fear for Elena's safety, but also for Damon because Stefan believes him to be a monster who must be stopped. I grieve for this rift between brothers and perhaps I grieve for my own hidden love—and fear it may never be requited. And I drive home, listening to Laura Dawn's voice and Moby's orchestration vibrate the walls of my car, as I delight in the raw emotion of his version of this song.

Music speaks the emotionally unspeakable, at least where words initially falter. Nussbaum connects music to "the perception of urgent needs and vulnerabilities that are often masked from view in daily life" (*Upheavals* 254), to "our inner world … not really translatable into words" (*Upheavals* 255), and to "our deepest strivings and most powerful emotions" (*Upheavals* 260). The music for these three series provides another layer of narrative and emotional complexity, and *TVD* goes the furthest in using music to infuse seemingly unredeemable characters with a vulnerability that reveals their ability to love. A hand literally and metaphorically capable of ripping out a heart tenderly strokes a cheek while a piano plays, and we forgive past transgressions and look forward to a kiss.

"Kiss Me or Kill Me. Which Will It Be? We Both Know You're Only Capable of One."

The previous section outlines how really looking and mutual attention over time initiates and leads to love. For the most part, these exchanged looks occur across distances as lovers lurk in alleys, hover in hallways, and watch through windows. In this section, the gaze moves closer and longing looks become kisses that reveal the monster in the man. Both *BtVS* and *TVD* continue the convention of distinguishing visually between the monstrous and human sides of vampires by showing how their faces change. In *BtVS*, vampires can put on their fighting face, a "vamp face," which includes a bumpy forehead, protruding brows, and extended incisors, but this face also emerges unbidden in moments of emotional upheaval, such as anger or passion. Vampires in Mystic Falls reveal themselves more subtly: the vessels beneath their eyes fill, and it appears as though rivers of blood flow beneath the skin on their cheeks. Curious humans often ask, "What's wrong with your eyes?" to a vampire who unknowingly reveals him or herself. Vampires in the *Twilight* saga do not morph when they feed or fight, so there are no warning signs when they verge on losing control or when their vampiric urges emerge; more often, they lunge toward or away from Bella before she has a chance to respond.

These three series continue to redefine the moment of the deadly kiss between vampire and human by portraying the kiss as a gesture of intimacy that still contains the possibility of danger. As Christopher Craft says about this ambivalence between desire and danger in *Dracula*, the vampiric kiss excites a "swooning desire for an overwhelming penetration and an intense aversion to the demonic potency empowered to gratify that desire" (169). Each series portrays the establishing kiss across two parallel scenes: the first establishes the man as a vampire and the second exhibits his control over the vampire aspects of himself. The kiss resembles the act of feeding, of opening one's mouth to consume, so when a vampire opens his mouth to his beloved, the difference between kissing and killing eliminates only the distance between her lips and neck and the depth of his incisors. Although in these series the vampire no longer kisses his beloved to kill her or to transform her into an immortal, his kiss awakens a desire that leaves him vulnerable. Angel, Edward, and Stefan all make a commitment to shun their vampire natures, which means maintaining control of their desire to feed on humans, and this control beats at the heart of this generic redetermination, which shifts the sympathetic vampire into a beloved. If love occurs despite will, as Nussbaum argues, then love threatens the very control these vampires work so hard to maintain.

Kisses between young people—especially a young male vampire and his female human beloved—exude a particular potency in their simultaneous reticence and hunger. In her essay "Of Kisses and Ellipses: The Long Adolescence of American Movies," Linda Williams charts the evolution of film kisses as "textual punctuation mark[s]" that show, refuse, and suggest sexual acts. Williams claims, "The movie kisses of the era before the 1960s sexual revolution were both more infantile and more adolescent than the kisses of today—infantile in their orality and adolescent in their way of being permanently poised on the brink of carnal knowledge" (289). She summarizes psychologist Richard

Alapack's essay "The Adolescent First Kiss" and "writes that a kiss is a transcendence of self through the connection to an other whom one both 'faces' and 'tastes' for the first time" (289). While Williams uses the term "adolescent" to characterize an era of kisses, she does not—for the most part—look at young people's kisses. Regardless, her analogy connects punctuation, youth, and kisses in film history and provides a useful framework in which to consider kisses between young beings. In the teen vampire series I study, kisses form brackets around ellipses that open and close trajectories of anticipation, realization, refusal, and repetition as human and vampire lips meet.

Although Angel and Buffy partake in many kisses, two kisses in particular puncture their relationship and mark it as a love-based connection as powerful as it is painful: their first kiss, before Buffy knows Angel is a vampire; and their second kiss, after Angel reveals himself as a vampire. These kisses take on a larger significance also because they initiate and redetermine future kisses between a vampire and his human beloved. Their first bedroom kiss establishes the semantics of a passionate moment that brings out the monster in the man, which we see replicated in *Twilight*. The second scene occurs in public under the watchful eyes of their friends, and this public moment causes a ripple effect that transforms the kiss from a moment of intimacy into a broader political gesture that undermines the notion vampires are always evil creatures.

Buffy waits a relatively long time for Angel's kiss. As I outline earlier, the first half of the twelve-episode Season One sets up Angel and Buffy's relationship as one in which Angel mostly watches Buffy and warns her about the Master, an ancient vampire who wants to bring about the apocalypse. Episode Seven, entitled "Angel," begins with the Master plotting with Darla—the blonde female vampire who attacks her date in the first scene of the pilot episode and who we discover in this episode used to be Angel's lover—about how to stop Buffy from killing their vampire crew and thwarting their plans. He decides to send the ambiguously-named The Three to eliminate her. The setting then shifts to the Bronze where Buffy and Willow sit on a couch talking about Angel. Buffy sums up their relationship: "He disappears! Every time. Tells me there's trouble then poof. Gone. But when he's around … It's like the lights dim everywhere else." Buffy acknowledges Angel's radiance, but then tires of infecting her friends with her brooding mood, and as she leaves, the camera tilts up to the balcony of the club and reveals Angel watching her. It appears as though this episode will continue to maintain the distance between them as Angel watches her and she longs for him.

The dynamic changes, however, when Buffy finds herself being attacked by The Three. Suddenly, Angel appears and, for the first time in the series, joins her in a fight. They do their best, but The Three threaten to overpower them, so when one of them slashes Angel in the ribs, Buffy and Angel run away. This fight demonstrates, again, how *BtVS* reworks a narrative trajectory: in most films, when a woman encounters danger, a man swoops in and saves her, but Angel never simply saves Buffy. Instead, he watches and when he decides she needs assistance, then he joins the fight. Significantly, they do not win their fight against The Three and Angel, not Buffy, sustains an injury. This fight models the mutual attention they develop in other aspects of their relationship; they attend to each other reciprocally, neither one overpowering the other.

This mutual attention continues in the next scene when Buffy and Angel escape The Three by running into Buffy's house. Concerned about the wound to Angel's side, Buffy tells Angel to remove his shirt, so she can bandage his wound. He lifts off his shirt, and we see Angel's naked torso for the first time, but certainly not the last. As I discuss in Chapter 2, Angel's shirtless body—often wounded—serves as a spectacle that directs the gaze to its beauty and functions as a metaphor for his tortured existence. In this scene, it also foreshadows their kiss, as applying first aid to Angel's cut requires Buffy to assume an intimate proximity to his body. The camera pulls in to a medium shot that positions Buffy's face next to Angel's naked chest, his nipple conspicuously and sensually in the foreground, as he gazes down at her. The atmosphere of intimacy permeates the room as thick as a vampire's rolling fog, so when Buffy's mother, Joyce, returns home, they pull away from each other like two teenagers caught in a compromising situation. That night, Angel sleeps on the floor next to Buffy's bed.

After dinner the next night, Buffy goes to her bedroom where Angel waits for her. She asks him how he spent the day and when she sees her open diary on the bookcase, she accuses him of reading it and rushes into a bumbling defence:

BUFFY: That is not okay, a diary is a person's most private place and you don't even know what I was writing about. "Hunk" can mean a lot of things, bad things, and where it says your eyes are "penetrating" I meant to write "bulgy." And for your information "A" does not stand for Angel, it stands for … Achmed, a charming foreign exchange student and so that whole fantasy part has nothing to do with—

ANGEL: Your mother moved your diary when she came in to straighten up. I watched her from the closet. I didn't read it. I swear.

BUFFY: Oh. Ohhhh.

ANGEL: I did a lot of thinking today. I can't really be around you … Because when I am …

BUFFY: Hey, no big. Water over the bridge—

ANGEL: all I can think about is how badly I want to kiss you.

BUFFY: It's under the bridge, over the dam. Kiss me?

ANGEL: I'm older than you and this can't ever … I better go.

BUFFY: How much older?

ANGEL: I really should …

BUFFY: Go, you said.

Their exchange reveals the depth of their attraction to each other, and although Angel opens the window to leave, he reaches for her rather than leaving. She moves into his arms, and they kiss. Their tender, tentative kiss grows more passionate, until, suddenly, Angel pulls away from Buffy. The camera follows Buffy's face and then swings back to Angel. In the dim light from outside, the horizontal blinds cast shadows, like bars—a technique the *Twilight* saga often employs—across Angel's face, which now contains the characteristics of a vampire. The camera pulls into a closer view of his vampire face and then swings back to Buffy, who screams, as Angel dives out her window (Figure 3.2).

Although it may be difficult to recall a time when *Buffy* fans did not know Angel is a vampire or to remember a time before vampires kissed humans without killing them, when this episode first aired in 1997, no one had a precedent for understanding someone could be a vampire and not be evil. Buffy, Giles, Willow, and Xander discuss this lack of precedent the next day when Buffy tells them what happened. Buffy asks Giles, "Can a vampire ever be a good person? Couldn't it happen?" Giles replies with a standard answer, "A vampire isn't a person at all. It may have the movements, the memories, even the personality of the person it takes over, but it is a demon at the core. There's no halfway." And as Darla insightfully asks Angel later in this episode, "What did you think? Did you think she'd understand? That she would look at your

Figure 3.2 Buffy and Angel's first kiss.

face—your true face—and give you a kiss?" It is a testament to Buffy's belief in the relationship of mutual attention she and Angel have established when she kisses him again later in this episode.

The episode ends where it began: back in the Bronze with Buffy and Willow talking about Angel. Not much time has passed, but much has happened. Angel reveals himself as a vampire; Darla bites Buffy's mother and makes it look like Angel did it; Buffy and Angel fight each other; Angel tells Buffy his history about killing his family, biting a Romani girl, being cursed with a soul; Angel and Buffy admit their love for the other; Angel kills Darla and then disappears. Now Willow asks Buffy, "No word from Angel?" and Buffy responds, "No. I don't think he'll be around. It's weird, though. In a way I feel like he's still watching me." Willow smiles and looks over Buffy's shoulder: "Well, in a way, he is. In the way of that he's right over there." This exchange, while light-hearted, also points to the connection between Angel and Buffy and how it is, in part, established through looking.

The closing scene recalls Nussbaum's claim one cannot choose the object of one's love or the goodness of that love, and it also foretells of the pain of loving and leaving that pervades Buffy and Angel's love, which I discuss in the next chapter. The public setting of the conversation and their kiss also relates to Nussbaum's idea, "Love does not occur without guilt, the fear of judgment, and the longing for reparation and salvation—and that all attempts to love are watched and judged ..." (*Love's Knowledge* 297). Buffy and Angel—despite their fear, despite Angel's striving for redemption, despite the way others judge their love—attend to and respond to each other's hearts. Together they create a model for a love-based justice that deepens through watchfulness, conversation, and, sometimes, a painful kiss:

ANGEL: Look, this can't ...
BUFFY: I know, ever be anything. For one thing, you're like two hundred and twenty-four years older than I am.
ANGEL: I just gotta ... I gotta walk away from this.
BUFFY: I know. Me, too.

This brief exchange employs metaphors of looking and leaving, yet neither of them walks away. Instead of leaving, Angel bends his head towards her, her arms go around his neck, and as the shooting script describes, "oh do they kiss." Buffy asks Angel if he is okay, and he starts to say, "It's just ..." and she finishes, "Painful, I know ... I'll see you around." Buffy turns and walks away, and Angel watches her with a pained expression on his face. The camera slowly pans from his face to his chest, where we see the imprint of Buffy's cross necklace burned into his flesh, their emotional pain made visible because of Angel's inescapable vampirism.

In the film version of *Twilight*, Edward makes visible his pain, too, the first time he kisses Bella, albeit in a less embodied way. Their first kiss takes place in Bella's bedroom in a scene that recalls the moment in which she believes she first dreamed of Edward Cullen before she knows he is a vampire. This first kiss also contains elements of the scene in the forest when Bella confronts Edward about his vampirism because both sequences rely upon and revise conventional cinematic semantics of a male vampire biting his female victim. Bella opens herself to his bite, and then protects herself by physically moving into his space. Her proximity, the way she looks at him and refuses to feel afraid, restructures their relationship and the second half of the film.

The forest scene occurs midway through the film and therein functions as a hinge that opens the door to Bella and Edward's relationship and allows them to move from primarily looking into really loving. The night before Bella confronts Edward, she dreams about him as a classic film Dracula, complete with black cape and blood dripping from the corner of his mouth, and herself as the swooning victim, seductively and willingly reclined beneath him to receive his bite to her neck. Her dream, therefore, sets up the vampire's desired and deadly kiss as an expected act. When she summons Edward with a look, and he follows her into the woods, her dream lingers and contributes to the atmosphere of suspense that hovers in the fog-filled forest.

The high establishing shot shrinks Bella and Edward to small players on nature's stage. She stands with her back to him, and her head hangs down as she speaks: "You're impossibly fast and strong." The camera then cuts in to the familiar close-up of Bella's face as she says, "Your skin is pale white and ice cold. Your eyes change color, and sometimes you speak like you're from a different time." As Bella continues, Edward draws ever closer to her until he stands ominously close to her, his eyes focusing on her neck. She finally asks, "How old are you?" to which he responds, "Seventeen." "How long have you been seventeen?" she pressures. "A while," he admits. The camera swirls around them, which contributes to the unsettled atmosphere, as she tells him she knows he is a vampire. The sound of her breathing fills the air. When he asks her if she is afraid, she finally turns to look at him to answer a firm "no." As she continues to assert her belief he will not hurt her, he grabs her wrist, lifts her onto his back, and runs with her through the forest to the top of the mountain, so she can see him in the sunlight.

Bella counteracts each one of Edward's attempts to prove himself as a monster she should fear. When the sunlight strikes his skin, Bella looks at him with wonder and awe, as I discuss in Chapter 2, but he scoffs, "Beautiful? This is the skin of a killer, Bella." He turns away and walks deeper into the forest. Bella stumbles over fallen logs and struggles to keep up, her clumsiness an obvious counterpoint to his ease. The forest serves as an appropriate backdrop to his assertions about his predatory nature, but Bella refuses her role as victim, even as he leaps to the top of a rock or hurls a tree to demonstrate his ferocity. It seems laughably ludicrous when he tells her he is designed to kill, and she shakes her head with a smile and proclaims, "I don't care." He continues to emphasize he has killed people and she continues to shrug her shoulders with a breathily naive nonchalance. He leans in towards her, touches his hand to her face, and says, "I wanted to kill you. I've never wanted a human's blood so much in my life." She never flinches, never waivers, and instead stands firm: "I trust you. … I'm here; I trust you." Unlike Buffy's initial reactionary scream in response to evidence of Angel's vampirism, Bella moves forward and begins to stalk Edward causing him to flee. Her belief in him and in her love for him invites viewers to follow her lead—as Carroll suggests—and to begin to trust him.

Bella alters the momentum of the scene, as she asserts the power of her love. He leaps away from her, maintaining his distance. When he worries about his ability to control himself with her, she climbs toward him, pushing into his space to prove her belief in him. She tells him she is not afraid of him—she fears only losing him. Here, the camera draws in for a close-up so their faces in profile fill the screen, eye to eye, nose to nose, open mouth to open mouth—the kiss waiting to happen. Instead, they acknowledge their love and the potential pain their love may entail. "You don't know how long I've waited for you," Edward confesses, as the camera follows his hand down to where he places it upon her heart, and then pans back to their faces. "And so the lion fell in love with the lamb, he says." "What a stupid lamb," she replies. "What a sick masochistic lion," he smiles, as the sequence swirls up to the treetops and into the meadow where they lie themselves down, curled towards, but not touching each other (Figure 3.3).

When the kiss finally does happen, it takes place in Bella's bedroom, backlit by the window in a similar framing to Angel and Buffy's first kiss. The scene begins with fear when Edward climbs in her bedroom

Figure 3.3 Bella and Edward's kiss waiting to happen.

window and catches Bella unaware, as she talks on the phone to her Mom. She startles and turns and her fear melts to a smile, as she hangs up the phone and asks Edward how he got into her room. When he tells her he enters the room through the window and she questions whether he does that a lot, he replies, "Just the last couple of months ... I like watching you sleep. It's kind of fascinating to me." Bella smiles and laughs softly, which operates as the visual and aural equivalent of her response in the novel, when she says she feels flattered.

This scene of Edward's confession continues into the moment of their first kiss, thus uniting the earlier dream scene with this one, and merging the possibility of the fatal kiss implied in the initial scene with its continued potential here. After Edward admits to watching her sleep, he whispers, "Bella, I just want to try one thing." The camera pulls back from Edward's face and swings out to position Edward and Bella in profile in the center of the frame. As Edward's face moves slowly towards Bella, so the camera inches towards them, pulling their faces closer and closer. Edward commands, "Don't move," and the sound of Bella's breath permeates the moment as the camera moves to a point of view shot over Edward's shoulder, then back to Edward's lips, and out to their profiles, as their lips meet. Their kissing is slow, hesitant, but like the scene in the forest when Edward admits he is a vampire and Bella takes control of the situation, so she moves toward him here. Their kissing increases in intensity, to a point where he lies on top of her on the bed.

In an inversion of the trope in romances when the girl tells the boy to stop and he apologizes for his urgency, here Edward tells himself to stop as he flings himself across the room and away from Bella. Instead, Bella apologizes, as she sits sheepishly yet invitingly on the bed, her bare legs bent but open, her hands placed between them, in a suggestive pose that both shields her groin from view and calls attention to it. Edward says, "I'm stronger than I thought," and Bella replies, "Yeah, I wish I could say the same." Edward turns away from Bella and towards the camera, so he shows his pained face to the viewer but hides it from Bella, as he states, "I can never lose control with you." Bella asks him not to go, and the following montage shows them sitting on her bed, talking, until Bella finally falls asleep and cuddles into Edward's chest, while he hesitates to touch her. This scene of their first kiss reconceives and reconstitutes the bedroom as a site of safety and intimacy, and although Edward does not show his vampire face, the monster in the man appears when he resists responding in kind to her overt desire for him.

The Vampire Diaries replicates this scene almost verbatim visually in an episode in which Stefan tries to maintain control of his yearning for human blood ("Under Control" 1018) after Elena feeds her blood to him in order to heal him ("Let the Right One In" 1017). I discuss this episode (1017) in more detail in Chapter 5, but it is worth mentioning here *TVD* draws upon the semantics of the dangerous and desirable bedroom kiss, but with a difference: unlike Bella, when Elena sees Stefan's vampire face, as he sits panting against the wall, she immediately calls Damon for backup. What she does not know, however, is Stefan unintentionally reveals his vampire face to Elena at the mere mention of passion in the pilot episode.

The scene unfolds around multiple references to sight and eyes, and attaches looking to passion. Elena and Stefan attend a party and discuss Elena's friends. Stefan sees Matt watching them and says to Elena, "Matt can't seem to take his eyes off of us." Elena responds, "Matt's that friend since childhood that you start dating because you almost owe it to yourselves to see if you can be more." "And?" Stefan urges. "And then my parents died. And everything changed. Anyway, Matt and I, together, we just … I don't know, it wasn't … it wasn't …" "Passionate," Stefan finishes. "No," Elena agrees, "No, it wasn't passionate." The held two-shot pans between Stefan and Elena as they gaze at each other with the implication that perhaps together they *would* be passionate. As the camera pulls in to Stefan's face, the music changes, becomes more foreboding, and the vessels under Stefan's eyes fill with blood. Elena looks closely at him and says, "Hey, uh, are you okay? Your eyes …" Stefan quickly looks away, rubbing his eyes, and then leaves her under the premise of going to get them some drinks. Stefan removes himself from a situation in which his eyes reveal his vampiric identity and his desire for Elena, and this first exit establishes Stefan's belief that leaving constitutes right action, which is the focus of the next chapter.

The endings of the first two episodes of the series parallel each other and introduce the house and porch as sites of emotional upheavals. They both begin with establishing shots of the exterior of a home, Elena's in the first episode and Stefan's in the second. One voice speaks over the extra-diegetic music and then a second joins the first. In the first episode, Elena shares what she writes in her diary: "Dear Diary, I couldn't have been more wrong. I thought that I could smile and nod my way through it. Pretend like it would all be ok." The background vocals by The Fray connect Elena's words to her ability to love and to anticipate Stefan's appearance: "Somethings we don't talk about. Rather do without. Just hold the smile. Falling in and out of love. Ashamed and proud of. Together all the while." Then Stefan's voice continues, "I had a plan. I wanted to change who I was. Create a life with someone new. Someone without the past." "Without the pain," says Elena. "Someone alive," they assert together, as The Fray sings, "You can never say never." "But it's not that easy. The bad things stay with you," Elena reflects while the setting shifts to Jeremy looking at a picture of their parents, and Stefan says, "They follow you. You can't escape them, as much as you want to" and the setting cuts to Damon—the bad who follows you—sitting in the Mystic Grill watching Caroline. "Don't let me go," croons The Fray, as the scene swings back to Elena writing in her diary. We hear her voice say, "All you can do is be ready for the good, so when it comes, you invite it in because you need it. I need it." Elena looks over her shoulder out the window and sees Stefan standing there—the good vampire ready to be invited in. The episode closes with Elena opening the door of her house and her heart to Stefan.

The end of the second episode ("Night of the Comet" 1002) sets up a reciprocity between Elena and Stefan, as they take turns approaching each other. At the end of this episode, Elena comes to Stefan's house, but instead of going inside as he did in the scene I discuss above, she leads him outside. The closing sequence uses piano chords to establish the mood when Stefan opens the door to Elena, as Sara Bareilles sings, "Something always brings me back to you." In an alteration of the previous episode that ends without a kiss, when Stefan asks Elena if she would like to come in, she points outside and says, "The comet's actually this way." She then explains her reason for being there:

> See the thing is, I got home tonight, planning on doing what I always do: write in my diary, like I have been since my Mom gave me one when I was ten. It's writing everything out, everything I'm feeling, it all goes in this little book ... but then I realized that I'd just be writing things that I should probably be telling you. ... I'm scared Stefan. I'm scared that if I let myself be happy for even one moment that the world's just going to come crashing down, and I don't know if I can survive that.

"Do you want to know what I would write?" asks Stefan before he repeats the same words Elena said to him earlier that day but with a different ending: "I met a girl. We talked. It was epic. Then the sun came up and reality set in. Well, this is reality. Right here." The piano music swells, as Stefan and Elena move together and kiss to the background lyrics, "I can't seem to let you go. The one thing that I still know is that you're keeping me down." The ambiguity of Bareilles "Gravity" lyrics, that someone keeps another person down, can be read both positively and negatively. To be untethered, unconnected to another being suggests the opposite of love, but to be kept down also implies not being able to realize one's own potential. Furthermore, Elena's fear of being "happy for even one moment" recalls Angel's curse.

The double meaning of the lyrics signals the doubleness of the scene. Stefan and Elena kiss tenderly under the night sky, and when they separate and gaze at each other, the camera pulls back to show Stefan's face, which maintains its human structure. They kiss more intensely, touching each other's faces, the vampire nowhere to be seen. The song continues while the setting shifts to show a close-up of the top of Damon's head and the swell of a hot-pink bra cup in the foreground. Damon looks up, and the camera moves to a medium profile of Damon kissing Caroline's belly as she moans blissfully on a bed, her arms above her head, her torso arching into his kisses. The juxtaposition between the exterior scene of Stefan and Elena's kisses and the interior bedroom eroticism shared by Damon and Caroline suggests the two moments occur simultaneously but also they could be substituted for each other. Stefan's eyes turn vampiric at the mention of passion, so when he now kisses Elena, he reigns in his own passion, while Damon revels in his. This potential becomes promise when the close-up on Caroline's face cuts to Damon's now blood-filled eyes. The episode ends with an abrupt end to the musical crooning as Damon plunges his fangs into Caroline's neck. Her screams echo into the closing credits.

This comparison between Stefan's controlled passion and Damon's use of passion to control continues two episodes later ("Family Ties" 1004). During the opening credits, the episode picks up this narrative thread that ties brother to brother via the beds they occupy. Stefan knocks on the front door of Elena's house, and she pulls him in and kisses him, and then leads him upstairs to her bedroom. They continue kissing, and as the kissing becomes more passionate, Stefan glances up and sees his reflection in the mirror: his vampire eyes betray his lust. He sits up and turns his back to Elena. She asks if he is okay, and as his eyes return to their human form, he tellingly responds, "I'm good." In other words, he connects goodness to his human and not his vampire nature.

Meanwhile, Damon reclines on Caroline's bed reading the *Twilight* saga while Caroline tries on party dresses. He compels her to ask him to her party, and then they riff off the *Twilight* saga to explicate the differences between vampire semantics: "What's so special about this Bella girl? Edward's so whipped," scoffs Damon. Caroline says, "You've got to read the first book first. It won't make sense if you don't." "I miss Anne Rice," sighs Damon. "She was so on it." "How come you don't sparkle?" asks Caroline. "Because I live in the real world where vampires burn in the sun," replies Damon before explaining the power of his daylight ring and how humans become vampires. "This book has it all wrong," he proclaims before playfully grabbing Caroline and pulling her on to the bed to kiss her. "You can be very sweet when you want to be," sighs Caroline succumbing to his kisses and agreeing to do anything for him, despite the fact he admits he is eventually going to kill her (although he never does). These two simultaneous bedroom scenes portray Stefan as the good vampire whose passion exposes his vampiric side and Damon as the bad vampire whose sweetness suggests his humanity.

The first season gradually reveals that love drives Damon's return to Mystic Falls. He believes his first love, Katherine, exists locked in a tomb beneath Mystic Falls and if he releases her from the tomb, then they can continue to live blissfully together. As the plot unravels, however, so does Damon, for he discovers Katherine escaped before being locked away and never looked for him. Elena sympathizes with Damon, as she does in episode three, wraps her arms around him and says, "I'm sorry" ("Fool Me Once" 1014). In this parallel scene, Stefan watches as Damon and Elena embrace, in the first of what will be many moments when Stefan bears witness to the growing affection between his brother and Elena.

Elena and Damon kisses mark surprising ends and hinging middles throughout the first four seasons: three out of four season finales include a momentous kiss and the fourth season smacks such a kiss in the middle of the season. Frequently interrupted—what Linda Williams calls *osculum interruptum* in her discussion of the frequent practice of interrupting code-era kisses—these kisses encompass the volatility that defines Elena and Damon's love, and their scarcity makes their presence all the more potent. Moreover, each kiss begins with a conversation between Elena and Damon, in which they acknowledge Damon's striving to act morally, thus linking the kiss to moral action. Finally, the kisses are themselves paired in order to complete or extend an interrupted act. In a subversion of the previous vampire-human first kiss scenes, these kisses rarely take place in a bedroom, as though to suggest Elena and Damon's relationship develops less through lust and more via a striving toward goodness and right action. In fact, the only kiss that occurs in a bedroom happens at the end of Season Two, when Elena cradles Damon in his bed and lightly kisses him goodbye when he verges on death ("As I Lay Dying" 2022).

The first and third kisses take place on the front porch of Elena's house, a full season and a half apart ("Founder's Day" 1022 and "The New Deal" 3010). In the first instance, Damon believes—as does the viewer—he kisses Elena, when, in fact, Katherine impersonates Elena. Katherine arrives on Elena's porch, just as Damon exits the house. She asks him what he is doing here, and he responds, "A failed and feeble attempt at doing the right thing. ... You know I came into this town wanting to destroy it. Tonight I found myself wanting to protect it. How does that happen? I'm not a hero, Elena. I don't do good. It's not in me." Damon thanks Katherine/Elena for finding him worth saving—a reference to convincing Bonnie to assist Stefan in rescuing Damon from a burning building—and kisses her lightly on the cheek. As he pulls away, he looks at her again and finds her returning his gaze. He kisses her on the lips this time, and as their kiss deepens, Jenna—Elena's aunt—opens the front door and interrupts them, watching and judging them. Although Damon misidentifies Katherine as Elena, the kiss originates from an acknowledgement of his moral worth and sets a precedent for future kisses.

This first kiss forks in two over two seasons: Damon confronts Katherine and asks her to validate her love for him ("The Return" 2001); and Damon kisses Elena on the front porch without interruption ("The New Deal" 3010). I discuss the first kiss in Chapter 2 because when Katherine rips open Damon's shirt to kiss him, his beautifully naked chest exposes his heart and reveals his vulnerability. The second moment that stems from Damon's mistaken-identity kiss begins again with Damon walking out the front door of Elena's house after trying to do the right thing by compelling Jeremy to forget about all the horrors that have befallen him ("The New Deal" 3010). This time, however, Damon acts on Elena's behalf and then follows her out the door, while Ross Copperman's non-diegetic song "Holding On and Letting Go" underpins their conversation: "It's everything you wanted. It's everything you don't. One door swinging open and one door swinging closed." Damon tries to comfort Elena, to let her know her decision will save Jeremy. She thanks Damon, "not just for this, but for everything. I don't know what I would do if you weren't here." In the pause where the possible kiss sits, Damon steps away from Elena and tells her although it appears as though Stefan has been lost to them, instead he has been acting to protect them from Klaus. When Elena questions what Stefan's actions mean, Damon replies, "It means I'm an idiot cuz I thought, for one second, that I wouldn't have to feel guilty anymore. ... For wanting what I want. ... Believe me, I get it. Brother's girl and all." The repetition of the compulsion conversation with Jeremy, the porch, the light, close-ups on their faces, but Elena standing in front of him instead of Katherine—all set the scene for another kiss. Instead, Damon expresses guilt, a love-based moral feeling, and he walks away leaving Elena standing perfectly still. He takes one step down off the porch and stops. "No," he says, "No, you know what? If I'm going to feel guilty about something, then I'm going to feel guilty about this." He walks back up the stairs to the sound of swelling music, and he takes her face in his hands and kisses her softly, sweetly. No one interrupts them. No one pulls away. And then he says goodnight and walks away leaving her breathless (Figure 3.4).

Figure 3.4 Elena and Damon's first kiss.

Their third kiss—and the last one I discuss in this chapter—confirms Elena's desire for Damon and links it to his ability to act morally. In "Heart of Darkness" (3019), Elena goes on a road trip with Damon to see Jeremy and to determine if he can talk to Rose's ghost, so she can provide them with crucial information about her past. As I discuss in my Introduction, Rose knows Damon intimately as a friend and as a lover, and Damon kills Rose as an act of love and mercy, but no one knows what he has done for her. Midway through the episode, Elena lies in a hotel room bed, trying to sleep but instead watching Damon, beautiful and sensual in his unbuttoned shirt that reveals his naked torso. He notices her watching, she meets his gaze, and he comes to lie beside her. She whispers, "You never told me about that. About what you did for Rose." He rolls over and stares at the ceiling, "It wasn't about you." She snuggles a bit closer to him and asks, "Why don't you let people see the good in you?" Still looking at the ceiling, he replies, "Because when people see good, they expect good." He turns his head to Elena and says, "And I don't want to have to live up to anyone's expectations." Elena sighs, rolls on her back, and the camera closes in on their intertwined fingers. Panicked, Elena walks away, walks outside, and when she hears Damon following her, she sighs, "Don't," and Damon questions, "Why not? Elena." She looks directly at the camera, breathing heavily, shaking her head, and then she turns, stalks towards him, and grabs him in a fierce kiss, as we hear Florence + the Machine singing, "Never let me go, never let me go." Their passion is fierce, voracious, uncontrolled, and the hotel lights flicker in the background, as though weakened under the power of Elena and Damon's desire.

Established through looking and an acknowledgment of Damon's good, their kiss ends only when Jeremy interrupts it—in another moment of watching and judging that mimics Jenna's interruption—to tell them Rose has information for them. As the four of them drive to Kansas together, Rose explains to Jeremy how she sees the love between Elena and Damon:

> I know you want to stop it. Protect her from it. But you're young. You don't see what I see. It's not just that she makes him a better person, and she does, but he changes her too. Damon challenges her. Surprises her. He makes her question her life. Beliefs. Stefan is different. His love is pure, and he'll always be good for her. Damon is either the best thing for her … or the worst.

Rose, the insightful ghost of a 500-year old vampire, sees the love between Elena and Damon and finds it to be the risky, mysterious, volatile relationship that can lead to a more just way of living by not simply following predetermined beliefs but by challenging oneself to go beyond the safety of purity.

As we follow the stories of Buffy and Angel, Bella and Edward, Elena and Stefan, and Elena and Damon, we practice falling in love. In *Love's Knowledge*, Nussbaum argues novels can be

> both friendly and erotic. They both enlist the reader as a participant by sympathy and compassion, and also lure her with more mysterious and romantic charms. They ask the reader to join in a public moral world and also, at times, lure her away from that world into a more shadowy passionate world, asking her to assent, to succumb. Allowing oneself to be in some sense passive and malleable, open to new and sometimes mysterious influences, is a part of the transaction and a part of its value. Reading novels ... is a practice for falling in love. And it is in part because novels prepare the reader for love that they make the valuable contribution they do to society and to moral development.
>
> (238)

Although Nussbaum discusses novels, looking closely at these three series invites the same effect. We desire Damon's passionate kisses over the purity of Stefan's controlled caresses. We imagine the pain of love searing itself into our exposed hearts. We hope we really look at our lovers in order to attend to their needs and to act morally based on our love.

This chapter traces moments of "really looking," that is, when the human sees the monster in the man—and loves him regardless of his vampiric undertones—and when the monster watches the woman and loves her regardless of his probable pain. The extended development of the relationship between Elena and Damon over eight seasons of *TVD* provides the most sustained model of mobility, volatility, and riskiness as necessary elements of love. The show encourages an emotional attachment to Damon, which refuses the seeming dichotomy between good and evil Stefan and Damon represent, and therein challenges simplistic ideas about romantic love. This chapter entwines love and looking as necessary to moral consideration, which prefaces and informs actions, such as those I discuss in the next chapter. To love someone, to feel love for someone other than oneself, means becoming vulnerable to him or her and therein, being more fully human.

Note

1 In the very witty episode "Buffy vs Dracula" (5001), Dracula compels Xander to do his bidding, and Buffy nearly succumbs to Dracula's thrall, so the series suggests a vampire's ability to compel people is limited to Dracula only. The *Twilight* saga reworks compulsion to provide certain vampires with supernatural gifts. For instance, Edward hears other people's thoughts; Alice sees into the future; Jasper changes the emotional tenor in a room; when Aro touches humans or vampires, he sees every thought they ever had; Jane uses her mind to inflict excruciating pain; and vampire Bella creates a protective shield, which explains why vampire power does not affect her when she is human.

Works Cited

"Angel." *Buffy the Vampire Slayer: the Complete First Season on DVD*. Writ. David Greenwalt. Dir. Scott Brazil. Twentieth Century Fox, 2001. DVD.

"As I Lay Dying." *The Vampire Diaries*. Writ. Turi Meyer, Al Septien, and Michael Narducci. Dir. John Behring. CWTV. 12 May 2011. Television.

Bareilles, Sara. "Gravity." *Careful Confessions*. Sarah Bareilles Music, 2004. Song.

Barrett Browning, Elizabeth. "Sonnet 43." *Sonnets from the Portuguese*. Project Gutenberg. Web. 13 November 2013.

"Bloodlines." *The Vampire Diaries*. Writ. Kevin Williamson and Julie Plec. Dir. David Barrett. CWTV. 21 January 2010. Television.

Browning, Tod. *Dracula*. Universal Pictures, 1931. Film.

Copperman, Ross. "Holding On and Letting Go." *Holding On and Letting Go*. Me and Yew, 2012. Song.

Craft, Christopher. "'Kiss Me with Those Red Lips': Gender and Inversion in Bram Stoker's *Dracula*." *Dracula: the Vampire and the Critics*. Ed. Margaret Carter. Ann Arbor, MI: UMI Research P, 1988. 167–194. Print.

Edwards, Kim. "Good Looks and Sex Symbols: the Power of the Gaze and the Displacement of the Erotic in *Twilight*." *Screen Education* 53 (2009): 26–32. Electronic.

"Family Ties." *The Vampire Diaries*. Writ. Kevin Williamson and Julie Plec. Dir. David Barrett. CWTV. 21 January 2010. Television.

"Fool Me Once." *The Vampire Diaries*. Writ. Brett Conrad. Dir. Marcos Siega. CWTV. 11 February 2010. Television.

"Founder's Day." *The Vampire Diaries*. Writ. Bryan Oh and Andrew Chambliss. Dir. Marcos Siega. CWTV. 13 May 2010. Television.

The Fray. "Never Say Never." *The Fray*. Epic, 2009. Song.

"Friday Night Bites." *The Vampire Diaries*. Writ. Barbie Kligman and Bryan M. Holden. Dir. John Dahl. CWTV. 1 October 2009. Television.

"The Harvest." *Buffy the Vampire Slayer: the Complete First Season on DVD*. Writ. Joss Whedon. Dir. John T. Kretchmer. Twentieth Century Fox, 2001. DVD.

"Heart of Darkness." *The Vampire Diaries*. Writ. Brian Young and Evan Bleiweiss. Dir. Chris Grismer. CWTV. 19 April 2012. Television.

"Helpless." *Buffy the Vampire Slayer: the Complete Third Season on DVD*. Writ. David Fury. Dir. James A. Contner. Twentieth Century Fox, 2002. DVD.

"Innocence." *Buffy the Vampire Slayer: the Complete Second Season on DVD*. Writ. and Dir. Joss Whedon. Twentieth Century Fox, 2002. DVD.

"Let the Right One In." *The Vampire Diaries*. Writ. Kevin Williamson and Julie Plec. Dir. Dennis Smith. CWTV. 8 April 2010. Television.

Mackey, Margaret. "Serial Monogamy: Extended Fictions and the Television Revolution." *Children's Literature in Education* 37 (2006): 149–161. Print.

Meyer, Stephenie. *Eclipse*. New York: Little Brown, 2007. Print.

———. *New Moon*. New York: Little Brown, 2006. Print.

———. *Twilight*. New York: Little Brown, 2005. Print.

Moby. "Temptation." *Hotel*. Little Idiot, 2005. Song.

Murdoch, Iris. *The Sovereignty of Good*. 1970. New York: Routledge, 2013. Print.

The National. *High Violet*. 4AD, 2010. Album.
———. *Trouble Will Find Me*. 4AD, 2013. Album.
"The New Deal." *The Vampire Diaries*. Writ. Michael Narducci. Dir. John Behring. CWTV. 5 January 2012. Television.
"The Night of the Comet." *The Vampire Diaries*. Writ. Kevin Williamson and Julie Plec. Dir. Marcos Siega. CWTV. 17 September 2009. Television.
Nussbaum, Martha C. *Love's Knowledge: Essays on Philosophy and Literature*. New York: Oxford UP, 1990. Print.
———. *Upheavals of Thought: the Intelligence of Emotions*. Cambridge: Cambridge UP, 2001. Print.
"Passion." *Buffy the Vampire Slayer: the Complete Second Season on DVD*. Writ. David Tyron King. Dir. Michael Gershman. Twentieth Century Fox, 2002. DVD.
"Pilot." *The Vampire Diaries*. Writ. Kevin Williamson and Julie Plec. Dir. Marcos Siega. CWTV. 10 September 2009. Television.
"The Return." *The Vampire Diaries*. Writ. Kevin Williamson and Julie Plec. Dir. J. Miller Tobin. CWTV. 9 September 2010. Television.
"Rose." *The Vampire Diaries*. Writ.Brian Young. Dir. Liz Friedlander. CWTV. 4 November 2010. Television.
Sumner, Brian. "Moby Meets New Order." *New York Times*. 3 April 2005. Web. 12 July 2013.
Twilight. Writ. Melissa Rosenberg. Dir. Catherine Hardwicke, 2008. DVD.
"Under Control." *The Vampire Diaries*. Writ.Kevin Williamson. Dir. David Von Ancken. CWTV. 15 April 2010. Television.
Velleman, J. David. "Love as a Moral Emotion." *Ethics* 109 (January 1999): 338–374. Print.
"Welcome to the Hellmouth." *Buffy the Vampire Slayer: the Complete First Season on DVD*. Writ. Joss Whedon. Dir. Charles Martin Smith. Twentieth Century Fox, 2001. DVD.
Williams, Linda. "Of Kisses and Ellipses: The Long Adolescence of American Movies." *Critical Inquiry* 32 (Winter 2006): 288–340. Print.
Wilson, Natalie. *Seduced by Twilight: The Allure and Contradictory Messages of the Popular Saga*. Jefferson, NC: McFarland & Co, 2011. Print.

4 "You Have a Heart?" Loving, Leaving, and Letting Go

the condition of incompleteness… is pain itself
—(*Love's Knowledge*, Nussbaum 256)

On 14 November 2013, Louis Peitzman ranked and summarized all 144 episodes of *Buffy the Vampire Slayer* on the popular entertainment website *BuzzFeed*, and social media went off. Within two days, the list received 53,000 likes on Facebook, and Sarah Michelle Gellar—Buffy herself—tweeted she thought "The Prom" (3020) episode should have ranked much higher than the 23rd place it received. I retweeted Gellar's comment and publically agreed, having already selected "The Prom" as one of the episodes to feature in this book. Peitzman summarizes the episode as follows: "Play the cover of 'Wild Horses' by The Sundays. See how fast you can get a *Buffy* fan to cry. This is such an emotional episode, with Angel breaking up with Buffy and then returning for one final dance. Buffy earning the Class Protector Award is one moment of sweetness amidst all the pain. So much pain." I tested Peitzman's claim and listened to "Wild Horses." I was crying within seconds.

Peitzman's summary of this Season Three penultimate episode links love, protection, and pain, three touch points for this chapter. As Nussbaum claims, "Love is grasped in the experience of loving and suffering. That pain is not some separate thing that instrumentally gives us access to the love; it is constitutive of loving itself" (*Love's Knowledge* 255). In this chapter, I ask, "What does it mean to love and act morally?" and my response links love and moral action to the pain and suffering that occurs through leaving. This chapter charts how leaving and letting go become gestures of love, which hook moments of open vulnerability to intense suffering that occurs in and after scenes of leaving. These departures signal not the end of love but evidence of its gravity. The three series represent leaving as a misguided but necessary step toward a fulfilling erotic love.

And my own tears? Nussbaum suggests audiences embrace stories that may return them to narratives of their own pasts, but this point takes me beyond the focus of this book, except as my occasional anecdotes creep into the corners of my analysis. Rather, I draw attention to how the three series represent pain and suffering as an aspect of love and learning. For instance, Nussbaum could be talking about Angel, Edward, Stefan, and Damon in the following passage:

> pain shows him something about his soul. And, as we are brought into intimate relation with our own most painful memories, we will… suffer violently as we suffered in some past, and feel, from the present, the power of the past upon us. This part of our psychological inquiry arrives at truth, if it does so, not by straightforwardly intellectual paths, but by way of a violent surge of recognition, in which what will be in our imaginations and hearts will be not a piece of knowledge, but the face and body of some particular recollected internal person; and we will feel anew our deep emotions concerning that person…. human learning proceeds through suffering.
> (*Love's Knowledge* 254)

Nussbaum's claim identifies pain as a potential aspect of memory, both for characters within a given narrative and for people engaging with that narrative. Peitzman gestures towards a united suffering when he suggests *BtVS* fans cry every time they remember Buffy and Angel's final dance in "The Prom," as though viewers mourn for their own lost love. Furthermore, the identification and recognition about which Nussbaum speaks recall Carroll's claim that monsters represent a belief more than a literal being. If so, then Angel as a beautiful tuxedo-clad man becomes a belief our lovers will attend to our needs even through the suffering of a final slow dance before a potential apocalypse.

This chapter builds upon Chapters 2 and 3 by showing how vampire-human relationships move from desiring a beautiful monster to mutual looking and kissing and then into what Murdoch calls "right action," without necessarily being a linear development:

> right action is important in itself, with an importance which is not difficult to understand. But it should provide the starting-point of reflection and not its conclusion. Right action, together with the steady extension of the area of strict obligation, is a proper criterion of virtue. Action also tends to confirm, for better or worse, the background of attachment from which it issues. Action is an occasion for grace, or for its opposite.
> (69)

In each of the three series, one or both of the beloveds sacrifice their love for each other in order to act justly. I consider these gestures of sacrifice as at least an attempt at right action, but I also follow Murdoch's suggestion that these actions begin and do not conclude reflection. Significantly, none of the break-ups occur at the conclusion of a series, although when Angel leaves Buffy at the end of Season Three, it does signal the end of their physical relationship, except for periodic trysts when she travels to Los Angeles or he returns briefly to Sunnydale.

This chapter analyzes significant scenes of leaving and letting go. It focuses on the episode in which Buffy sends Angel to Hell ("Becoming, Part Two" 2022); the conversation when Angel tells Buffy about his impending departure ("The Prom" 3020); the scene when Edward leaves Bella in *New Moon* and the repercussions of his absence; the two episodes that depict the first break-up between Elena and Stefan ("Lost Girls" 1006 and "Haunted" 1007); and the moment when Damon erases Elena's memory after the first time he professes his love to her ("Rose" 2008). The syntax of the break-up carries through the three series, although the semantics vary: Angel embodies the stoic, unemotional moral vampire who contains his emotions in order to act for the greater good, and Stefan continues this stoicism. Edward and Damon, however, exude their pain as evidence of their love.

A metaphor of being broken reverberates throughout the three series as relationships break up and leave broken bodies in their wake. While I focus primarily on the speech acts that assert leaving or letting go as a right action because it protects a beloved, I also analyze the physical pain that results from these break-ups. In each case, pain occurs on the body as a metaphoric wound but also as embodied pain, usually portrayed as tears or as an ache in the chest where the heart exists. I agree with Nussbaum's identification of grief as a love-based emotion and her reflection, pain "probably is necessary for grief: namely, the pain *that an important element of one's life is gone*" (*Upheavals* 64, italics in original). Also significant to this chapter is Nussbaum's rationale for the importance of tragic narratives: "its forms are well suited for generating experiences that cut through the dullness of everyday life and show us something deep about ourselves and our actual situation.... we seek out painful literary experiences... for the understanding of self and the world that they offer" (*Upheavals* 243). In other words, bearing witness to a character's pain tells us something about how we might love and grieve.

Perhaps more than any other episode I discuss in this chapter, "Becoming" links love with loss, letting go, and leaving. Peitzman is not wrong when he ranks "Becoming, Parts One and Two" as number one, for as he says, "There were many great episodes after *Buffy*'s second season finale, but none broke our hearts like 'Becoming' did. Angelus is finally re-ensouled, but just as he reunites with Buffy—she's forced to put a sword through him. While the entire episode is brilliant, it's that final scene that leaves you broken." Peitzman implies the final scene of the episode is the scene in which Buffy kisses Angel and then sends him to hell with a sword through his chest, but in fact the final scene follows Buffy as she watches the Scooby Gang on the front lawn of the high school from across the street before catching a bus out of Sunnydale, while Sarah McLachlan sings "Full of Grace" in the background. Buffy chooses to save the world instead of saving Angel, but her love—or perhaps obligation—means she loses Angel, lets go of her friends and her Slayer duties, and leaves Sunnydale and all her loved ones behind.

Parts one and two of "Becoming" (2021 and 2022) highlight how one's decisions and actions shape the being one becomes. Part one alternates between the present and various phases of Angel's past—from when he first becomes a vampire, to when he meets Drusilla, to when his soul is cursed, and finally to watching Buffy be called to be the Slayer and deciding to help her. Although part one begins with Buffy's voice-over saying, "I can't hold onto the past anymore. Angel is gone. Nothing is ever going to bring him back," the narrative arc of these two episodes demonstrates how the past informs the present and how the present may mirror the past. For instance, when—in a flashback to Galway, 1753—Darla approaches Angel and he asks her to show him her world, she tells him to close his eyes just before she bites him. In this scene of Angel's transformation into a vampire, Darla says the same words Buffy does before she sends Angel to hell. In the moment Angel receives his soul, Buffy unknowingly utters Darla's exact words. After almost 250 years, Angel forgets not to trust a beloved who says, "Close your eyes," as he opens himself to Buffy and her sword.

After the first flashback shows how Angel becomes a vampire, the scene returns to the present where Angel, now Angelus, lurks in the shadows and watches Buffy fight and kill three vampires. After she stakes the final one, she helps Xander to his feet and says to him soon it will be over. Angelus whispers to himself, "Yes, my love, it will." That Angelus still refers to Buffy as his love, even though she cannot hear his words, rankles because he knows he can hurt her by drawing upon his intimate knowledge of her. The narrative then turns to the discovery of an ancient relic unearthed by construction workers, which we later learn is the demon Acathla, who was turned to stone when a virtuous knight plunged his sword into Acathla's heart before Acathla could swallow the world. Angelus and Drusilla work together to awaken Acathla, so "every creature living on this planet will go to hell."

In the meantime, Buffy and Willow discover a file that contains the spell for returning Angel's soul to him. When they bring the spell to Giles and tell the rest of the Scooby Gang about their discovery, Xander and Buffy debate the right course of action to take:

XANDER: So this spell might restore Angel's humanity? Well, here's an interesting angle… Who cares?!

BUFFY: I care.

XANDER: Is that right?

GILES: Let's not lose our perspective here, Xander.
XANDER: I'm perspective guy. Angel's a killer.
BUFFY: It's not that simple.
XANDER: What? All is forgiven? I can't believe you people… Angel needs to die.
GILES: Curing Angel seems to have been Jenny's last wish.
XANDER: Yeah, well, Jenny's dead.

…

WILLOW: What do you want to do?
BUFFY: I don't know. What happened to Angel isn't his fault.
XANDER: But what happened to Ms Calendar is. You can paint this any way you want, but the way I see it is that you want to forget all about Ms Calendar's murder so you can get your boyfriend back.

This conversation cuts to the heart of a debate about right action and demonstrates a difference between love-based action and action that stems from vengeance. Xander's questions—"who cares" and "Is that right?"—can be read on one level as colloquialisms, but Buffy responds from a place of love, when she affirms she does still care about Angel. Xander's taunts her with his responding question—"Is that right?"—and the tone implies he tries to make her feel guilty for still caring. On another level, however, his question can be heard as a moral position that asks if it is right for her to care.

Furthermore, Buffy responds to Willow's question not by saying what she wants to do, but by drawing on one of the criteria for compassion: Angel's situation arises through no fault of his own. I discuss compassion more fully in the next chapter, but Buffy and Xander's exchange also relates to how their ethical stances determine right and later action, and the background of attachment from which action issues, to return to Murdoch's claim. Xander's lack of attachment to Angel, and his unwavering position Angel should die because of his vampirism, leads him to withhold crucial information—when Buffy goes to the mansion to stop Angelus from awakening Acathla, Willow performs the spell to restore Angel's soul—which may change Buffy's course of action and save Angel.

"Becoming: Part One" ends with Angelus drawing Buffy out of the high school and into a fight with him, so Drusilla and her minions can kidnap Giles, who they hope can provide information to help them awaken Acathla. During the fight, Willow and Xander are injured, and Drusilla kills Kendra—another Slayer. "Becoming: Part Two" opens with Buffy on the run from the police after they discover her at the school crouched over Kendra's dead body. With Willow unconscious in the hospital, Kendra dead, Xander suffering a broken arm, and Giles missing, Buffy strengthens her resolve to kill Angelus. When Buffy looks for Giles at his home, she finds Whistler—a good demon who takes Angel to see the moment when Buffy is called to be the Slayer—instead:

WHISTLER: It wasn't supposed to go down like this. Nobody saw you coming. I figured this for Angel's big day, but I thought he was here to stop Acathla, not to bring him forth. Then you two made with the smoochies, and now he's a creep again. Now what are you going to do? What are you prepared to do?
BUFFY: Whatever I have to.
WHISTLER: Maybe I should ask: what are you prepared to give up?

In this exchange, Whistler identifies a direct link between sacrifice and right action, a connection he links later in the episode to loss. When Buffy returns to Giles's apartment to ask Whistler for more information about how to stop Angelus, she learns Angel's blood is the key both to awakening and stopping Acathla. As soon as Angel completes the ritual, Acathla opens his mouth and creates a vortex that will suck everyone into hell. Whistler suggests Buffy arrives before "that happens, because the faster you kill Angel, the easier it's gonna be on you." Buffy says, "Don't worry about me.... I can deal. I got nothing left to lose," and Whistler sadly replies to her once she is out of earshot, "Wrong, kid. You got one more thing." Whistler's statement hangs forebodingly in the empty room and creates a tension and fear for Buffy's future suffering.

After Buffy leaves Whistler, she goes to Angelus's mansion and greets him as he has addressed her in the past, "Hello lover." Fighting ensues and while Buffy battles with another vampire, Angel pulls the sword out of Acathla to awaken him. In the meantime, Willow begins the spell to return Angel's soul, and Xander rescues Giles. The following scene switches between Angel and Buffy's vigorous sword fight, Willow's spell, Acathla's slowly-opening mouth, and Spike escaping with Drusilla. The intensity builds between Willow's words and the vicious sound of blades until finally the orb with Angel's soul glows, Willow finishes speaking, and Buffy swings her sword back to deal the final blow to close the vortex and send Angelus to hell. The music crescendos and suddenly Angel gasps for air. The camera slams in to a close-up on Angel's face to reveal his open mouth and glowing eyes. Then, his eyes soften in confusion and he bends forward on the ground out of breath. The camera shifts upward to show Buffy hesitate, her sword still raised as she gazes down at Angel and listens to the sounds of his gasping. The fighting music switches to the soft mournful sound of the song that has provided the backdrop to their first kiss—heart-wrenchingly titled "Close Your Eyes"—and Angel, still on his knees, slowly looks up, tears moistening his eyes. "Buffy?" he whispers, "What's going on?" He looks around confused and Buffy warily lowers her sword. Angel struggles to his feet, and Buffy looks him up and down and finally asks, "Angel?" Angel notices she is hurt and pulls her into his arms: "Oh Buffy. God, I feel like I haven't seen you for months.

God, everything's so muddled." The camera nudges closer to them and alternates between Angel and Buffy's tear-filled eyes as they desperately embrace each other. Buffy closes her eyes and gives herself over to him, but when she opens her eyes, her expression turns from bliss to horror as she stares into the opening maw of Acathla. As dread crosses Buffy's face, so Whistler's words resound, a reminder of who Buffy has to lose: Angel.

The next sequence pulls at the gut and stops breath. It is the scene that breaks hearts and opens tear ducts. Buffy slowly pulls from Angel's embrace, and as he asks what is happening, she says, "Shhhh, don't worry about it." Their faces fill the screen, as Buffy gently touches Angel's lips with her fingertips and then leans in to kiss him deeply. As they kiss, the camera pulls back to show Buffy and Angel kissing in front of the slowly-opening vortex that threatens to suck them into hell. Buffy again withdraws from Angel's arms, and the camera moves in to a close-up on Buffy's face as she whispers, "I love you." The camera shifts to Angel's face as he replies in kind, "I love *you*." Then Buffy says softly, "Close your eyes." Angel trustingly obliges, and we watch, horrified, as Buffy tearfully kisses him one last time. She then moves back and thrusts the sword through Angel's chest, impaling him into Acathla. In shock and pain, Angel gasps, looks down at the sword, and then up at Buffy, reaching his arm out to her. The camera again moves in to an extreme close-up to show his shocked eyes and his open mouth. The vortex swirls around him, he whispers her name, and she steps back and watches as he disappears into the dark cavity of hell, the cross necklace he gave her huge against her heart (Figure 4.1).

Figure 4.1 Buffy sends Angel to hell.

As I mention earlier, the episode ends not here but with a closing sequence set against Sarah McLachlan singing "Full of Grace," and the lyrics link pain with loss, love, and the courage and strength it takes to let go:

> Everything we say and do, hurts us all the more. It's just that we stayed too long, in the same old sickly skin. I'm pulled down by the undertow, I never thought I could feel so low, and, oh, darkness, I feel like letting go. If all of the strength and all of the courage, come and lift me from this place. I know I could love you much better than this. Full of grace. I know I can love you much better than this. It's better this way.

"Full of Grace" recalls Murdoch's words: "Action is an occasion for grace, or for its opposite." The song suggests Buffy's action is an occasion for grace, but it also demonstrates grace—with its roots in love—comes with great pain. The *Oxford English Dictionary* outlines eighteen definitions of the word *grace*, but sub-section c under the first definition specifically defines the term *full of grace* to imply "a quality possessed by human beings: benevolent divine influence regarded as an enduring force in the individual human, having its seat in the soul. Sometimes personified." Although this definition implies a religious history often associated with the Virgin Mary, Buffy's actions realign the notion of grace and hinge it both to human love for an individual and to humankind. In Buffy's final speech to her mother during this episode in which she tries to explain her lack of choice in being the Slayer, she says, "Do you think I chose to be like this? Do you have any idea how lonely it is? How dangerous? I would love to be upstairs watching tv or gossiping about boys or, God, even studying! But I have to save the world. Again!" Buffy understands her responsibility, her duty, as a Slayer is to serve humankind—to save the world—even if it means loneliness and alienation. Although she walks away from her mother, Buffy does not yet realize the extent of her sacrifice. When she plunges the sword into Angel, she both avenges Angel and is an avenging angel who stops the world from being swallowed into hell.

Additionally, the song provides a backdrop to the scene that follows Buffy as she walks down the street back home; as Buffy's mother goes to Buffy's bedroom and reads a note left on the bed; as the Scooby Gang gathers outside school to reflect upon the previous day's events; and as Buffy watches them from behind a tree before taking a bus out of Sunnydale. The final line of McLachlan's song, "It's better this way," corresponds with the closing shot of the bus driving past the "Now Leaving Sunnydale. Come back soon!" sign and implies Buffy's act of letting go and leaving is the right action to take—at least for now.

In addition to the song itself, some of the paratexts surrounding this episode and the song highlight its emotional impact. Firstly, each episode of

Buffy ends with the closing credits and then the Mutant Enemy monster crossing the screen with his arms outstretched uttering, "Grrrr argggh." At the end of this episode, however, the monster whimpers, "Ohhhh, I need a hug," effectively summarizing the collective need of an unknown audience. The second paratext exists beneath the lyrics of McLachlan's song. Comments on various websites including YouTube and sing365.com link "Full of Grace" explicitly to *Buffy* and to the emotional resonance between the song and the show. For instance, a 2005 comment by Jade says simply, "When I heard it on Buffy the Vampire Slayer; the last episode of season two I cried my eyes out it was the saddest song ever and I loved it!" Other comments also link the song to crying, but Kate Hartman goes into greater detail in her "Sweet Sadness" post on March 22, 2007:

> First, I have to say that if you ever watch that episode, always have a box of tissues handy. It is acclaimed by many for being one of the saddest moments in Television history, and the haunting Sarah Mclachlan song enhances the final moments like no other song really can.... But I have to say, no matter how many times I watch Becoming, pt. II, I always cry. It never gets old, and although I've seen it about 100 times and will probably see it 100 times again, I'll always end up a basketcase at the end, and most of that has to do with the tone set by this remarkable song.

While many of the comments reflect primarily upon the song's ability to infuse the episode with even more pain, a few comments come closer to Nussbaum's assertion that pain begets pain as we remember our own suffering:

> Before I watched it I wrote the show off as a joke. People don't understand that the thing that made this show awesome had nothing to do with vampires. It was how well the emotions of the characters hit home. My parents died and I was having trouble relating to anyone. In the show Buffy felt similar emotions and went through similar circumstances and it help me to understand my own feelings. Sometimes its the weirdest things in life that can speak to you.
>
> (www.youtube.com/watch?v=L3sjSnhZJk0)

While Nussbaum discusses how pain begets pain, this comment also identifies the importance of representing complex emotions that allow for audiences to recognize themselves in this pain. Although the above comment speaks about parental love and loss, Buffy's pain relates to the loss of her lover but also how the depth of her pain emanates outwards and affects the circle of her other relationships.

These examples of emotional resonance are not restricted to *Buffy* but instead connect to a larger repository of paratexts in which audiences reflect upon and share their pain. One particularly apt example can be found in Mark Slutsky's *Buzzfeed* article and blog "Sad YouTube," in which Slutsky analyzes the comments section of YouTube and reprints some of the comments, so they do not disappear. He states,

> Dig deep into comments—particularly on pop songs—and you'll see that buried beneath the hate speech, the poorly formulated insults, and the Obama conspiracy theories are countless amazing nuggets of humanity. You'll find stories of love and loss, perfectly crystallized moments of nostalgia and *saudade* (a Portuguese word meaning an ineffable longing for something lost in time). It's a repository of memories, stories, and dreams, an accidental oral history of American life over the last 50 years written by the site's millions of visitors every day.

In the case of "Full of Grace," one need not dig very deep at all to find these stories of love and loss, perhaps because people connect the song so explicitly to this particular episode of *BtVS* and to the moment—or moments—they watched and re-watched that episode. This concept of *saudade* embraces the viewer's moment of watching but also Buffy's own longing and loss.

Buffy's physical loss of Angel manifests into possibly an even deeper emotional loss in Season Three, which follows Buffy's return to Sunnydale, Angel's return from hell, and their subsequent attempts to reunite as a romantic couple. Despite their love for each other, Angel decides he must leave Buffy and Sunnydale on the cusp of Buffy's high school graduation, so Buffy has a better chance at a normal life ("The Prom" 3020). The episode begins sweetly enough. Angel and Buffy awake in Angel's bed after a night of slaying. The "subtle interplay," to use Winnicott's important phrase about loving attention (qtd. in *Upheavals*, Nussbaum 196), of their conversation portrays their casual intimacy, as Buffy worries about her bed head and Angel tells her he thinks she looks perfect. The synchronicity of the interplay takes a turn, however, when their embodied differences appear. Buffy flings open the curtain to reveal the sunshine, and Angel leaps out of bed into a corner to avoid being incinerated by its rays.

These differences become both irrelevant and meaningful when Buffy's mother, Joyce, comes to visit Angel at his mansion the next day. While the conversation about what he drinks and his limited movements during the day signal her acknowledgement of his vampirism, Joyce expresses her concerns not about his vampire nature but about Buffy's future and the repercussions of Buffy's love for Angel. She says, "when it comes to you, Angel, she's just like any other young woman in love. You're all she can see of tomorrow. But I think we both know that there are some hard choices ahead. If she can't make them, you're going to have to. I know you care about her. I just hope you care enough." Joyce implies that "caring enough" means loving her enough to let her go. Joyce acts upon her own love for Buffy, and she moves Angel to respond in kind. She links Angel's love for Buffy to his ability to perform the right action for Buffy's future.

Unbeknownst to Joyce, she seconds what the Mayor foretells for Buffy and Angel's future in the previous episode ("Choices" 3019). In a confrontation with the Mayor when the Scooby Gang meets with him to save Willow, the Mayor says to Buffy and Angel:

> I wish you kids the best, I really do. But if you don't mind a bit of fatherly advice, I just don't see much of a future for you two. I don't sense a lasting relationship.... You're immortal, she's not.... And let's not forget the fact that any moment of true happiness will turn you evil. I mean, come on. What kind of a life can you offer her? I don't see a lot of Sunday picnics in the offing. I see skulking in the shadows, hiding from the sun. She's a blossoming young girl and you want to keep her from the life she should have until it has passed her by. My God! I think that's a little selfish. Is that what you came back from Hell for? Is that your greater purpose?

Although the Mayor functions as the big bad evil for Season Three, his insights into Buffy and Angel's future relationship come from his own experience as an immortal who loved a human. Furthermore, his opening comment about offering them "fatherly advice" is not out of character with his role as a father figure to Faith, and, therefore, does not sound like only the rantings of a mad man. All the questions he asks, all the potential scenarios he poses ring true, and Angel references them in his break-up conversation with Buffy. Finally, the Mayor succinctly links the love Angel feels for Buffy to Angel's ability to act morally. When he questions Angel about his "greater purpose," he touches the heart of Angel's worries about what it means for him to live well.

The Mayor's observations, Angel's conversation with Buffy, Joyce's visit, a notebook he finds in his mansion upon which Buffy has scrawled "Buffy & Angel 4-Ever"—all lead Angel to think more deeply about the feasibility of a romantic future for him and Buffy. The undertone of the "The Prom" episode simmers with Angel's growing unease, as he sidesteps Buffy's inquiries to him about setting up his home with mirrors and a drawer for her. The more evidence he finds about her imagining them into the future as a romantic couple, the more troubled he becomes. Angel rarely verbalizes his emotions, so his concern for Buffy's safety manifests in a dream, in which he watches helplessly as Buffy bursts into flames after their wedding ceremony. Unlike the opening scene in which the sun symbolizes their differences and depicts him as the vulnerable one, his dream illuminates his fear their relationship may lead to Buffy's demise.

Act Two, which follows immediately on from Angel's dream, opens with Angel lowering Buffy into the sewers in search of a vampire who eludes them. This change from the radiant but harmful sun to the bowels of the earth seems the appropriate setting to have a conversation that will cause both of them pain:

ANGEL: I've been thinking... about our future. And the more I do, the more I feel like us, you and me being together, is unfair to you.
BUFFY: Is this about what the Mayor said? Because he was just trying to shake us up.
ANGEL: He was right.
BUFFY: No. No, he wasn't. He's the bad guy.
ANGEL: You deserve more. You deserve something outside of demons and darkness. I mean, you should be with someone who can take you into the light. Someone who can make love to you.
BUFFY: I don't care about that.
ANGEL: You will. And children.
BUFFY: Children? Can you say jumping the gun? I kill my goldfish.
ANGEL: Today. But you have no idea how fast it goes, Buffy. Before you know it, you'll want it all. A normal life.
BUFFY: I'll never have a normal life.
ANGEL: Right, you'll always be a Slayer. But that's all the more reason why you should have a real relationship instead of this, this freak show... I'm sorry. Buffy, you know how much I love you. It kills me to say this.
BUFFY: Then don't. Who are you to tell me what's right for me? You think I haven't thought about this?
ANGEL: Have you, rationally?
BUFFY: No. No, of course not. I'm just some swoony little schoolgirl, right?
ANGEL: I'm trying to do what's right here, okay? I'm trying to think with my head instead of my heart.
BUFFY: Heart? You have a heart? It isn't even beating!
ANGEL: Don't.
BUFFY: Don't what? Don't love you? I'm sorry. You know what? I didn't know that I got a choice in that. I'm never going to change. I can't change. I want my life to be with you.
ANGEL: I don't.
BUFFY: You don't want to be with me? I can't believe you're breaking up with me.
ANGEL: It doesn't mean that I don't...
BUFFY: How am I supposed to stay away from you?
ANGEL: I'm leaving. After the Ascension... I'll go.

Buffy and Angel rehearse a debate about the nature of love and the way it emanates outward to another. Using metaphors of sunlight and procreation, his gestures of love relate to his concern for her flourishing. He begins his statements with Buffy as the subject: you, you, you. Buffy, on the other hand, acknowledges the mystery of love, and the lack of choice in who one loves. Her retorts relate to her own ability to define her happiness, but when she tells Angel she wants her life to be with him, and he replies, "I don't," she has no response, except to repeat his statement back to him in a horrified whisper.

The conversation proceeds through an exchange of "dos" and "don'ts." Angel asserts his position through positives: the more he thinks, the more his thinking leads to appropriate action. Buffy, on the other hand, responds through negatives: she stipulates she does not care about the absence of physical intimacy and commands him to cease with his words. The conversation lurches to a painful pace when Angel switches his tactics to include the negative. When he says, the single word, "Don't," he asks her not to be angry and hurtful, and she rightly links her anger to her love. Her anger projects her love outward, but her anger quickly becomes grief when Angel says he no longer wants their lives to be intertwined. When Angel uses the negative to end their relationship, but begins to link that ending to his love for her, Buffy holds up her hand to stop the words, so the space between them suspends the expression of his love.

His stoicism, his lack of emotion, stand in stark contrast to Buffy's pain. Vulnerable, open to the other, her tears welling in her eyes, Buffy casts aside the practical limitations of their love and rebels against Angel's reasoning, his ability to "think with [his] head instead of his heart." When he utters, "Buffy, you know how much I love you. It kills me to say this," his words fail him, for how can words kill an already dead vampire? Significantly, the word "right" occurs five times, as both Buffy and Angel talk about right action and about the Mayor's correct assessment of their relationship. When Buffy asks Angel, "Who are you to tell me what's right for me?" a justifiable response would be, "I am your beloved, whose love is based on your wellbeing."

Although Buffy rails against Angel's impulse to put his heart aside in his ethical evaluations, in the conversation she has with Willow about Angel's decision, Buffy agrees with him and refers back to ideas about what is right:

BUFFY: But he's right. I think, maybe, in the long run—that he's right.
WILLOW: Yeah. I think he is. I mean, I tried to hope for the best, but…

With painful precision, Buffy acknowledges how right action for the future translates into suffering in the present. When Willow empathizes with Buffy about the horror of the break-up, Buffy responds by repeating the transition phrase "right now": "I think horrible is still coming. Right now, it's… worse. Right now, I'm just trying to keep from dying.

I can't breathe, Will. I feel like I can't breathe." Buffy reiterates Angel's previous stance that ending their romantic relationship kills him, but Buffy's breakdown, her sobbing collapse into Willow's lap portrays her grief as an upheaval of emotion in a way Angel's silence does not.

But Angel has never been a creature of language or tears. He expresses his love through his repeated actions, through his willingness to help, indeed through his unwavering commitment to acting virtuously. When Angel and Buffy accidentally meet in the days after their break-up and Buffy tells him about the hellhounds she must stop in order to ensure the safety of everyone at the prom, Angel pleads with her, "Let me help you." She tells him, "I'm ok," and he reasserts his offer, "If you ever need my help…" In line with Angel's ability to express his love through gestures and not words, he appears at the prom in a tuxedo, and asks Buffy to dance with him. As they dance to "Wild Horses," we understand that painful irony of the lyrics: wild horses may not drag a beloved away, but sometimes lovers leave each other all by themselves. For all of Buffy's abilities to protect her classmates, she cannot protect her heart.

Unlike Buffy's expression of disbelief when Angel tells her he is leaving her, when Edward breaks up with Bella in *New Moon*, she understands it as the logical ending to their relationship. Bella's disbelief resides in her inability to understand why Edward—a creature of such beauty and perfection, in her eyes—would ever find her to be an appealing beloved. Katie Kapurch usefully analyzes Bella's suffering and links it to melodrama. In her article "'Unconditionally and irrevocably': Theorizing the Melodramatic Impulse in Young Adult Literature through the *Twilight Saga* and *Jane Eyre*," Kapurch analyzes how "occasions of exaggerated suffering prior to a joyful reunion, speak to contemporary readers" (164). Kapurch draws upon *The Melodramatic Imagination* by Peter Brooks in order to highlight the significance of suffering and excess and to relate these aspects of melodrama to the appeal of the *Twilight* saga to young people. She writes,

> just as suffering is necessary for the happy resolution offered by melodrama, so, too, is excess, which Brooks relates to the meaningful way in which melodrama speaks to the ordinary and contemporary: "those melodramas that matter most to us convince us that the dramaturgy of excess and overstatement corresponds to and evokes confrontations and choices that are of heightened importance, because in them we put our lives—however trivial and constricted—on the line."
>
> (Brooks qtd. in Kapurch 178)

Kapurch's argument about the melodramatic similarities between *Jane Eyre* and the *Twilight* saga provides a useful way for thinking about another generic intersection that Meyer's texts invoke, especially given melodrama's reliance upon excessive emotion. Bella's heightened emotions manifest most overtly when Edward tells her he does not love her and then leaves her. Bella spirals into pain she characterizes repeatedly, perhaps excessively, as a hole in her chest (*New Moon* 118, 123, 193, 228, 233, 235, 254, 263, 267, 273, 276, 298, 314, 347, 355, 452, 507, 551). In the next section, I analyze their break-up conversation and the scene of their reconciliation in order to establish Edward's belief that lying and leaving constitutes loving.

The event that seemingly instigates the break-up takes place on Bella's birthday. Bella accidentally gives herself a paper cut, which sends Jasper into a blood frenzy. In his attempt to protect Bella from Jasper, Edward knocks Bella backwards into a table where she cuts herself more seriously on broken glass. Carlisle stitches her wound and while he does, he explains to her Edward believes vampires to be damned, to be without a soul, which enlightens her as to why Edward does not want to turn her into a vampire. I quote at some length from the novel here to show the semantic and discursive similarities between this conversation and the break-up dialogue between Angel and Buffy. As with the break-up conversation between Angel and Buffy, when Edward tells Bella he and his family are leaving Forks, the discussion hinges on questions of rightness and goodness and on repetitions of negatives:

> "Where we're going… It's not the right place for you."
> "Where you are is the right place for me."
> "I'm no good for you, Bella."
> "Don't be ridiculous." I wanted to sound angry, but it just sounded like I was begging. "You're the very best part of my life."
> "My world is not for you," he said grimly.
>
> ….
>
> "You promised! In Phoenix, you promised that you would stay—"
> "As long as that was best for you," he interrupted to correct me.
> "*No!* This is about my soul, isn't it?" I shouted, furious, the words exploding out of me—somehow it still sounded like a plea. "Carlisle told me about that, and I don't care, Edward. I don't care! You can have my soul. I don't want it without you—it's yours already!"
>
> ….
>
> "Bella, I don't want you to come with me." He spoke the words slowly and precisely, his cold eyes on my face, watching as I absorbed what he was really saying.
> There was a pause as I repeated the words in my head a few times, sifting through them for their real intent.

> "You… don't… want me?" I tried out the words, confused by the way they sounded, placed in that order.
>
> "No."
>
> ….
>
> He looked away into the trees as he spoke again. "Of course, I'll always love you… in a way. But what happened the other night made me realize that it's time for a change. Because I'm… *tired* of pretending to be something I'm not Bella. I am not human." He looked back, and the icy planes of his perfect face were *not* human. "I've let this go on much too long, and I'm sorry for that."
>
> "Don't." My voice was just a whisper now; awareness was beginning to seep through me, trickling like acid through my veins. "Don't do this."
>
> He just stared at me, and I could see from his eyes that my words were far too late. He already had.
>
> "You're no good for me, Bella." He turned his earlier words around, and so I had no argument. How well I knew that I wasn't good enough for him.
>
> (61–63)

The film condenses this conversation but the focus on rightness and goodness remains. In a similar rhetorical gesture to Angel, Edward shifts his argument from a position about what is right for Bella to what is good for him, therein effectively ending the argument and drawing upon Bella's insecurity about not being good enough for Edward and about the lack of reciprocity in their relationship.

This break-up scene in the film version of *New Moon* refers visually back to the courtship settings in *Twilight*. Bella sits with her friends in the cafeteria and gazes over her shoulder at the now-empty table where the Cullens once sat. When Bella returns home from school, she finds Edward waiting for her. He leads her into the forest in a scene reminiscent of when she confronts Edward about being a vampire. Now, however, the scene reverses as Edward leads Bella into the forest to break-up the relationship she begins. The two-shot scene moves back and forth between Edward and Bella, the camera held still on Edward, but slanting and unsteady when it looms above Bella, implying her own emotional unsteadiness. Edward, however, faces Bella, stoic, unmoving, and seemingly unmoved, until the final gesture when he says goodbye and kisses her on the forehead. As he kisses her, his eyes tightly squeeze shut in a grimace of agony, the only clue he feels pain (Figure 4.2).

He verbalizes his pain near the end of the film and book after Bella travels to Italy with Alice to stop Edward from killing himself because he believes Bella died. Bella still believes Edward does not love her and

Figure 4.2 Edward breaks up with Bella.

understands his action to kill himself as a gesture based on guilt. When he explains why he acted as he did, he again returns to words based on right action as a way of protecting Bella:

> "You weren't going to let go," he whispered. "I could see that. I didn't want to do it—it felt like it would kill me to do it—but I knew that if I couldn't convince you that I didn't love you anymore, it would just take you that much longer to get on with your life. I hoped that, if you thought *I'd* moved on, so would you."
>
> "A clean break," I whispered through unmoving lips.
>
> "Exactly.... I lied, and I'm so sorry—sorry because I hurt you, sorry because it was a worthless effort. Sorry that I couldn't protect you from what I am. I lied to save you, and it didn't work. I'm sorry. But how could you believe me? After all the thousand times I've told you I love you, how could you let one word break your faith in me?" (509–510)

Edward uses a similar expression to Angel when he says his words felt like they would kill him, and Bella aptly uses a metaphor of brokenness when she understands his actions. The main difference between Angel and Edward stems from Edward's use of a lie about his love as a means to achieve what he believes to be right action. Whereas Angel says he loves Buffy and therefore has to leave her, Edward cites the absence of his love as a reason for leaving.

This action of lying as a gesture of love appears again in *The Vampire Diaries* when Elena and Stefan repeatedly lie to their friends and family and each other in order to protect them and when Damon's actions frequently contradict his words, which I discuss in Chapter 3 and expand upon shortly. Murdoch claims, "It is what lies behind and between actions and prompts them that is important" (65), and I want to test this statement in order to determine the appropriateness of a lie disguised as protection. If the lie is the action, then what exists behind and between the lies? The situations that follow from a lie rarely result in the desired outcome, so I question why characters believe lying—or at least withholding information—to be the right action. Why does Edward repeatedly try to keep information from Bella, even after he sees that lying and leaving do not protect her? Why does Elena continue to lie to Jeremy and to erase his memories as an attempt to relieve him of his pain? And why does Damon insist upon lying about his feelings for Elena—at least for most of the first two seasons? I answer these questions by pointing to pain as that which exists behind and between the lies. Each of these characters must learn pain exists as part of love, so no one can be protected from it.

Elena and Stefan learn this lesson about pain in a six-episode story arc that follows them as they break up and reunite and break up and reunite again. This repetition of the break-up semantics condenses the show's overall imperative that history repeats itself, especially given the centuries-long fated, "epic" love between Stefan and Elena and their doppelgängers. The arc begins with "Lost Girls" (1006) when Elena deduces the mystery about Stefan's identity and then confronts him about being a vampire. He confirms her suspicions and asks her to give him one day to show her his history, so she can make an informed decision about being with him. During this one day, Damon bites Vicky Donovan—Matt's sister—and then feeds her his blood, which begins her transformation process from human to vampire. Seemingly, this drama of the day informs Elena's decision because unlike Angel and Edward, Elena gives Stefan no reasons for their break-up.

The final two minutes of the episode take place on the porch where she first kissed Stefan, and therein repeats the semantics of the *Twilight* saga in which an early courtship moment and a break-up scene occur in the same setting, which deepens the pain of the exchange. Elena sits on the chair awaiting Stefan's arrival with news about Vicky. He climbs the steps and the tell-tale sound of a non-diegetic piano note signals an impending emotional upheaval. Stefan reveals he could not stop Vicky from drinking human blood and therein completing the process to become a vampire. Elena panics and Stefan tries to comfort her by telling her he will teach Vicky how to live as a moral vampire, to live as he does without hurting people. Elena asks him what she will tell Jeremy and Matt, and Stefan replies, "We'll come up with a story," to which Elena responds, "You mean we'll come up with a lie." Stefan says, "I'm so sorry," and Elena states, "I gave you today, just like you asked. And I understand that you would never do anything to hurt me, and I promise that I will keep your secret, but—I can't be with you, Stefan. I'm sorry, I just can't." The full moon overhead shines as a spotlight on their pain, marking the space between them.

In the silence of their pain, Jason Walker's voice enters over the piano, "I shot for the sky" and then Molly Reed joins the song, "I'm stuck on the ground, so why do I try, I know I'm gonna fall down. I thought I could fly, so why did I drown. I'll never know why. It's coming down down down." These two voices, male and female, could be Stefan and Elena voicing the pain that results from their striving towards love and right action. Forebodingly, the lyrics also predict Stefan's repeated death by drowning in Season Five, after Elena chooses to be with Damon and not Stefan. Here and now, however, in this moment, Elena walks away from Stefan and through the front door of her house. As the music crescendos, she leans her back against the door, clutches at her belly, and slides down the door to sit sobbing on the floor. Perhaps Stefan would never physically hurt Elena, but her refusal to lie to the people she loves means she will suffer emotional pain we see as she clutches at her stomach and then her head and, finally, her heart.

The next episode ("Haunted" 1007) continues the narrative thread—seemingly from the same night—but initiates an overt storyline about morality and action and the events that lie between actions. Stefan and Damon find Vicky, stop her from attacking Tyler, and then take her back to their mansion in order to help her with the transition phase:

VICKY: Why can't I have people blood?

STEFAN: Because it's wrong to prey on innocent people, Vicky.

DAMON: You don't have to kill to feed. Just find someone really tasty and then erase their memory afterwards. It's so easy.

STEFAN: No no no. There's no guarantee that you can control yourself, ok? It takes years to learn that. You could easily kill somebody and then you have to carry that with you for the rest of your life, which if I haven't made clear, is eternity.

DAMON: Don't listen to him. He walks on a moral plane waaaaay out of our eyeline. I say, snatch, eat, erase.

STEFAN: Hey, look at me. We choose our own path. Our values and our actions, they define who we are.

DAMON: Okaaay, Count Deepak.

Stefan and Damon rehearse their versions of moral action: Stefan errs on the side of caution and control, and Damon leans toward more volatile and risky action. What emerges at the end of this season, however, is Stefan's choice not to drink human blood is based upon his addictive personality and not wholly upon his morality.

Furthermore, unlike in *BtVS* and the *Twilight* saga, choosing a lifestyle which consists of not feeding on humans weakens a vampire's powers. Damon repeatedly lords both his physical and compulsion strengths over Stefan, which become significant at the end of this episode. When Vicky manages to sneak away from Damon and Stefan, she contacts Jeremy and asks him to meet her at the school Halloween party. They start kissing, she bites his lip, and then she loses control, as Stefan predicts. Her face turns vampiric, and she attempts to feed on him. Elena finds them, yells at Vicky to stop, and hits her with a plank of wood. Stefan arrives to break up the fight, and then Vicky disappears. As Elena and Jeremy try to escape, Vicky reappears, throws Jeremy aside, and attacks Elena. Feeding on Elena, Vicky does not notice Stefan behind her until he drives a piece of wood through her heart, killing her, in order to protect Elena.

Elena tells Stefan to take Jeremy away from Vicky's corpse, and as Stefan leaves, he telephones Damon and asks for his help. When Damon arrives to dispose of Vicky's body, he tells Elena to leave, and she accuses him of being responsible for Vicky's death. While it is the case that turning Vicky into a vampire in effect killed her, Stefan is the one who drove the stake through her heart, which does not seem like the only possible course of action open to him. Regardless, Damon does not shun his part in her death, and instead quips, "You confuse me for someone with remorse." Elena punches him, and as he grabs her hand to stop her, he says, "None of this matters to me. None of it." She responds angrily, "People die around you. How could it not matter? It matters and you know it." Damon looks at her and ponders, "hmmm." They stare at each other for a long moment, and then he tells her again to leave, which she does. This moment continues to establish a connection between Elena and Damon because she accuses him of knowing his actions have consequences and knowing they affect him. In a similar scenario to the one that occurs in "Friday Night Bites" (1003), which I discuss in Chapter 3, Elena acknowledges a contradiction between Damon's words and actions, and he internalizes her words and responds accordingly.

In this episode (1007), his response occurs when he offers to erase Jeremy's memory of the evening because Stefan cannot. In another parallel scene that takes place on Elena's porch in the final two minutes of an episode, Elena changes her mind about her refusal to lie and makes a decision to try to protect Jeremy from feeling pain. In the previous episode, Elena waits on the porch to hear news from Stefan about Vicky, and in this episode, Stefan waits for Elena. She goes inside to talk to Jeremy and finds him crying and confused. "Make it stop. It hurts," Jeremy weeps. Elena holds him as he continues to cry, and the scene cuts to show Stefan sitting on the porch listening to Jeremy's sobs. Elena comes back outside and asks if Stefan's okay:

STEFAN: I wanted to help her—but instead.... How's he doing?

ELENA: He's a mess. I don't want him going through this again. He's just a kid.

STEFAN: Elena, what can I do to help? I'll do anything.

ELENA: Can you make him forget? Stefan, please, I don't know how he'll ever get past this. I just want him to forget everything that happened.

STEFAN: If I did it, there's no guarantee that it would work because of who I am. Because of how I live, I don't have the ability to do it right.

A two-shot establishes this scene, and when Stefan utters these final words about rightness, the camera closes in on Elena's face, and we hear from behind her Damon's voice: "I can do it. If this is what you want—I'll do it." Damon enters the scene and interrupts the couple, waiting for Elena's answer. When Elena confirms, "It's what I want," she looks at Stefan in her response to Damon, therein effectively establishing a tension between the three of them, which continues for the rest of the series: she turns to Damon to take away a pain Stefan cannot and he does so because of his growing love for Elena, which he finally admits to her a full season later ("Rose" 2008).

Damon goes inside the house to compel Jeremy to forget the evening's events and to tell him Vicky left town and is not coming back. Stefan sits, deflated, on the porch bench, and Elena goes to sit beside him:

ELENA: Part of me wishes that I could forget too. Forget meeting you. Finding out what you are and everything that's happened since.
STEFAN: That's what you want?
ELENA: Yes, it is. Because I don't want it to be like this. I don't want to feel like this. But I can't. With everything that's happened. I can't lose the way I feel about you.

Significantly, Elena emphasizes she does not want to lose the *feeling* of falling in love with Stefan; she does not say she cannot lose Stefan himself. The implication of this distinction leaves a space for her to have this feeling for someone else, perhaps Damon. Regardless, Stefan's chagrined face turns to hope, and as they pause to look at each other, Damon enters the screen, filling the rest of the frame. "It's done," he states. Elena looks at Stefan, stands up, goes into the house, and leaves both Damon and Stefan looking after her, alone on the porch, the two brothers in love with the same woman again, trying to act morally.

Over the next four episodes, Stefan and Elena continue to struggle with their feelings for each other. Like with Angel and Buffy, Stefan and Elena are drawn to each other, but they believe their relationship harms others, so they try to stop spending time together. In "162 Candles" (1008), Stefan turns 162-years old and his best friend Lexi comes to town to help him celebrate. On that same day, Matt, Jeremy, Stefan, and Elena provide statements to Sheriff Forbes about Vicky's disappearance, and as Elena leaves the police station, she says to Stefan, "I can't do this Stefan.... Around you people get hurt and people die, and I can't, it's just too much.... Stefan, you have to stay away from me." Elena's statement foretells the horrific moment when Damon stakes Lexi later in the episode—which I discuss in Chapter 1—and leads to Stefan's analogous response, after he and Elena witness Lexi's murder:

STEFAN: He killed her. He killed Zach. He killed Tanner. He turned Vicky. I have to kill him.
ELENA: No, you can't do that.
STEFAN: Why are you trying to save him, Elena? He's never going to change. Don't you see that? He's never going to change.
ELENA: I'm not trying to save him. I'm trying to save you. You have no idea what this will do to you. Please, Stefan.
STEFAN: Everywhere that I go, pain and death follow. Damon follows me. No more.
ELENA: Stefan, please. Please, just talk to me. Let me be here for you. Talk to me.
STEFAN: No. You were right to stay away from me.

Stefan draws on their earlier conversation and repeats Elena's sentiments that pain and death surround him. He personifies pain and death by equating them with Damon, and when Elena tries to convince him not to kill Damon, Stefan concedes Elena's earlier action was right. He walks away from her, goes home, stakes Damon—intentionally missing his heart—and says, "You saved my life. I'm sparing yours. We're even. And now we're done." Stefan refuses to become like Damon, to become death, but he equates pain with justice, as he leaves Damon gasping on the floor.

It soon becomes apparent that strong speech acts, which seemingly sever ties between lovers and brothers, portray an emotional upheaval rather than an irreparable break. Stefan's claim he and Damon are "done," for instance, does not carry through for even one episode, or one day. The following morning ("History Repeating" 1009), Damon wakes Stefan up, apologizes for killing Lexi, and promises not to feed on a human for at least a week. Stefan shows exasperation rather than anger towards Damon, but he does not repeat the previous night's claim their relationship is done. Instead, they engage in a rather humorous exchange in which they mimic each other, with Stefan highlighting Damon's proclivity for nefarious activities and Damon emphasizing Stefan's brooding nature.

Stefan does, however, reaffirm his intention to stay away from Elena. When Elena emerges from school, she finds Stefan waiting for her:

STEFAN: I'm going to back off and keep my distance. It's the right thing to do.
ELENA: Back off from school or from me? Thank you for telling me.
STEFAN: It's better this way.
ELENA: Yup, I got it.
STEFAN: You're angry. That's good. It'll be easier if you hate me.

This dialogue draws on earlier conversations about right actions, but it also introduces a new aspect to their dynamic: for the first time, Elena exhibits anger towards Stefan, which expresses the value she places on her relationship with him, for as Nussbaum states, "Anger requires the thought that I have suffered not trivial but important damages at another's hand" (*Love's Knowledge* 293). As with Buffy and Bella's expressions of anger towards Angel and Edward, however, Elena's anger does nothing to change Stefan's actions. Instead, Stefan names Elena's anger as good, as a proper response.

This episode also reveals Damon's reason for returning to Mystic Falls: he believes Katherine exists imprisoned in a tomb, and he intends to free her from this tomb, so they can resume their romantic relationship. The tomb is sealed by a spell created by Emily Bennett, one of Bonnie's ancestors from the Civil War period and "handmaiden" to Katherine. Emily takes possession of Bonnie's body in order to destroy a crystal Bonnie wears around her neck, a crystal required to open the tomb. When Emily/Bonnie performs the spell that shatters the crystal and releases Bonnie from Emily's possession, Damon reacts with pain and grief, thinking he has lost Katherine forever. Fuelled by rage, he attacks Bonnie, viciously biting her on the neck.

The most overt adherence to the genre's break-up semantics occurs after Elena witnesses Stefan feeding Bonnie his blood in order to save her life after Damon bites her. Deep in the forest, Stefan and Elena hold a conversation that parallels the discussion and setting in which Edward tells Bella he has to leave:

ELENA: I'm sorry Stefan. I thought that I couldn't be with you, but I can. You don't have to push me away. I can do this.
STEFAN: I can't. I have to leave, Elena. Too many people have died. Too much has happened.
ELENA: What? No! I know you think that you're protecting me, but...
STEFAN: I have to. Coming home. It was a mistake. I can't be a part of your life anymore.
ELENA: Don't go, Stefan. Please. You don't have to. This is your home. Just please don't go.
STEFAN: Goodbye Elena.
ELENA: You're just going to walk away? Don't walk away, Stefan. Stefan!

This scene of leaving echoes the rhetoric of Angel and Edward's stoic positions, and Buffy and Bella's responses of disbelief. Elena's repeated use of the word "don't" echoes Buffy's use of the negative to try to convince her beloved to stay. Their commands not to leave hurl ineffectually against the backs of their departing beloveds.

The Vampire Diaries continues to follow the semantics by moving from the break-up conversation to the scene in which the human lover suffers. As Buffy does before her, Elena sits on her best friend's bed and tearfully recounts the event. *TVD* departs from the semantics of the break-up, however, by showing Stefan's pain, and indeed by amplifying his pain with non-diegetic music. At first, Stefan seems in control, as he sits on his bed, pen in hand, his journal open to a blank page, the only sign of his pain a small muscle movement as he clenches his jaw. Slowly, he gets up, and then hurls his journal across the room. Barcelona croons, "Come back when you can. You've done nothing at all to make me love you less," and Stefan grabs the back of his head, his face a mask of pain, as he cries. For both beloveds, the break-up leads to a painful breakdown.

Both *BtVS* and the *Twilight* saga draw out this break-up period to demonstrate how the couples deal with an end to the relationship, but in *TVD*, Elena refuses to let Stefan use her safety as a reason for his actions. Although both Stefan and Damon say they are leaving, a new vampire in town provides the impetus for them to remain in Mystic Falls: Damon to find a new way to open the tomb; and Stefan to protect Elena ("The Turning Point" 1010). After a day of dealing with the vampire, who kidnaps Caroline and tortures Damon, Stefan tries to reason with Elena, so she agrees with their separation:

STEFAN: You saw what happened tonight. I mean you understand why we can't be together. You see it.
ELENA: Yeah, I'm starting to see a lot of things, Stefan.

Both Stefan and Elena connect seeing with understanding, which, as I discuss in Chapter 3, also signifies an aspect of love: this idea of really looking. Although Elena's comment may be read in multiple ways, one implication suggests she starts to see Stefan's pattern of pulling away from her, regardless of the intensity of his love for her.

Elena counters Stefan's resistance by offering to drive him home, an offer he accepts. They pull up outside Stefan's house, and Elena turns off the engine. In the conversation that ensues, Elena tries to show Stefan she does not hold him responsible for the pain in her life:

ELENA: I know you think that you brought all this bad stuff into my life, but my life already had it. I was buried in it.
STEFAN: This is different.
ELENA: It doesn't make it any less painful.
STEFAN: I know that it's hard to understand, but I'm doing this for you.

Stefan then turns from Elena and gets out of the vehicle. A close-up of Elena's face shows her staring after him and then looking down, thoughtful. It appears this exchange will be another instance in which a moral vampire leaves his beloved because he believes it is the right action.

Instead, Elena's face changes, hardens, moves from hurt to resolve. Elena follows Stefan and confronts him, opposing his logic, much in the same way Buffy challenges Angel when he tells her they should not be together. Rather than challenging him with anger though, Elena uses love: "No. You don't get to make that decision for me. If you walk away, it's for you because I know what I want. Stefan, I love you." The establishing shot shows Elena standing beside the car, talking to Stefan across the space he has already crossed. The shot/reverse shot closes in on Stefan's face, as Elena begins talking. The scene switches to a close-up of Elena's face as she admits her love for him, and then in an unusual and tense moment, the camera holds a point of view shot of the back of Stefan's head. In this frozen moment, this moment of agonized waiting, when the viewer sees through Elena's eyes, the semantics shift because Elena's love overpowers Stefan's resistance. Stefan turns—a visual metaphor that embodies the episode's title, "The Turning Point"—with a pained, disbelieving look on his face. He closes his eyes, swallows, crosses the distance between them, takes Elena's face in his hands, and kisses her deeply. Cue music.

Against a piano backdrop, Elena and Stefan kiss, as Plumb sings, "Not a stranger. No, I am yours. With crippled anger and tears that still drip sore. A fragile frame aged with misery. And when our eyes meet, I know you'll see." The ambiguous "I" of the lyrics attaches to both Stefan and Elena, as they let go of their hesitation and stumble passionately into the house, kissing and loving each other in those kisses. Perfectly timed, the lyrics, "And when our eyes meet, I know you'll see" correspond with the moment when Stefan's vampire eyes emerges with his growing passion. In another turning, he turns away from Elena, so she cannot see his changed face.

The final turning of this scene—perhaps *the* turning point—occurs in a tender moment when Elena encourages Stefan not to hide from her. Gently, she reaches around his body, cups his face in her hand, and turns him to face her. In an over-the-shoulder shot, Stefan turns to Elena, to the camera, so the viewer shares the moment when Elena sees his full vampire face. The shot reverses to show Elena's face gazing lovingly at Stefan, her fingers still brushing his jaw. In this moment, recalling Carroll's argument that characters cue the audience's emotive response, the viewer watches Elena's loving expression and aligns with her love and even wonder, as her fingers lightly touch his vampire eyes and as she kisses—for the first time—his vampire face. Plumb sings, "I do not want to be afraid," and the lyrics seem to embrace Stefan's emotional fear rather than Elena's fear of physical harm (Figure 4.3).

Elena's certainty about her desire, about knowing what she wants, to use her earlier phrasing, flows into the next shot, as she leads Stefan by the hand up the stairs to his bedroom. Unlike the beginning of this sequence when their passion rules their actions, here they walk at a

Figure 4.3 Elena kisses Stefan's vampire face.

measured pace up the stairs, stopping only at the top to kiss. This kiss initiates the scene of their love-making, for the extreme close-up of this kiss becomes the next, now in Stefan's bedroom. Tender kisses, careful touches, and loving looks punctuate this scene, and the lyrics with which this sequence started return at the end, "Not a stranger. No, I am yours." A close-up of Elena's face, eyes blissfully shut as Stefan kisses her neck, reaffirms her trust in him, as a piano trills into the final shot of the exterior of Stefan's house.

As with Buffy and Bella, Elena's post-coital bliss is short-lived. Stefan neither turns evil like Angelus, nor withdrawn like Edward, however; rather, the human lover, Elena, breaks the bliss, albeit due to Stefan's error of omission. The scene opens with Elena and Stefan chatting in bed, and Elena commenting she has never been in Stefan's room before. He tells her this room "is the only place that has remained constant. This room holds every memory that I ever thought was important enough to hold on to." When Stefan leaves the room to bring Elena a glass of water, she happily looks around the room, seemingly interested in learning more about what Stefan values. Tyrone Wells's upbeat song "This is Beautiful" accompanies Elena as she joyfully moves through Stefan's room, "I never could have seen, never could have seen this coming. You are here with me, I'm alive all of a sudden." The peppiness of the song matches Elena's mood, until she, and the music, stops. Her face changes, the music becomes instrumental and foreboding, and in a point-of-view shot, we see Elena holds a picture of Katherine in her hand. Stefan returns to the room to find Elena gone, and her Vervain necklace on top of Katherine's picture. The episode ends with Elena driving out of town on a foggy night. A figure suddenly looms in front of her, reminiscent of the pilot episode of the series. She crashes into it, loses control of her vehicle, and as she struggles to free herself from the ravaged vehicle, the figure gruesomely unhinges itself from the road and stalks towards her. Her screams echo into the closing credits.

The final episode in the narrative arc of Stefan and Elena's first series of break-ups and reunions ("Bloodlines" 1011), opens with the same sequence that closes the previous episode. Exactly halfway through the first season, this episode connects the two halves of the season by revealing the origin of Elena's relationship with Stefan while bringing Damon and Elena closer together. In other words, it provides a gateway between brothers, as Elena draws upon her time with Damon to confront Stefan. The two opening scenes show the distinction and connection between the two brothers: Stefan leaves an ineffectual, disembodied message for Elena on her phone imploring her to call him; and Damon rescues her from the supernatural creature stalking towards her while she hangs trapped upside down in the vehicle.

This connection with Damon and separation from Stefan continues throughout the episode when Elena awakes after fainting and finds herself in a car with Damon driving in Georgia. Stefan's voice messages follow them on their adventure, but when Elena uses her knowledge of Lexi's love and goodness to convince Lexi's grieving vampire beloved to spare Damon's life, it becomes clear Elena believes Damon to be worth saving. When Elena returns to Mystic Falls, she confronts Stefan about his feelings for her and interrogates him about why he never told her about her resemblance to Katherine:

ELENA: I can accept the fact that the world is a much more mysterious place than I ever thought possible, but this, this lie I cannot take. What am I to you? *Who* am I to you?

STEFAN: You are *not* Katherine. You are the opposite of everything that she was.

ELENA: And when did you figure that out? Before you kissed me? Before we *slept* together?

STEFAN: Before I met you.... The first day of school when we met. It wasn't for the first time, Elena.

Significantly, but rather disturbingly, Stefan responds to Elena's question by describing Elena in the negative—as not Katherine, as the opposite of Katherine. Thus, even though he means to comfort her that their intimacy does not depend upon her physical resemblance to Katherine, the dialectic remains: Stefan defines Elena in relation to Katherine, not for herself.

Stefan proceeds to tell Elena he rescued her from the car crash that killed her parents and tried to go back to save them. When Elena pushes him further, he also reveals he discovered she is adopted, and there are no records of her mother being pregnant. He then tries to comfort her by saying, "Listen to me. It doesn't matter. You are the woman that I love. I love you." Elena looks at him and kisses him, and they embrace as Elena cries against his chest. Through this speech act, Stefan constructs Elena through his love for her, effectively erasing her history by implying his love for her defines her identity. If we recall Nussbaum's normative criteria for love—compassion, reciprocity, and individuality—then Stefan remains unconvincing in the individuality category, which opens the door to Elena finding a more fulfilling love with Damon.

Although his actions make it clear Damon feels deeply about Elena, he resists verbalizing his love for her until well into the second season. One of Damon's most painful and loving acts occurs when he mercifully kills Rose in order to deliver her from suffering a long excruciating death from a werewolf bite, which is fatal to a vampire. As I discuss in the Introduction, Rose's story arc occurs over five episodes, during which time she becomes Damon's lover and teaches him about the necessity of living a loving life. In the first episode in which Rose appears ("Rose" 2008), Rose kidnaps Elena in order to negotiate a pardon for herself and her long-time friend Trevor, who defied the Originals 500 years ago by helping Katherine escape from them. Damon and Stefan drive three hundred miles together to save Elena and during the drive, Stefan confronts Damon about his feelings for Elena:

STEFAN: Thank you. For helping me.
DAMON: Can we *not* do the whole road trip bonding thing? The cliché of it all makes me itch.
STEFAN: Oh, come on Damon. We both know that you being in this car has absolutely nothing to do with me anyway.
DAMON: The elephant in the room lets out a mighty roar.
STEFAN: Well, it doesn't have to be an elephant. Let's talk about it.
DAMON: There's nothing to talk about.
STEFAN: That's not true. Sure there is. Just get it out. I mean are you in this car because you want to help your little brother save the girl that he loves or is it because you love her too? I mean, come on, express yourself. I happen to like road trip bonding.
DAMON: Keep it up, Stefan. I can step out of helping as easily as I stepped in.
STEFAN: Nope. See that's the beauty of it. You can't.

Stefan's final comment draws attention to the continuing discrepancy between Damon's words and actions, which Elena also recognizes. Stefan understands and acknowledges how Damon's love for Elena informs his right action. Although Damon says he can stop helping protect Elena, Stefan articulates Damon's double lie: Damon loves Elena and because of his love, he will do whatever he can to protect her.

After Stefan and Damon return from rescuing Elena, Stefan initiates another bonding conversation with Damon which models an apology as a moral action that counteracts selfishness:

STEFAN: You know the only way we're going to be able [to keep Elena safe] is if we're not fighting each other. We let Katherine come between us, if we let that happen with Elena, we're not going to be able to protect her.

DAMON: Yes, Stefan. Heard it all before.

STEFAN: I'm sorry.

DAMON: About what?

STEFAN: For being the guy who made you turn a hundred and forty-five years ago.

DAMON: Enough Stef. It's late. No need to rehash that.

STEFAN: Well, you know what, I've never said it out loud. I guess I just need to say it and you need to hear it. I'm sorry. What I did was selfish. I didn't want to be alone. Guess I just needed my brother.

Stefan's apology and admission of fraternal love models for Damon the possibility of right action within romantic love, especially in relation to speech acts.

Typically, Damon's words and actions contradict each other. He verbally denies having positive loving feelings for other people, but he acts in order to care for and protect Stefan and Elena. One of Damon's most revealing acts of love occurs in this same episode after he and Stefan return from rescuing Elena and following from Stefan's apology. Elena emerges from the bathroom into her bedroom and finds Damon seated on the window bench with her Vervain necklace in his hands, which he recovered after Elijah—one of the Originals—ripped it from her neck. He extends his arm to give it to her and then pulls his hand back in order to speak:

DAMON: I just have to say something.

ELENA: Why do you have to say it with my necklace?

DAMON: Because what I'm about to say is probably the most selfish thing I've ever said in my life.

ELENA: Damon, don't go there.

DAMON: I just have to say it once. You just need to hear it. I love you, Elena. And it's because I love you that I can't be selfish with you. Why you can't know this. I don't deserve you. But my brother does. God, I wish you didn't have to forget this. But you do.

Damon uses the same phrases Stefan utters to apologize to Damon for being selfish: I have to say it and you need to hear it. Damon's declaration and gestures of love recall his earlier moment in Elena's bedroom when he touches her cheek while she sleeps. As he did then, here he gently caresses the side of her face. Elena neither flinches nor pulls away when he touches her hair or kisses her forehead, in a gesture similar to Edward kissing Bella goodbye. Indeed, her lips part slightly, as though in anticipation of his kiss. Instead, he compels her to forget his admission of love, and as he does so, a single tear drops from his eye. Although Elena may not remember this moment, the viewer becomes an intimate voyeur and witness to his pain. His future actions will forever be informed by this moment when he put his love for his brother ahead of his love for Elena, when he lets go of Elena. No longer shall he be seen as the bad boy brother who acts for himself only. When he mercifully kills Rose four episodes later and cries while doing so, the viewer again bears witness to his pain, as he lets go of another lover ("The Descent" 2012).

The importance of love between men—literal and metaphoric brotherhoods—repeats throughout the series, but manifests most significantly in the final episode of Season Two. This episode concludes with a reciprocal gesture of fraternal love—expressed in part through leaving—that will alter the course of the series. In the season finale ("As I Lay Dying" 2022), Stefan makes a pact with Klaus in order to save Damon's life, and, like Damon does earlier, he does so by letting go of his love for Elena and by departing from his moral code not to drink human blood as part of the agreement. The title of the episode invokes both William Faulkner's novel of the same name and Book XI of *The Odyssey*, in which Agamemnon says, "As I lay dying, the woman with the dog's eyes would not close my eyes for me as I descended into Hades." At first glance, the title appears to refer to Damon only, who suffers as a werewolf bite slowly seems to kill him. Stefan learns Klaus's blood can heal Damon, but Klaus will provide a vial of his blood only if Stefan agrees to do everything Klaus says, which means drinking human blood and then leaving town with Klaus. As the episode progresses, it becomes apparent the title also relates to the death of Stefan's moral principles.

The thematic backdrop to this episode circulates around the importance of family by drawing parallels between two examples of brotherly love. Klaus and Elijah function as a cautionary tale about how romantic love can destroy fraternal love, for both of them loved Elena's doppelgänger, Katerina Petrova, which places a rift between the brothers. Stefan and Damon's prior love for Katerina/Katherine causes a similar animosity, but in this episode, Stefan chooses his love for Damon over his love for Elena. This choice serves as a moral action that foregrounds brotherly attachment cloaked as obligation. Speech acts that cite obligation bookend the episode, as both Stefan and Katherine claim to act out of obligation to Damon for previous actions that caused him harm. At the beginning of the episode Stefan says, "Whatever Damon's done.

Whatever's led him here. I'm the one who made him become a vampire in the first place, so if there's a chance for a cure, I owe it to him to find it." Correspondingly, at the end of the episode, Katherine brings the vial of Klaus's blood to Damon when she could have run away with it. When Damon questions her about her decision to bring it to him, she responds by saying that she "owed [him] one."

While the next chapter will focus primarily on Season Three and acts of compassion and forgiveness, I conclude this chapter with a brief analysis of the first episode of Season Three ("The Birthday" 3001) because it joins loving to leaving and letting go in specific speech acts. At the end of Season Two, when Katherine delivers the vial of Klaus's blood to Damon, Elena asks her where Stefan is, and Katherine responds, "He's paying for this. He gave himself over to Klaus..... He just sacrificed everything to save his brother. Including you. It's a good thing you have Damon to keep you company. Goodbye Elena. Oh, it's ok to love both of them. I did." In other words, the season ends by connecting Stefan's departure with the potential arrival of a romance between Elena and Damon. Stefan loves Damon enough to let go of Elena, to leave Mystic Falls, and to let go of his own moral code.

Episode One of Season Three takes place on Elena's eighteenth birthday ("The Birthday" 3001), but, similar to "As I Lay Dying," as the episode unfolds, it becomes apparent the title functions in at least two ways: as Elena's symbolic birth into adulthood; and also as Stefan's birth—or rebirth—into The Ripper, a violent, vicious vampire who literally rips his victims apart. Unbeknownst to Elena, Damon and Alaric have been trying to track Stefan and Klaus by mapping reports of suspicious and violent deaths across nearby states. When they go to the site of a particularly gruesome double murder and find two women's bodies whose heads have been ripped off and then put back on top of their seated bodies, Damon confirms this practice of putting together ripped apart bodies is Stefan's signature, for after he kills people, he feels remorse and tries to provide a semblance of normality.

While the evidence seems to point to Stefan for these grisly deaths, no one—including the viewer—bears witness to these crimes, so there remains a glimmer of hope that Klaus and not Stefan committed the murders. In a horrific scene that solidifies Stefan's capacity for cruelty, Stefan returns to Mystic Falls to warn Damon to stop tracking him and Klaus. Since midway through Season Two, after Damon tells Elena he loves her and then compels her to forget his declaration, Damon has been dating Andie, a reporter, who he says is his distraction from Elena, but for whom he seems to care quite deeply. When Damon goes to the news studio to pick up Andie to bring her to Elena's birthday party, he finds Stefan waiting for him. Stefan tells Damon to stop following him, and when Damon says, "I'm supposed to care what [Klaus] thinks?" Stefan replies, "What you're supposed to do is let me go." Damon ignores Stefan and initiates a slightly different line of conversation:

DAMON: Saw your latest artwork in Tennessee. You're walking a fine line there, my friend. Keep that up and there *will* be no saving you.
STEFAN: See the thing is, I don't need any saving. I just want you to let me go.
DAMON: No, I got a birthday girl at home whose not gonna let me do that.

In this role reversal, Stefan becomes the brother who needs saving, but Damon uses Elena as the reason for his actions. Stefan's actions to save his brother repeatedly connect to his own obligation to and love for Damon, but Damon seems unable to admit he acts out of his own love for Stefan.

When Damon shrugs off Stefan's suggestion, Stefan attempts to demonstrate the seriousness of his demand that Damon let him go. He directs Damon's attention to a catwalk suspended high about the floor where Andie stands compelled to remain still. Stefan then commands Andie to move, and at the same time grabs Damon and shoves him across the room, so he cannot catch Andie. Andie's body crashes sickeningly to the floor, while Stefan growls at Damon, "I *said* let me go." Damon pushes Stefan away and rushes to Andie's dead body, too late to save her. He quickly looks over his shoulder and finds Stefan gone. He turns, touches Andie, and sits back on his heels, deflated and defeated. Back at the party, he tells Elena Stefan is gone: he has "flipped the switch" to turn off his emotions and to become a "full blown ripper."

In this episode, Stefan repeatedly threatens Damon to let him go, Klaus warns Stefan that letting go of family will keep Damon safe, and Elena uses these very words to try to save Stefan by giving him hope. After Klaus warns Stefan he needs to stop caring for his family and claims feeding on human blood "makes it easier to let go," Stefan stumbles outside of the bar where he and Klaus have been torturing a werewolf for information. He slowly takes his phone out of his pocket and makes a call. A series of cross-cuts move between Elena in her bedroom and Stefan in the parking lot. The first cut shows "Caller Unknown" ringing Elena's phone and then switches back to a close-up of Stefan's face, holding a phone against his ear but saying nothing. Elena picks up her phone and says hello. When no one responds, she asks, "Stefan? Stefan, if this is you, you'll be ok. I love you, Stefan. Hold onto that. Never let that go." He nods his head as she speaks, tears well in his eyes, and, like Damon's tears in previous episodes, Stefan's tears reveal a disconnect between his actions, his words, and his feelings. While it may appear he has shut off his emotions, his tears in this scene flow symbolically through the remainder of Season Three reminding viewers, if not the characters, Stefan's moral compass still functions, if not fully, then possibly justifiably.

In each of the three series, the vampire beloveds end the romantic relationship with their human lovers because they believe letting go of their lovers will allow them to live a better life. To recall Nussbaum's claim, "we can't choose to fall in love with someone; it simply happens to us. And we can't altogether govern the way in which, or the goodness with which, it will happen" (*Love's Knowledge* 336), each vampire tries to govern the way in which he loves by refusing that very love and in the process suffers for it and causes pain more than relief. Even in the case of Buffy and Angel in which it appears the end of their romantic relationship does serve a greater good, neither Angel nor Buffy ever love again with the goodness that infuses their love for each other. As the season finale implies, their hope for a future love together continues even beyond the potential apocalypse. Each series suggests one cannot let go of love easily or even with intention without causing deep pain to oneself and one's lover. To try to end a romantic relationship while still being in love seems an injustice because it betrays a moral emotion that can lead to right action. Nonetheless, as the next chapter examines, each vampire lover does attempt to let go of his beloved, and then seeks forgiveness for acting wrongly and for causing pain.

Works Cited

"162 Candles." *The Vampire Diaries*. Writ. Kevin Williamson and Julie Plec. Dir. Rick Bota. CWTV. 5 November 2009. Television.

"As I Lay Dying." *The Vampire Diaries*. Writ. Turi Meyer, Al Septien, and Michael Narducci. Dir. John Behring. CWTV. 12 May 2011. Television.

Barcelona. "Come Back When You Can." *Absolutes*. Universal, 2008. Song.

Beck, Christophe. "Close Your Eyes [Angel & Buffy Love Theme]." *Buffy the Vampire Slayer: the Album*. TVT, 1999. Song.

"Becoming, Part One." *Buffy the Vampire Slayer: The Complete Second Season on DVD*. Writ. and Dir. Joss Whedon. Twentieth Century Fox, 2002. DVD.

"Becoming, Part Two." *Buffy the Vampire Slayer: The Complete Second Season on DVD*. Writ. and Dir. Joss Whedon. Twentieth Century Fox, 2002. DVD.

"The Birthday." *The Vampire Diaries*. Writ. Kevin Williamson and Julie Plec. Dir. John Behring. CWTV. 15 September 2011. Television.

"Bloodlines." *The Vampire Diaries*. Writ. Kevin Williamson and Julie Plec. Dir. David Barrett. CWTV. 21 January 2010. Television.

"Choices." *Buffy the Vampire Slayer: The Complete Third Season on DVD*. Writ. David Fury. Dir. James A. Contner. Twentieth Century Fox, 2002. DVD.

"The Descent." *The Vampire Diaries*. Writ. Sarah Fain and Elizabeth Craft. Dir. Marcos Siega. CWTV. 27 January 2011. Television.

"Friday Night Bites." *The Vampire Diaries*. Writ. Barbie Kligman and Bryan M. Holden. Dir. John Dahl. CWTV. 1 October 2009. Television.

"Haunted." *The Vampire Diaries*. Writ. Andrew Kreisberg and Brian Young. Dir. Guy Ferland. CWTV. 29 October 2009. Television.

"History Repeating." *The Vampire Diaries*. Writ. Bryan M. Holdman and Brian Young. Dir. Marcos Siega. CWTV. 12 November 2009. Television.

Kapurch, Katie. "'Unconditionally and irrevocably': Theorizing the Melodramatic Impulse in Young Adult Literature through the *Twilight Saga* and *Jane Eyre*." *Children's Literature Association Quarterly* 37.2 (Summer 2012): 164–187. Print.

"Lost Girls." *The Vampire Diaries*. Writ. Kevin Williamson and Julie Plec. Dir. Marcos Siega. CWTV. 15 October 2009. Television.

McLachlan, Sarah. "Full of Grace." *Surfacing*. Arista, 1997. Song.

Meyer, Stephenie. *Breaking Dawn*. New York: Little Brown, 2008. Print.

———. *Eclipse*. New York: Little Brown, 2007. Print.

———. *New Moon*. New York: Little Brown, 2006. Print.

Murdoch, Iris. *The Sovereignty of Good*. 1970. New York: Routledge, 2013. Print.

Nussbaum, Martha C. *Love's Knowledge: Essays on Philosophy and Literature*. New York: Oxford UP, 1990. Print.

———. *Upheavals of Thought: The Intelligence of Emotions*. Cambridge: Cambridge UP, 2001. Print.

Peitzman, Louis. "Ranking Every Episode of *Buffy the Vampire Slayer*." *BuzzFeed Entertainment*. 14 November 2013. Web. 14 November 2013.

Plumb. "Cut." *Chaotic Resolve*, Curb, 2006. Song.

"The Prom." *Buffy the Vampire Slayer: The Complete Third Season on DVD*. Writ. Marti Noxon. Dir. David Solomon. Twentieth Century Fox, 2002. DVD.

"Rose." *The Vampire Diaries*. Writ.Brian Young. Dir. Liz Friedlander. CWTV. 4 November 2010. Television.

Slutsky, Mark. "Sad YouTube: The Lost Treasures of the Internet's Greatest Cesspool." *BuzzFeed Entertainment*. 20 January 2014. Web. 23 January 2014

The Sundays. "Wild Horses." *Blind*. Parlophone, 1992. Song.

"The Turning Point." *The Vampire Diaries*. Teleplay Kevin Williamson and Julie Plec. Story Barbie Kligman. Dir. J. Miller Tobin. CWTV. 19 November 2009. Television.

The Twilight Saga: New Moon. Writ. Melissa Rosenberg. Dir. Chris Weitz, 2009. DVD.

Walker, Jason. "Down." Ft. Molly Reed. *Jason Walker*. Word, 2009. Song.

Wells, Tyrone. "This is Beautiful." *Remain*. Universal Republic, 2009. Song.

5 "I Know I Don't Deserve Your Forgiveness, But I Need It"

Vengeance, Compassion, and Forgiveness

This chapter links compassion and forgiveness to love and to a love-based justice. If the previous chapter suggests pain exists in love, then this chapter demonstrates how acts of compassion and forgiveness alleviate such pain. This chapter analyses two aspects of compassion: it forms one of the key components of love; and it "pushes the boundaries of the self further outward than many types of love" (*Upheavals*, Nussbaum 300). The main aspects of compassion hang on the perception that the beloveds have become vampires through no wrongdoing of their own, and their monstrous existence expands their lovers' own sense of well-being. For instance, as I discuss in Chapter 3, Buffy defends Angel when Xander insists Angelus must die for killing Jenny Calendar. Buffy argues being a vampire is not Angel's fault, but Xander counters that killing Jenny is ("Becoming: Part Two"). Similarly, Elena feels compassion for Stefan in relation to his addiction to human blood, and she forgives him for his behavior when he acts irrationally due to his addiction.

Furthermore, all three series pit passion against compassion and demonstrate how the two feelings bind. As far back as the tenth century, passion refers to suffering, often the suffering of a saint or martyr, which links to my discussion of torture and suffering in Chapter 2. The word's meaning shifts, however, in the thirteenth century to apply to any strong feeling or impulse (*OED*). In the fourteenth century, the word *compassion* first came into usage in order to conjoin suffering with togetherness. In other words, to feel passion is to suffer alone and to feel compassion means to suffer with another. And to suffer with another sounds an awful lot like love.

As I summarize in the Introduction, Martha Nussbaum argues love should contain three positive normative criteria: compassion; reciprocity; and individuality (*Upheavals* 478–81). In the previous three chapters, I outline how the three series demonstrate a reciprocal love based on close looking and mutual concern and how this reciprocity relies upon each beloved's uniqueness. In this chapter, I focus on the concept of compassion, which Nussbaum defines as follows:

> Compassion… has three cognitive elements: the judgment of *size* (a serious bad event has befallen someone); the judgment of *nondesert*

> (this person did not bring the suffering on himself or herself); and the *eudaimonistic judgment* (this person, or creature, is a significant element in my scheme of goals and projects, an end whose good is to be promoted). The Aristotelian *judgment of similar possibilities* is an epistemological aid to forming the *eudaimonistic judgment*—not necessary, but usually very important. Finally, let us recall that, like all emotions directed at living beings, compassion frequently either contains or is closely linked to a non-eudaimonistic element of *wonder*.
> (*Upheavals* 353)

Similar possibility means the observer must identify with the sufferer and must believe it is possible for him or herself to be in the position of the sufferer (*Upheavals* 339). Nussbaum stipulates she does not emphasize similar possibility as much as Aristotle and Rousseau's account of compassion, but this element looms large in vampire texts because the possibility of becoming a vampire opens to everyone.

For the most part, a vampire's very existence satisfies the first two cognitive elements of size and nondesert: being turned into a vampire classifies as a "serious bad event"; and Angel, Edward, Stefan, and Damon did not bring their transformation into vampires—and its attendant suffering—upon themselves. Damon and Bella's situations may vary slightly because both of them desire to become vampires, although the moment of their transformations does not proceed as they intend, and, arguably, their love for Katherine and Edward respectively occurs through no fault of their own. The final element, eudaimonistic judgment, throbs at the heart of the matter. To feel compassion for another being means an admission this person—human, vampire, or any other creature—matters for one's own flourishing. Epiphanic moments often occur when it becomes apparent one feels compassion and/or acts compassionately because another being suffers. Compassion, in other words, reveals and constitutes love. Of the three series, *The Vampire Diaries* uses such moments the most frequently in order to reveal the love behind words that seem to contradict love, especially between Stefan and Damon, and Damon and Elena.

But what does it mean to act compassionately, and what does one do when compassion grates against evil and/or hurts someone beloved? Buffy feels love and compassion towards Angel in the moment when his soul returns to him, but she still thrusts a sword into his chest and sends him to hell. Bella feels compassion for Jacob, but she still chooses to be with Edward. Elena feels compassion towards Damon each time he mourns for Katherine, but she resists admitting she loves him, for most of four seasons. At least part of acting compassionately means behaving in ways that benefit a beloved. When such action seems impossible because it means harm to others, then one seeks and provides pardon or forgiveness.

Nussbaum's definition of compassion can fruitfully be supplemented here with Richard Kearney's threefold approach to "acknowledge the enigma of evil... while addressing the unavoidable question: *what is to be done*?" (100). Kearney's approach includes practical understanding; working-through; and pardon. Practical understanding includes a process of deliberation that "operates on the conviction that evil is something that must be actively *contested*.... For how could we *act against* evil if we could not *identify* it, that is, if we could not *in some way* discern between good and evil" (101). The second stage, working-through, means understanding how suffering may be a response to acting against evil (103). Pardon or forgiveness constitutes the third and final stage. Kearney argues, "Against the Never of evil, which makes pardon impossible, we are asked to think the 'marvel of a once again' which makes it possible.... [P]revention often requires pardon as well as protest in order that the cycles of repetition and revenge give way to future possibilities of non-evil" (105). This final statement seems most significant here because in these three series repeated actions can result in either redemption or condemnation. Buffy and her friends must learn this model of forgiveness, for instance, as Angel repeatedly performs good acts, including saving their lives.

Each series sets up revenge or vengeance as incorrect action. While initiating with love, vengeance morphs from grief into anger and then hatred. In *BtVS*, a gypsy clan curses Angel by returning his soul to him, so he suffers for all the pain he has inflicted on others, and especially on their people when he murders one of their daughters. The curse, however, contains a clause that if Angel experiences even one moment of true happiness, then the curse lifts and his soul disappears. Jenny Calendar, a descendant of this gypsy clan, has been sent to Sunnydale to watch Buffy and Angel—and to intervene in their relationship if necessary—so Angel does not feel happiness. When the clan senses the curse weakens, they charge Jenny's uncle Enyos with disciplining Jenny about her duty:

ENYOS: You know what it is, this thing vengeance?
JENNY: Uncle, I have served you. I have been faithful. I need to know...
ENYOS: To the modern man, vengeance is a verb, an idea. Payback. One thing for another. Like commerce. Not with us. Vengeance is a living thing. It passes through generations. It commands. It kills.

....

JENNY: Angel could be of help to us. I mean, he may be the only chance we have to stop the Judge.
ENYOS: It is too late for that.
JENNY: Why?
ENYOS: The curse. Angel is meant to suffer, not to live as human. One moment of true happiness, of contentment, one moment where the

soul that we restored no longer plagues his thoughts, and that soul is taken from him.

JENNY: Then, if somehow, if it's happened, then Angelus is back.
ENYOS: I hoped to stop it. But I realize now it was arranged to be so.
JENNY: Buffy loves him.
ENYOS: And now she will have to kill him.

("Innocence" 2014)

In this conversation, Enyos distinguishes between vengeance as a verb and vengeance as a noun, a living thing. In this personification, vengeance acts but is not the action itself. This nuanced definition moves beyond a transaction in which one death exchanges for another; it hangs on ideas of suffering and torment rather than on capital punishment. Regardless, Enyos's opening and closing statements connect vengeance to killing, and the ambiguity of his first statement solidifies in his second when he implies Buffy becomes vengeance.

In one of the most moving episodes of Season Two, "I Only Have Eyes for You" (2019), Buffy embodies forgiveness so she might learn to cast aside her vengeful nature. In this episode, a poltergeist seeks forgiveness for killing his lover and then himself. Possessed by the ghosts of these two lovers, Angelus and Buffy re-enact the scene of the lovers' deaths, with Buffy cast in the role of the killer seeking forgiveness. By working through why a killer might seek forgiveness, Buffy moves from a position of assertion that the killer does not deserve forgiveness to an understanding of why he—or she—might need it in order to move to a pardoned future. When Buffy symbolically kills Angel at the end of the season by sending him to a hell dimension, she must learn to forgive herself for her actions, and when Angel returns from hell, then the Scooby Gang is repeatedly called upon to forgive him for the torments he inflicted upon them as Angelus. In this episode, however, Buffy and Angelus perform a "marvel of a once again"—to recall Kearney—and learn the importance of pardon as prevention against future evil.

The episode begins on the eve of the school's annual Sadie Hawkins dance. Buffy leans against a balcony railing in the Bronze, overlooking the dance floor. A band plays, and the lead singer croons, "The way you love. Have you got a name for it? Cause I don't understand it. Language is an annoying necessity and I depend on all the regular things. Got a list tattooed on my memory of how our tryst should unfold" (Splendid). Ben, a boy from her school, approaches her and asks her if she might consider asking him to the Sadie Hawkins dance. Buffy replies, "You seem like a really great guy. It's me. I'm not seeing anybody. Ever again, actually." The episode's title "I Only Have Eyes for You," and Buffy's response she is never "seeing" anybody ever again, links back to my discussion about the importance of looking, of seeing, as a key element to loving. A twist, of course, lingers in the modifier "only," which implies the subject only has eyes—and no other body parts—for the you and/or suggests the subject sees only you.

Dejected, Buffy leaves the balcony and meets Willow, who chastises her gently for rejecting Ben. Buffy defends her decision by summarizing what happened with her last boyfriend:

BUFFY: Do you remember my ex-boyfriend the vampire? I slept with him, he lost his soul. Now my boyfriend's gone forever and the demon that wears his face is killing my friends.
WILLOW: Ok, the Angel thing went badly. I'm on board with that, but that's not your fault. And anyways, love isn't always like that. Love can be nice.

By reminding Buffy that Angel's transformation into Angelus is not Buffy's fault, Willow signals one element of compassion: judgment. This element becomes significant in the next scene, in which a tragedy between two lovers unfolds for the first time in the episode.

After Willow's words, the scene cuts to a hallway in the high school, where two people fight. Willow's claim, "love can be nice," grates uneasily against the confrontation between the lovers:

YOUNG MAN: Come back here! We're not finished. You don't care anymore, is that it?
YOUNG WOMAN: It doesn't matter. It doesn't matter what I feel.
MAN: Then tell me you don't love me. Say it!
WOMAN: Will that help? Is that what you need to hear? I don't. I don't. Now let me go.
MAN: No. A person doesn't just wake up one day and stop loving somebody. Love is forever.

As the young man says, "Love is forever," he slowly raises a gun and points it at the woman. The scene ends, and the credits roll. Unlike the conversation between Buffy and Ben, this exchange hinges on hearing rather than seeing. Following the trope of the break-up I outline in the previous chapter, but in a gender reversal, the woman seems to be fighting her love for the man and acting in a way that denies her love in order to perform a right action. Her repetition of "I don't" tellingly avoids the full claim, "I don't love you." The confrontation continues after the credits, but Buffy arrives and stops the fight, kicking the gun out of the man's hands. Buffy's interruption seemingly diffuses the situation as the couple shakingly tell her they do not know what happened because they were not fighting moments before. Buffy challenges the man by asking him why he had a gun, but when they look for the gun, it is no longer there.

As the episode unfolds, different people re-enact the same situation, with each repetition providing more information about a forbidden love affair that occurred in 1955 between a student, James, and his teacher, Grace Newman, whose very name implies forgiveness and renewal, and, moreover, foreshadows the season's closing song "State of Grace," which I discuss in Chapter 4. Buffy's first response to the discovery James killed Grace and then himself condemns James without mercy, but Willow tries to see the nuances of the situation and Xander states the obvious:

BUFFY: He couldn't make her love him, so he killed her. Sicko.
WILLOW: He looks so normal in this picture. He was smart, too. He made the Honor Roll.
BUFFY: Smart?
XANDER: He killed a person and killed himself. Those are pretty much two of the dumbest things you could do.
WILLOW: I know, but... Well, don't you feel kinda bad for them?
BUFFY: Sure I feel lousy. For her. He's a murderer and he should pay for it.
WILLOW: With his life?
BUFFY: No, he should be doing sixty years in prison, breaking rocks and making special friends with Roscoe the Weightlifter.
XANDER: Yikes. The quality of mercy is not Buffy.

Although Xander's observation resonates as typical Buffyspeak, it also echoes Enyos's statement in "Passion" that Buffy personifies vengeance and not the mercy or sadness Willow advocates. Tellingly, Buffy also names him "murderer" rather than "killer," which signals an intent that defies justification.

Buffy voices her strident position even more overtly when the Scooby Gang tries to determine what James's poltergeist desires, and Buffy identifies it as forgiveness:

GILES: He's trying to resolve whatever issues are keeping him in limbo. What exactly those are, I'm not...
BUFFY: He wants forgiveness.
GILES: Yes. I imagine he does. But when James possesses people, they act out exactly what happened that night. So he's experiencing a form of purgatory instead. He's doomed to kill his Miss Newman over and over and over again, and... forgiveness is impossible.
BUFFY: Good. He doesn't deserve it.
GILES: To forgive is an act of compassion, Buffy. It's not done because people deserve it. It's done because they need it.
BUFFY: No. James destroyed the one person he loved the most in a moment of blind passion. And that's not something you forgive. No matter why he did what he did. And no matter if he knows now that it was wrong and selfish and stupid. It is just something he's going to have to live with.
XANDER: He can't live with it, Buff. He's dead.

Giles rightly connects forgiveness with compassion, but Buffy remains immovable and ties James's wrong action to passion and love. Revealingly, she characterizes James's act as a moment of "blind passion," a moment of not seeing. The more she talks, the more it becomes apparent she equates James's violence with Angel's actions, and the poltergeist's repetition of killing parallels Angel's past violence and recent murder of Miss Calendar. Moreover, she also implies her moment of blind passion with Angel killed him metaphorically, and she is living with her role in his death.

This second layer becomes more apparent when Angelus and Buffy meet in the school and are possessed by the lovers, and James chooses Buffy to play the role of the killer seeking forgiveness. Suddenly, the gender reversal takes on new meaning, as the scene cuts between Buffy and Angelus in the present and James and Miss Newman in 1955:

BUFFY: You can't make me disappear just because you say it's over.
ANGELUS: Actually I can. In fact [then the spirit of Grace possesses him] I just want you to be able to have some kind of normal life. We can never have that, don't you see?
BUFFY: I don't give a damn about a normal life! I'm going crazy not seeing you. I think about you every minute.
MISS NEWMAN: I know. But it's over. It has to be.
BUFFY: Come back here! We're not finished!
[Buffy catches up with Angelus, grabs his arm, and turns him to face her]
BUFFY: You don't care anymore, is that it?
ANGELUS: It doesn't matter. It doesn't matter what I feel.
BUFFY: Then tell me you don't love me.

With metaphors of sight and seeing, this heart-breaking moment anticipates the break-up scene between Buffy and Angel that takes place in Season Three ("The Prom" 3020), when Angel tells Buffy he must leave her, even though he loves her. Significantly, the scene shows Miss Newman, and not Angelus, saying "it's over. It has to be," for the relationship between Buffy and Angelus does not end here. Leaving and letting go demonstrates an attempt at right action, but James's inability to do so, torments him for decades after his death. Only when Grace forgives him does his ghost stop its hauntings.

This act of forgiveness occurs when Angelus/Miss Newman does not die after being shot by Buffy/James. Instead, Angelus finds Buffy in the music room, where James killed himself after shooting Miss Newman. A record player scratches out the lyrics that add depth to the title of the episode and to the narrative's focus on seeing and blindness: "My love must be a kind of blind love. I can't see anyone but you" (The Flamingos). As Buffy raises her arm, gun still in hand, Angelus reaches out and lowers her arm:

ANGELUS: Don't do this.
BUFFY: But, I killed you.
ANGELUS: It was an accident. It wasn't your fault.
BUFFY: It is my fault. How could I…
ANGELUS: Shhh. I'm the one who should be sorry, James. You thought I stopped loving you. But I never did. I loved you with my last breath.

As Grace and James kiss, as Buffy and Angelus kiss, a column of light sweeps up from them, a symbol that the spirit of the poltergeist departs. Angelus and Buffy slowly stop kissing, Buffy whispers Angel's name, and Angelus growls and pushes Buffy away. The scene cuts to Buffy and the Scooby Gang back in the library, when Buffy confesses to Giles she cannot understand why Grace forgives James, but she accepts that maybe she does not need to understand the reasons why; she just needs to have experienced the feeling of being forgiven. By accepting she is not to blame for killing Angel metaphorically and turning him back into Angelus, she opens herself to the possibility she can forgive herself and, perhaps, in turn, others who commit evil acts. As for Angelus, he returns to his mansion, and the next scene shows him shirtless, washing himself frantically, trying to cleanse himself of feeling love. Angelus feels dirtied by love, and Buffy feels confused by forgiveness; together they rehearse a compassionate response based on similar possibility that transcends death and frees lovers into a peaceful wonder (Figure 5.1).

Figure 5.1 Buffy and Angel kiss the poltergeist away.

The *Twilight* saga—both the novels and the films—builds vengeance even more fully into its story arc as an example of wrong action. *Twilight* introduces a group of wandering vampires—Laurent, Victoria, and James—as an antithesis of the Cullen family, and when James becomes obsessed with tracking and killing Bella, Edward and his family work together to thwart his attempts. When James finally traps Bella, Edward and his family arrive in time to rescue Bella and kill James. In *New Moon*, Victoria begins plotting to avenge her beloved James's death, and her vengeance culminates in *Eclipse*, when she builds an army of newborn vampires to attack Bella and the Cullens. Victoria and James's actions function as an example of wrong behavior, and as the opposite of Bella and Edward; Victoria expresses her love through the intensity of her vengeance whereas Bella and Edward show their love through gestures of forgiveness.

When it becomes clear, in *Eclipse*, the newborns intend to fight the Cullens, Jasper explains to Bella his own history of training newborns in order to teach her about the difficulties of acting with forgiveness. Jasper joined the Confederate Army in 1861 and was turned into a vampire shortly thereafter (temporally making him a comrade of Damon Salvatore). Jasper explains while the Civil War raged, wars once being fought over territory now became feuds fuelled by vengeance for lost loves: "So many had lost their partners, and that is something our kind does not forgive..." (*Eclipse* 298). Victoria's quest for vengeance, and her reliance upon newborns to join her in this battle, has historical precedence bathed in an ideology about power through violence and a disregard for humanity, an ideology Jasper eventually deserts.

Victoria errs not only because she seeks to avenge her lost love by killing Bella but also because she misuses love. Victoria creates a newborn vampire, Riley, who she lures with declarations of love to act on her behalf, so Alice cannot see that Victoria leads and instructs the newborn army to kill the Cullens. During the battle, Edward hides Bella away from the main fighting, but Victoria and Riley find them, and Edward tries to reason with Riley by showing him how Victoria uses him to serve her own vengeance:

> "She doesn't love you, Riley.... She never has. She loved someone named James, and you're no more than a tool to her."... "She knows that I will kill you, Riley. She *wants* you to die so that she doesn't have to keep up the pretense anymore. Yes—you've seen that, haven't you? You've read reluctance in her eyes, suspected a false note in her promises. You were right. She's never wanted you. Every kiss, every touch was a lie."
>
> (*Eclipse* 543–544)

Although Victoria disputes Edward's claim and tells Riley she loves only him, her actions expose her. In the novel, Bella observes, "Victoria did not spare one glance for the boy she'd just pledged her love to" (545); and in the film, Victoria ignores Riley's pain and fate as he is slowly dismembered in the battle.

Against the ferocity of Victoria's vengeance nuzzles an antagonism between Edward and Jacob, almost a living thing—to return to Enyos's characterization of vengeance in *BtVS*. *BtVS* includes a model for compassion and forgiveness in which a lover reveals the mystery of love by being unable to stop loving, even if she believes that love to be flawed; Buffy does not stop loving Angel, even when he morphs into the soulless Angelus. The *Twilight* saga takes this model and tests it in slightly different circumstances by portraying a lover who loves two different people, rather than two opposites contained in one body. When Edward leaves Bella in *New Moon*, Jacob and Bella's friendship deepens, and Bella ruminates internally about the differences between her platonic love for Jacob and her romantic love for Edward. She does not deny to herself she loves Jacob, but she distinguishes between the two types of love calling her love for Jacob a "weak echo" (*New Moon* 375) of the "truest of true loves" (*New Moon* 397) she feels for Edward.

Given the bond that forms during Edward's absence, Jacob repeatedly tries to convince Bella a relationship with him would be better than one with Edward, and she does not deny his argument has merit:

> "I'm exactly right for you, Bella. It would have been effortless for us—comfortable, easy as breathing. I was the natural path your life would have taken..." He stared into space for a moment, and I waited. "If the world was the way it was supposed to be, if there were no monsters and no magic..."
>
> I could see what he saw, and I knew that he was right. If the world was the sane place it was supposed to be, Jacob and I would have been together. And we would have been happy. He was my soul mate in that world—would have been my soul mate if his claim had not been overshadowed by something stronger, something so strong that it could not exist in a rational world.
>
> (*Eclipse* 598–599)

Bella's acknowledgement that the love she and Edward share belongs in an irrational world unsettles because it suggests a love like theirs cannot exist in the world in which readers live, since our world purports to have neither monsters nor magic. Their love, in other words, is a fantasy, which implies people in a sane world choose comfortable soul mates, partners who fit into a rhythmic, unthinking existence, "as easy as breathing"—Nussbaum's "detached thinking" rather than "passional response," which I discuss in Chapter 3. In other words, they choose

Team Jacob. If, however, we recall Kearney's claim that monster myths provide a way for us to solve the mysteries of our lives, then we *do* live in a world of monsters and magic, an insane and irrational world.

In this world, who and how we love remains mysterious and to stop such a love requires what Murdoch calls "reorientation":

> Consider being in love. Consider too the attempt to check being in love, and the need in such a case of another object to attend to. Where strong emotions of sexual love, or of hatred, resentment, or jealousy are concerned, "pure will" can usually achieve little. It is small use telling oneself, "Stop being in love, stop feeling resentment, be just." What is needed is a reorientation which will provide an energy of a different kind, from a different source.
>
> (54)

In *BtVS*, Buffy attends to her fate to continue to save the world, and in the *Twilight* saga, Bella shifts her attention to Jacob after Edward leaves her. This reorientation towards Jacob manifests most fully in *New Moon*, but it continues to inform the dynamic between Edward, Bella, and Jacob in *Eclipse*, as Edward tries to make amends for leaving Bella, and Jacob tries to convince Bella that their love benefits her more than her love for Edward.

Edward's love for Bella shines through in his ability to forgive Bella for her indiscretions and to be compassionate towards Jacob. Jacob, on the other hand, struggles to express anything but disdain for Edward, at least throughout the first three novels and films before he imprints on Renesmee. Perhaps the clearest example of this distinction between Edward and Jacob's compassion appears in a humorous scene in *Eclipse*—in the chapter titled "Fire and Ice"—when Bella, Edward, and Jacob camp in an unexpected snowstorm the night before the anticipated battle against the newborn vampires. Unprepared for the weather, Bella lies huddled in a tent, while Edward's cold body fails to provide the heat necessary to warm her. Enter Jacob, whose body temperature "run[s] at a toasty one-oh-eight point nine these days" (*Eclipse* 490). The novel and the film align in this scene, but a voyeuristic pleasure exists in watching the film version of Jacob's smugness and Edward's scowl, as Jacob slides his half-naked body into the sleeping bag with Bella, while Edward glares at him from a corner of the tent (Figure 5.2).

As Bella drifts in and out of sleep, Edward and Jacob discuss their feelings for her and towards each other, and Edward thanks Jacob for keeping Bella warm. Jacob takes the opportunity to ask Edward what he would do if Bella chose Jacob instead of Edward. Edward admits it would be difficult, but he would let her go and keep watch in case Jacob

Figure 5.2 Jacob keeps Bella warm while Edward watches.

ever left her. Jacob reciprocates Edward's gratitude and thanks him "for letting me in your head" and Edward replies,

> "As I said, I'm feeling oddly grateful for your presence in her life tonight. It was the least I could do... You know, Jacob, if it weren't for the fact that we're natural enemies and that you're also trying to steal away the reason for my existence, I might actually like you."
>
> "Maybe... if you weren't a disgusting vampire who was planning to suck out the life of the girl I love... well, no, not even then."
>
> (*Eclipse* 497–503)

Speckled with metaphors of battle, this conversation exemplifies the contrast between Edward and Jacob's model for love. Edward seems to set aside his own suffering and anger in order to ensure Bella's wellbeing. Although he learns leaving her does not constitute right action—as I discuss in Chapter 4—he still believes letting her go would be morally right, if she chooses Jacob as her lover. Edward's closing statement to Jacob, in which he extends a verbal olive branch, may be read as a sign of compassion because he understands Jacob's unrequited love for Bella constitutes a serious bad event (judgment of size); this love occurs through no fault of his own (judgment of non-desert); and Jacob himself is important to Edward's own wellbeing (eudaimonistic judgment) because of Jacob's importance to Bella. Given similar possibility informs this final judgment, it makes sense Edward—perhaps more than anyone else—understands that a similar bad event could happen to him because he can imagine a world in which Bella chooses Jacob instead of him.

Jacob, on the other hand, still has to learn about compassion, and, in part, this inability stems from the way he characterizes Bella as the woman he loves, whereas Edward positions her as the reason for his existence. This seemingly minor distinction grows larger alongside Edward's reminder that Jacob might leave Bella someday because he imprints on someone else, as Sam and Emily do. Indeed, the way Jacob explains imprinting to Bella earlier in *Eclipse* comes closer to Edward's way of situating Bella as the reason for his existence. Jacob struggles to describe imprinting to Bella: "It's not like love at first sight, really. It's more like... gravity moves. When you see *her*, suddenly it's not the earth holding you here anymore. She does. And nothing matters more than her. And you would do anything for her, be anything for her... You become whatever she needs you to be, whether that's a protector, or a lover, or a friend, or a brother" (*Eclipse* 176). Although Jacob theoretically understands imprinting because he can hear it through the minds of other wolves in his pack, he does not comprehend it at an emotional level until he imprints on Renesmee in *Breaking Dawn*. *Eclipse* introduces the models for love and compassion Jacob needs to learn, and *Breaking Dawn* follows Jacob as he internalizes them.

Acts of compassion and forgiveness track through *Eclipse*: Edward admits he will never forgive himself for leaving Bella (33); Bella claims Edward's departure was because he believed he was acting justly and therefore requires no forgiveness (102); Bella forgives Jacob (209) for saying she would be better as a dead human than alive as a vampire (183); and, finally, Edward extends compassion towards Jacob and Bella (534) after Bella admits the depth of her love for Jacob by asking him to kiss her (525). In the following conversation between Bella and Edward, Edward's responses exemplify compassion as a component and demonstration of love:

> "when I left you, Bella, I left you bleeding. Jacob was the one to stitch you back up again. That was bound to leave its mark—on both of you. I can't blame either of you for something I made necessary. I may gain forgiveness, but that doesn't let me escape the consequences. [...] I can be noble, Bella. I'm not going to make you choose between us. Just be happy, and you can have whatever part of me you want, or none at all, if that's better. Don't let any debt you feel you owe me influence your decision."
>
> [...]
>
> "What happened to fighting back? Don't start with noble self-sacrifice now! Fight!"
>
> "How?" he asked, and his eyes were ancient with their sadness.
>
> I scrambled into his lap, throwing my arms around him.
>
> "I don't care that it's cold here. I don't care that I stink like a dog right now. Make me forget how awful I am. Make me forget him. Make me forget my own name. Fight back!"

> I didn't wait for him to decide—or to have the chance to tell me he wasn't interested in a cruel, faithless monster like me. I pulled myself against him and crushed my mouth to his snow-cold lips.
>
> (534–535)

Edward articulates how his attempt at right action in *New Moon* ultimately harms Bella and leads her to reorient herself towards Jacob. He sees Bella and Jacob's marked and damaged bodies and does not look away from their wounds, even though seeing causes him pain. His eyes reflect this pain, but his love for Bella constitutes an aspect of his compassion for her and for Jacob. In the face of his compassion, Bella names herself monster, as she acts on her passion.

Breaking Dawn harnesses passion to compassion as Bella decides to sacrifice herself—one might argue, martyr herself—in order to allow her unborn fetus to survive. Bella's physical suffering, however, diminishes beside Edward's emotional suffering, and Jacob begins to learn compassion when he bears witness to Edward's pain. *Breaking Dawn* diverges from the narrative structure of the previous three novels through its use of multiple narrators. The novel divides into three books: Bella narrates books one and three; and book two contains Jacob's first-person narration. By providing Jacob's perspective, the novel demonstrates his emotional shift from hating Edward to feeling some compassion for him. For this reason, I focus on the novel rather than the film in the next section about Jacob's shift towards compassion.

The epigraph to Jacob's section refers back to Jacob and Bella's conversation in *Eclipse* when Bella acknowledges she and Jacob would be together in a rational world. Tellingly, the epigraph is taken from *A Midsummer Night's Dream*, one of Shakespeare's most magical plays: "*And yet, to say the truth, / reason and love keep little company together nowadays*" (Act III, Scene i). In Shakespeare's play, Bottom speaks these words to Titania, after she professes her love for Bottom because Oberon has cast a spell upon her that makes her love whomever she sees when she first awakens. This emphasis on a love that stems from sight comments ironically on the colloquialism "love at first sight," but it also recalls how Jacob describes imprinting to Bella (*Eclipse* 176) and anticipates Jacob's moment of imprinting upon Bella and Edward's child as soon as he sees her, and against all reason.

More importantly for my argument here, Jacob's compassion for Edward also initiates from a moment of seeing. In the chapter entitled, "Sure as hell didn't see that one coming," Jacob decides to confront the Cullens and Bella after he learns they have returned to Forks after Bella and Edward's honeymoon. Fuelled by anger and vengeance because he believes Bella has been transformed into a vampire, Jacob arrives at the Cullens' house ready to challenge Edward to a duel (168). Instead, Bella invites Jacob to join them. As Jacob walks into the room he sees Edward:

> I'd seen him angry, and I'd seen him arrogant, and once I'd seen him in pain. But this—this was beyond agony. His eyes were half-crazed. He didn't look up to glare at me. He stared down at the couch beside him with an expression like someone had lit him on fire. His hands were rigid claws at his side.
>
> I couldn't even enjoy his anguish. I could only think of one thing that would make him look like that, and my eyes followed his.
>
> (170–171)

Jacob's eyes track down to where Bella lies on the couch emaciated, but more than this moment of seeing her, Edward's pain freezes Jacob's anger and stops him from taking pleasure in Edward's suffering.

Edward's pain—even more than Bella's body—shifts Jacob's vengeance towards compassion, although not fully. After this scene in which Jacob first sees Bella's pregnant body, damaged from the fetus feeding on her, Edward asks Jacob to speak with him outside. Jacob follows him, and again confronts Edward's agony:

> He stopped without warning and pivoted to face me. His expression froze me again.
>
> For a second I was just a kid—a kid who had lived all of his life in the same tiny town. Just a child. Because I knew I would have to live a lot more, suffer a lot more, to ever understand the searing agony in Edward's eyes.
>
> He raised a hand as if to wipe sweat from his forehead but his fingers scraped against his face like they were going to rip his granite skin right off. His black eyes burned in their sockets, out of focus, or seeing things that weren't there. His mouth opened like he was going to scream, but nothing came out.
>
> This was the face a man would have if he were burning at the stake.
>
> For a moment I couldn't speak. It was too real, this face—I'd seen a shadow of it in the house, seen it in her eyes and his, but this made it final.
>
> (*Breaking Dawn* 176–177)

Now Jacob sees a serious bad event befall Edward, and he comprehends the similar possibility between himself and Edward, made explicit in the realization that his face reflects a "watered-down echo" (179) of Edward's expression. He still blames Edward for Bella's condition, though, so he has yet to be fully compassionate.

Jacob's compassion finally reveals itself—and Carlisle names it as such—when Jacob refuses to follow Sam's order to destroy Bella's fetus and, therein, Bella herself. In a move that splits the wolf pack in two, Jacob claims his birthright as Alpha in order to act morally to protect Bella and, by default, the rest of the Cullens. After Jacob breaks from the pack, he warns the Cullens about Sam's plan and then spends the next day patrolling the perimeter of the Cullens' home in order to protect them from attack. That night, Jacob goes to check on Bella's health and finds Carlisle waiting for him: "'I didn't get a chance to thank you last night, Jacob. You don't know how much I appreciate your… compassion. I know your goal was to protect Bella, but I owe you the safety of the rest of my family as well'" (*Breaking Dawn* 233). Carlisle hesitates to call Jacob's act compassionate, but the naming fits Jacob's actions because his move to sever ties from Sam's pack in order to act morally depends upon a compassionate judgment of Bella and the Cullens' situation.

While both *BtVS* and the *Twilight* saga incorporate vengeance, compassion, and forgiveness into their larger narrative arcs, *The Vampire Diaries* repeats this pattern of action throughout each season. Damon most frequently lapses into wrong action and then receives compassion and forgiveness from Stefan and Elena, but Stefan and Elena also spiral into harmful action, which complicates rigid concepts of good and evil. Significantly, when one of these characters causes harm to another being, the act usually stems from love. For instance, in the episode in which Bonnie—possessed by her ancestor Emily—destroys the crystal that assists in breaking the tomb's seal, Stefan confronts Damon about his plan to open the tomb and therein release twenty-seven vampires:

STEFAN: This isn't about love is it? This is about revenge.
DAMON: The two aren't mutually exclusive.
STEFAN: Damon, you can't do this.
DAMON: Why not? They killed twenty-seven people and they called it a war battle. They deserve whatever they get.
STEFAN: Twenty-seven vampires. They were vampires. You can't just bring them back.
DAMON: This town deserves this.
STEFAN: You're blaming innocent people for something that happened 145 years ago.
DAMON: There is nothing innocent about these people.
("History Repeating" 1009)

In this exchange, Damon refuses to separate love from vengeance and implies one may enact vengeance because of love, which occurs in *BtVS* and the *Twilight* saga. As I discuss in the next chapter, Damon's comment also provides insight into how murder moves beyond an individual act to group killing sanctioned by the state as war.

In this final section of the chapter, I analyze significant moments of vengeance, compassion, and forgiveness in *TVD* that establish a pattern of protest and pardon as prevention against evil and future wrong action. The pattern in Season One begins in the exchange between Stefan and Damon I quote above ("History Repeating" 1009); continues into the scene when Elena convinces Lexi's boyfriend to pardon Damon, which leads Elena to forgive Stefan for lying to her about Katherine ("Bloodlines" 1011); includes Elena's compassion for and forgiveness of Damon when he discovers Katherine is not buried in the tomb ("Fool Me Once" 1014); crescendos when some of the tomb vampires seek vengeance against the Salvatore brothers ("Let the Right One In" 1017); and concludes with Damon moving from a position in which he says he "doesn't do forgiveness" ("Miss Mystic Falls" 1019) to apologizing to Jeremy and seeking Jeremy's forgiveness ("Founder's Day" 1022).

As I discuss in Chapter 4, "Bloodlines" concludes the narrative arc of Elena and Stefan's first break-up and reunion. Before their reunion, however, the episode initiates a pattern of pardon instead of vengeance as right action. Elena and Damon travel to Georgia and stop at a bar owned by Bree, a witch and one of Damon's ex-lovers. Bree assumes Elena and Damon are lovers, and Elena starts to correct her, but Bree interrupts her protestation and says, "Honey, if you're not roped, you're whipped. Either way, just enjoy the ride." Bree's words reiterate Nussbaum's point that we do not choose who we love or the manner in which we love, but we accept and find pleasure in it, despite the fact it may hurt and control us. Part of the enjoyment comes when a lover recognizes the pain caused and asks for forgiveness. When Elena says, "Ok" to Bree, she implicitly agrees with Bree's assessment of love and furthermore suggests she may, at least at some level, love Damon.

Later in the episode, this admission is confirmed when Elena pleads for Damon's life to be spared, which reveals her compassion and love for him, even if she does not recognize it as such. The scene begins when Damon and Elena talk outside the bar, and Bree calls Lexi's boyfriend, Lee, to tell him Damon is at the bar. Later, Lee lures Damon outside and proceeds to beat him and pour gasoline on him, while Elena watches helplessly. When Elena asks what Damon did to deserve such a beating, Lee tells her Damon killed his girlfriend. Elena deduces Lee is Lexi's boyfriend and pleads, "She loved you. She said that when it's real, you can't walk away.... Don't. Don't. Please don't hurt him.... Lexi loved you and she was good and that means you're good too. Be better than him. Don't do this. I'm begging you. Please." Lee reads her pleas as the words of a lover asking for her beloved's life, and while he continues to beat Damon, he does not light him on fire as he first intends, and instead throws him one last time against a wall. Elena thanks Lee, and he turns to her with tears in his eyes, and whispers, "It wasn't for you." The scene ends with him running away, and Elena running to Damon. Lee's decision not to kill Damon reads less as a pardon and more as a demonstration of his goodness and his love for Lexi. He does not forgive or pardon Damon, but he does walk away from vengeance.

At this stage half way through Season One, vengeance still drives Damon, who does not learn from Lee's model of withdrawing from it. Instead, he goes back into the bar to confront Bree, who says, "She was my friend. How could you?" Bree tries to bargain with Damon by telling him there is another way to open the tomb: to reverse the spell using Emily Bennett's spell book. When Damon asks where it is and she claims not to know, Damon touches her face and says, "And I believe you. My dear sweet Bree, that's why I'm sorry." He then calmly, vengefully plunges his hand into her chest and rips out her heart before he returns to the car to drive Elena back to Mystic Falls. His apology to Bree drops onto the floor, as lifeless as Bree's no-longer beating heart, and his cold, calculated killing of Bree travels uncomfortably in the car with him and Elena, as they banter back and forth. Elena's playful words, as she reminds Damon she saved his life, seems cruelly naïve, for, unbeknownst to her, her plea for forgiveness results in Bree's death.

Damon's act of vengeance leads to his own suffering from a wound he cannot avenge when he discovers Katherine has thwarted his love by escaping from the tomb without telling him. The next three episodes focus on Damon's efforts to open the tomb in order to release Katherine, and Stefan's attempts to stop Damon. A narrative of revenge as wrong action continues, as more and more vampires leave the tomb and find their way to an abandoned farmhouse outside of town where Pearl and her daughter Anna teach them about how the world has changed in the 145 years since their entombment. As the oldest and strongest of the vampires, Pearl leads the group and sets rules about not leaving the house in order to keep a low profile. Contrary to Stefan's concerns, Pearl wants to live a normal life in Mystic Falls, running her shop and caring for her daughter. Few tomb vampires seem intent on revenge against the townspeople, although they do not seem opposed to feeding on them. Rather, a small faction of vampires seeks vengeance against the Salvatore brothers, blaming their capture on Katherine's infatuation with Stefan and Damon. Frederick, the vampire most dissatisfied with Pearl's rules, disobeys them and with his girlfriend attacks Stefan and Damon. Frederick's girlfriend dies in the fight, which leaves Frederick even more intent on revenge ("There Goes the Neighborhood" 1016).

Frederick personifies vengeance in a way that recalls Enyos's position in *Buffy* that vengeance is a living thing, while Pearl features as a voice of reason. The night of the attack, Frederick returns to the farmhouse and asks Pearl if he can go into town the next day to pick up more blood from the hospital:

PEARL: I'm afraid not. Not after your stunt at the Salvatore house tonight.
FREDERICK: He and his brother deserved it.
PEARL: And where did that get you? Your girlfriend, Bethanne, is dead. And you have no one to blame but yourself. We cannot live our lives about revenge. We have to have better control of our emotions.

FREDERICK: I understand, Miss Pearl. I just wish I knew what you were up to.

PEARL: I'm going to make an exploratory visit into town tomorrow to assess who is under the influence of Vervain and who isn't. Anna tells me that the players haven't changed much. It's still the Lockwoods, the Forbes, the Fells.

FREDERICK: We should kill every last one of them.

PEARL: We are smarter than that, Frederick. These people are not our enemies. We don't hold grudges and resentments. We'll get our town back. We just have to have patience.

("Let the Right One In" 1017)

Although Frederick's words seem relatively calm, the conversation takes place while Frederick sits in front of a fireplace sharpening a stake. He repeatedly pulls the knife down the stake, so his aggressive, measured actions punctuate his words, keeping time like a metronome, each slash a gestural protest.

Private protest becomes public performance in the next scene when Frederick plunges the stake into Stefan's belly. When Stefan fails to return from the woods, Damon goes to the farmhouse looking for him. Frederick opens the door to reveal Stefan, wounded and barely able to stand. Unable to enter the house because the human who owns the house will not invite him in, Damon leaves to go enlist the help of Alaric. In the meantime, the scene cuts to Stefan, strung up in the basement, being tortured by Frederick, who asserts, revenge is "exactly what [they] are here for." Frederick achieves a measure of revenge when he impales Stefan with a tree branch, saying, "This is for Bethanne." As he verges on killing Stefan with a stake to the heart, Elena stabs Frederick with a Vervain-filled dart, which incapacitates but does not kill him. Too quickly, Frederick gains consciousness, while Stefan lies wounded. Desperate for Stefan to heal himself, Elena convinces him to drink blood from her wrist, so he will be strong enough to kill Frederick. Stefan resists and tells her to run, but Elena refuses and Stefan capitulates.

Elena cannot anticipate, however, the effect her blood has on Stefan. When Frederick attacks him, Stefan growls and stakes him again and again with a tree branch. Disturbed, Elena runs to Stefan and grabs his arm. He turns to her, and his face shifts back from a vicious vampire to a remorseful Stefan. Later, at home, Stefan apologizes to Elena for his actions: "I'm sorry that you had to see it." Tellingly, he does not apologize for this viciousness of his attack, only that she saw it. Damon, Alaric, and Elena rescue Stefan, but the fallout permeates the rest of the Season One and forewarns of Stefan's fall from grace in Season Three, for the episode ends as Damon finds Stefan drinking bags of human blood, its evidence smeared over his face.

Repeatedly, Season One demonstrates that acting out of vengeance is wrong. By Season Two, Damon seems to have learned this lesson, and while he still resorts to killing, he acts to protect Elena. Sometimes, however, Damon's actions to protect Elena also cause her harm. The strongest example occurs when Damon forces Elena to drink his blood, so she will become a vampire if she dies during a ritual to break Klaus's werewolf curse ("The Last Day" 2020). Damon never wavers on his stance to protect Elena, even when it means acting on her behalf against her will. Stefan, however, supports Elena's choices to determine her own fate, even if it means her death. A philosophical debate about one's right-to-life extends beyond the scope of this book, but the question about the soundness of each brother's moral judgment invites consideration.

More significant for this chapter, however, is Elena's ability to forgive Damon's actions. Later in this same episode, in another attempt to protect Elena and her friends, Damon sustains a werewolf bite, which kills a vampire slowly and painfully, as we know from Rose's death. He withholds this information from Elena and asks Stefan to do the same. Using similar phrasing to Giles explanation to Buffy about forgiveness, Damon says to Elena at the beginning of the episode, "I know I don't deserve your forgiveness, but I need it" ("As I Lay Dying" 2022). Elena responds by telling Damon she needs more time, not knowing about Damon's immanent death. As the episode progresses, Stefan works with Bonnie to try to find a cure and finally discovers Klaus's blood heals a werewolf bite. I discuss Stefan's sacrifice for Damon in the next chapter, so here I attend to Damon's apology and Elena's pardon.

In previous episodes in Season Two, Stefan apologizes to Damon for being the reason Damon becomes a vampire, and in this final episode of the season, Damon apologizes and seeks forgiveness for his previous actions and the choices he made. As he lies dying, Damon takes responsibility for his actions and for death as their outcome, but he expresses no regret because his past actions result in his love for Elena:

DAMON: I've made a lot of choices that have gotten me here. I deserve this. I deserve to die.
ELENA: No. You don't.
DAMON: I do, Elena. It's ok. Cuz if I'd have chosen differently I wouldn't have met you. I'm so sorry. I've done so many things to hurt you.
ELENA: It's ok. I forgive you.
DAMON: I know you love Stefan. And it will always be Stefan. God, I love you. You should know that.
ELENA: I do.
DAMON: You should have met me in 1864. You would have liked me.
ELENA: I like you now. Just the way you are.

Elena kisses Damon softly, and then Katherine enters the room with Klaus's blood, paid for by Stefan, who gives himself over to Klaus in exchange for Damon's life (Figure 5.3).

Figure 5.3 Damon asks for Elena's forgiveness.

On a seemingly endless loop, right action based on love begets wrong action that requires forgiveness based on love, which initiates right action and so on. Buffy sends Angel to a hell dimension, and when he returns, their love returns, which worries everyone. The more they fight against demons together, the closer they become, the more Angel approaches happiness and the loss of his soul. Edward gains Bella's forgiveness for the right action of leaving, which turns out to be wrong action that leads to harming Bella, who, in turn kisses Jacob, which harms Edward, who forgives Jacob, and Jacob learns compassion from bearing witness to Bella and Edward's pain. Stefan saves Damon's life, and in exchange he shuts off his emotions, so he can commit wrong actions for the right reason. Damon loves Elena and tries to protect her, but when his protection becomes control, then Elena angers and acts to hurt. Damon loves too much. Stefan refuses to show he cares because it means pain. Love initiates right action and lovers forgive wrong action. And in between those moments, lovers strive to live well.

Works Cited

"As I Lay Dying." *The Vampire Diaries*. Writ. Turi Meyer, Al Septien, and Michael Narducci. Dir. John Behring. CWTV. 12 May 2011. Television.

"Becoming, Part One." *Buffy the Vampire Slayer: The Complete Second Season on DVD*. Writ. and Dir. Joss Whedon. Twentieth Century Fox, 2002. DVD.

"Becoming, Part Two." *Buffy the Vampire Slayer: The Complete Second Season on DVD*. Writ. and Dir. Joss Whedon. Twentieth Century Fox, 2002. DVD.

"Bloodlines." *The Vampire Diaries.* Writ. Kevin Williamson and Julie Plec. Dir. David Barrett. CWTV. 21 January 2010. Television.

The Flamingos. "I Only Have Eyes For You." *Flamingo Serenade.* End, 1959. Song.

"Fool Me Once." *The Vampire Diaries.* Writ. Brett Conrad. Dir. Marcos Siega. CWTV. 11 February 2010. Television.

"History Repeating." *The Vampire Diaries.* Writ. Bryan M. Holdman and Brian Young. Dir. Marcos Siega. CWTV. 12 November 2009. Television.

"I Only Have Eyes For You." *Buffy the Vampire Slayer: The Complete Second Season on DVD.* Writ. Marti Noxon. Dir. James Whitmore Jr. Twentieth Century Fox, 2002. DVD.

"Innocence." *Buffy the Vampire Slayer: The Complete Second Season on DVD.* Writ. and Dir. Joss Whedon. Twentieth Century Fox, 2002. DVD.

Kearney, Richard. *Strangers, Gods, and Monsters: Interpreting Otherness.* New York: Routledge, 2003. 1–20. Print.

"The Last Day." *The Vampire Diaries.* Writ. Andrew Chambliss and Brian Young. Dir. J. Miller Tobin. CWTV. 28 April 2011. Television.

"Let the Right One In." *The Vampire Diaries.* Writ. Kevin Williamson and Julie Plec. Dir. Dennis Smith. CWTV. 8 April 2010. Television.

Meyer, Stephenie. *Breaking Dawn.* New York: Little Brown, 2008. Print.

———. *Eclipse.* New York: Little Brown, 2007. Print.

———. *New Moon.* New York: Little Brown, 2006. Print.

———. *Twilight.* New York: Little Brown, 2005. Print.

"Miss Mystic Falls." *The Vampire Diaries.* Writ. Kevin Williamson and Julie Plec. Dir. Marcos Siega. CWTV. 22 April 2010. Television.

Murdoch, Iris. *The Sovereignty of Good.* 1970. New York: Routledge, 2013. Print.

Nussbaum, Martha C. *Love's Knowledge: Essays on Philosophy and Literature.* New York: Oxford UP, 1990. Print.

———. *Upheavals of Thought: The Intelligence of Emotions.* Cambridge: Cambridge UP, 2001. Print.

Splendid. "Charge." *Buffy the Vampire Slayer: the Album.* TVT Records, 1999. Song.

"There Goes The Neighbourhood." *The Vampire Diaries.* Writ. Bryan Oh and Andrew Chambliss. Dir. Kevin Bray. CWTV. 1 April 2010. Television.

Twilight. Writ. Melissa Rosenberg. Dir. Catherine Hardwicke, 2008. DVD.

The Twilight Saga: Breaking Dawn—Part 1. Writ. Melissa Rosenberg. Dir. Bill Condon, 2011. DVD.

The Twilight Saga: Breaking Dawn—Part 2. Writ. Melissa Rosenberg. Dir. Bill Condon, 2012. DVD.

The Twilight Saga: Eclipse. Writ. Melissa Rosenberg. Dir. David Slade, 2010. DVD.

The Twilight Saga: New Moon. Writ. Melissa Rosenberg. Dir. Chris Weitz, 2009. DVD.

6 "But How Do I Stop a Monster without Becoming One?"

War and Killing

This chapter responds to a question Stefan asks himself as he contemplates how he should respond to Damon's actions early in Season One of *The Vampire Diaries*: "But how do I stop a monster without becoming one?" Angel, Edward, Stefan—and at times, Damon—all choose not to kill humans because they believe such action to be wrong, but they rarely hesitate to kill another monster if that death serves a larger purpose. More radically, Damon—once a soldier in the Civil War—justifies killing almost anyone as long as the death will protect Elena and/or the larger community. Each series provides a seemingly-ethical rationale for killing: *BtVS* exists within a context of saving the world; the *Twilight* saga frames its defense within a familial structure; and *TVD* stands as a metonym for a divided America in need of protection from itself. In each series, discourses of war and scenes of battles suggest ethical love emanates out from the romantic couple to a larger concept of the greater good.

So far, this book analyzes how the romantic love between a male vampire and a female human initiates a love-based ethics. The moral vampire acts justly because he loves and is loved. This right action often translates into protection of his beloved and, at times, her friends and family. In this chapter, I suggest this romantic love also models right action to and for a larger community. In her discussion about the different ways Spike and Anya express their love in *BtVS*, Carolyn Korsmeyer provides a useful analysis of passion and action. She values Spike's love for Buffy above Anya's love for Xander because Anya expresses her love only for Xander whereas the messiness of Spike's love for Buffy exists in a history of Spike being a loving, sensitive human and an obsessively loving vampire. Korsmeyer extends her analysis of these two characters to claim more generally, "it would seem that although romantic love demands that we love only one person, forsaking all others, we may not properly be said to love truly if one person is all that we are capable of loving" (169–170). This chapter expands upon this idea of how to "love truly" by opening one's romantic love to embrace and defend a group of others.

As I discuss in Chapter 3, Angel decides to help Buffy slay demons while watching her struggles, so from the outset, Buffy and Angel align in their commitment to protect the people of Sunnydale according to a

Kantian state of right. In his "Kantian Analysis of Moral Judgment in *Buffy the Vampire Slayer*," Scott R. Stroud analyzes Buffy's actions at individual and systemic levels using Kant's philosophy on moral judgment and right action, and I employ his distinction between individual and systemic action throughout this chapter. Stroud defines Buffy's struggle to act morally given a tension between her individual desire to deny her slayer duties and her moral systemic duty to be the slayer. Ultimately, however, Buffy and Angel work together to uphold what Kant calls a "state of right," which is "created when equal agents act in such a way as to not harm the capability of other agents to act" (Stroud 191). Kant believes freedom is the only innate right and the state is obligated to uphold this right: "Freedom (independence from being constrained by another's choice), insofar as it can coexist with the freedom of every other in accordance with a universal law, is the only original right belonging to every man by virtue of his humanity" (*Metaphysics of Morals* 6:238). In this chapter, I discuss not only Buffy's actions but analyze primarily the actions of moral vampires, all of whom choose to shun their individual vampire impulses in order to act justly for a larger good, in other words, to sustain a state of right. The three series present this action as both epic and personal.

BtVS goes the furthest of the three series in aligning the protection of a community with love. Analyzing friendship—or reciprocity, to use Nussbaum's term—as an aspect of love, Melissa M. Milavec and Sharon M. Kaye argue Buffy and Angel satisfy the requirements for Aristotle's highest level of friendship, which includes utility and pleasure as well as valuing "the other for his or her own sake" (174). Importantly for my analysis, Milavec and Kaye link the love between Buffy and Angel to their mental and physical fighting. They fight demons together, but they also use their will to help each other survive and flourish. According to Milavec and Kaye, "Buffy's relationship with Angel demonstrates complete friendship.... Angel helps Buffy accomplish her goal of protecting Sunnydale, and Buffy provides Angel with inspiration to make amends for the evil deeds he committed in the past" (180). The *Twilight* saga draws upon a similar syntax in which Jacob satisfies the characteristics of a utility friendship, which Riley—Buffy's boyfriend in Seasons Four and Five—fills in *BtVS*, but Edward embodies both pleasure and complete friendship, which means Bella has no need for a Spike-type passion outside her relationship with Edward. In *The Vampire Diaries*, Stefan and Damon tag-team utility, pleasure, and complete friendship with Elena, which makes an attempt to categorize their friendship delightfully messy.

For all their attempts at morality, however, these vampires struggle with the murderer at the core of their impulses. As Jules Zanger argues in his essay "Metaphor into Metonymy: The Vampire Next Door," vampires slide from metaphor into metonymy when they move from being a metaphysical monster embodying evil to an individual entity who commits an evil act: "One function of the new vampire's contiguity is not so much to make clear as it is to conceal, to obscure, to misdirect our attention from his most salient characteristic as murderer, while at the same time retaining that characteristic for its essential, defining function" (20). All three series engage with this slippage by resignifying the moral vampire as protector—and often soldier—rather than murderer, a moral agent who kills in order to protect the community rather than for his own pleasure.

To get to the heart of this matter regarding the extent to which romantic love—or complete friendship—protects a state of right by justifying killing, I analyze key battle scenes in which the moral vampires fight alongside everyday citizens in order to protect people from an enemy who seeks to "radically harm the external freedom of agents in the community" (Stroud 191). Often these battles mark the end of a season or a series, such as at the end of Season Three and Season Seven of *BtVS*, and at the end of *Breaking Dawn* in the *Twilight* saga. *The Vampire Diaries*, however, resists this syntax and instead uses references to the American Civil War to infiltrate and inform moral judgments about right action. In this chapter, the focus on the moral vampire and his human beloved expands to include a larger community, as the moral vampires become part of a collective. The community shares the responsibility for making moral judgments that justify killing, so while the romantic relationship initiates reflections about right action, it no longer stands as the primary basis for action.

In each of the seven seasons of *Buffy the Vampire Slayer*, Buffy and the Scooby Gang battle to save the world from an evil entity determined to change the world as they know it. In Season One, The Master attempts to escape from his subterranean cell in order to create a world in which vampires reign supreme, a vision brought to life in one episode in Season Three when Cordelia wishes that Buffy had never come to Sunnydale ("The Wish" 3009). In Season Two, Angel loses his soul and becomes Angelus, who reawakens The Judge in order to suck the world into a hell dimension. Season Three brings forth the Mayor, whose Ascension and transformation into a demon would destroy the world. Season Four's monster, Adam, resembles Frankenstein's monster in its assemblage of demons constructed by Maggie Walsh, leader of an army called the Initiative. In Season Five, Buffy battles the god Glory, who seeks to open a portal to a hell dimension. Season Six abandons the monsters metaphor in order to reveal humans as perhaps the most monstrous of all creatures. In the final season, The First, the origin of evil—introduced in Season Three—succeeds in winning the battle to destroy Sunnydale, but Buffy and her army win the war by changing the rules of destiny to empower all nascent slayers.

While fighting forces of evil punches through each season, Season Three and Season Seven explicitly deploy war rhetoric and large-scale battles to stage scenarios in which a community bonds together to protect a populace, ordinary citizens become combatants and probable killers, and moral vampires fight alongside them all. Season Three funnels the focus into the final two-part episode—once Buffy realizes the size of the demon into which the Mayor transforms means she requires reinforcements to defeat him. The entirety of Season Seven, however, queries the moral responsibility of, and the extent to which, each individual can help and protect others. The season suggests right action occurs on a daily basis and makes this point explicit as early as the fourth episode in which Buffy tries but cannot help a student who foresees her own death ("Help" 7004). In this episode, Buffy saves Cassie from being sacrificed in a ritual, and then saves her again from death when Cassie triggers a trap that shoots an arrow at her head, but she cannot stop Cassie's premature death from a genetic heart condition. In the final exchange of the episode, Buffy responds to her sister Dawn's statement, "sometimes you can't help" by asking, "So what then? What do you do when you know that? When you know that maybe you can't help?" The episode ends with Buffy answering her own question: she goes back to work as a counselor in the high school the next morning, back to her desk to try to listen and help again. By moving from seemingly small individual acts that attempt to save the life of one person to large systemic actions that seek to save the lives of many, Season Seven presents a range of circumstances in which characters must make moral judgments about upholding a state of right for the many, even if it means the death of some.

Buffy and the Scooby Gang confront such moral judgments in Season Three when the Mayor threatens to bring about an apocalypse on the cusp of their graduation from high school. If the etymology of apocalypse suggests destruction or disclosure (*OED*), then end-of-the-world-as-we-know-it scenarios occur across the two-part episode that ends Season Three—"Graduation Day"—in several ways: Buffy and the Scooby Gang graduate from high school; Angel leaves Buffy and the series to move to Los Angeles and to his own spin-off show; Buffy graduates from being a slayer ruled by the Council to a slayer no longer in need of a Watcher; and the students of Sunnydale High School band together to create an army to defeat the Mayor, which results in the literal destruction of the high school.

Part One of the episode opens with a conversation between Xander and Cordelia while they pick up their graduation gowns and caps, and Xander's military metaphor constructs the day as equivalent to going into battle:

XANDER: I'm telling you. I woke up the other day with this feeling in my gut. I just know there's no way I'm getting out of this school alive.
CORDELIA: Wow, you've really mastered the power of positive giving-up.
XANDER: I've been lucky too many times. My number's coming up. And I was short! One more rotation and I'm shipping stateside, you know what I mean?
CORDELIA: Seldom, if ever.

Xander's colloquial phrase "shipping stateside" originates with the United States military and was first used in 1942 in the midst of World War II (*OED*). In standard Joss Whedon style—who wrote and directed both parts of the episode—a seemingly innocuous exchange, couched in humor, arms the viewer for the season finale, as does Buffy's very next conversation with Willow in which she reflects that the senior class's nostalgia reminds her of the Sixties, "or what the Sixties would have been like without the war and the hairy armpits."

Buffy names her battle against the Mayor explicitly a war in "Graduation Day—Part Two" after she recovers from a fight with Faith. Still dressed in the infamous red leather pants and black tank top in which she fought Faith, she finds Giles, Xander, Willow, and Oz in the hallway outside her hospital room. She asks them to get Angel and get everyone because she is ready for "war." As the episode progresses, the scenes cut between the school and the Mayor's office where Buffy and the Mayor each gather their troops to discuss strategy. When the Mayor finally transforms into the demon Olvikan and therefore can be killed, all members of the graduating senior class open their graduation gowns to reveal weapons. Buffy creates an army of citizens to defend their state of right, and although they suffer casualties, in the end, as Giles says, Buffy runs "a good campaign" (Figure 6.1).

Figure 6.1 Buffy leads a graduation-day army.

Season Three ends with the destruction of Sunnydale High School and Season Seven begins with its grand reopening, thus returning to the high-school-as-hell metaphor. As Buffy says, "Being in high school can feel like being at war. Now it's true" ("Storyteller" 7016). This metaphor equates war with hell, and manifests itself as the origin of all evil threatens to overtake the world by releasing an army of Ubervampires from the Hellmouth, a sealed cavern located beneath the high school. Season Three introduces this evil in an episode in which Angel receives visitations from The First—who takes the form of dead people Angel has killed ("Amends" 3010), and Season Seven expands this rumination on evil by asking how one might keep evil at bay. When The First tries to convince Angel to feed on Buffy in "Amends," Angel decides to kill himself so he no longer feels tempted to be with Buffy—and therein lose his soul again—or to kill her. Buffy's words to Angel serve as a prologue to the message that underlies Season Seven: "Strong is fighting! It's hard and it's painful, and it's every day. It's what we have to do. And we can do it together" ("Amends" 3010). Although Angel appears only briefly in the final episode of the series, this strategy to work together to stop evil by acting justly remains the same whether the fight be against a spell that causes Buffy, Dawn, Willow, and Anya to compete with each other for the love of the same boy ("Him" 7006); or against one's own demons ("The Killer in Me" 7013); or against the Harbingers, who are the minions of The First; or against Caleb, the vessel of The First; or against an army of Ubervampires.

Season Seven delves into a debate about justified killing in "Selfless" (7005), and, as the title of the episode suggests, the debate hinges upon right action as it connects to the self and to love. The episode pivots upon Anya's actions as a vengeance demon, who seemingly suffers remorse for the pain she inflicts. Trying to shun her reputation as "Miss Softserve" in the vengeance order, Anya kills twelve frat boys because a college student who was tormented by them wishes that they could "feel what it's like to have your hearts ripped out." When Willow finds the bodies and tells Buffy and Xander about Anya's actions, Buffy states reluctantly that she has to kill Anya. Xander tries to convince Buffy she should spare Anya's life because he still loves her, but Buffy holds her line that killing Anya is justified because Anya is a demon who harms others:

XANDER: Buffy, you wanna kill Anya!
BUFFY: I don't want to.
XANDER: Then don't! This isn't new ground for us. When our friends go all crazy and start killing people, we help them.
WILLOW: Sitting right here.
XANDER: I'm sorry. But it's true.
BUFFY: It's different.

XANDER: Because you don't care about her the same way I do. Buffy, I still love her.

BUFFY: I know. And that's why you can't see this for what it really is. Willow was different. She's a human. Anya's a demon.

XANDER: And you're the slayer. I see now how it's all very simple.

BUFFY: It is never simple.

XANDER: No, of course not. You know, if there's a mass-murdering demon that you're, oh, say boning, then it's all gray area.

BUFFY: Spike was harmless. He was helping.

XANDER: He had no choice.

BUFFY: And Anya did! She chose to become a demon. Twice.

XANDER: You have no idea what she's going through.

BUFFY: I don't care what she's going through!

XANDER: No, of course not. You think that we haven't seen all this before? The part where you just cut us all out. Just step away from everything human and act like you're the law. If you knew what I felt—

BUFFY: I killed Angel! Do you even remember that? I would have given up everything I had to be with—I loved him more than I will ever love anything in this life. And I put a sword through his heart because I had to.

This exchange mirrors the argument Buffy and Xander have in Season Two, in which Xander defends the other side of the debate and tries to convince Buffy that killing Angelus is the right action to take. In both instances, choice—or what we might think of here as moral judgment—influences action. Willow, Anya, Spike, and Angel all kill humans, but Buffy bases her decision to kill Anya on Anya's choice to become evil and on the possibility she will continue to cause harm. These small-scale judgments at the personal level inform the decisions Buffy, the Scooby Gang, and the potential slayers make at the systemic level.

Perhaps Spike, more than any other character in Season Seven, embodies the torment love inflicts when it affects and justifies moral judgment. Season Six ends with Spike receiving his soul back, so Buffy "can get what she deserves" ("Grave" 6022), and Season Seven deals with Spike's remorse over his past evil acts and his attempts to be a good man for Buffy. With Spike's decision to seek the return of his soul based upon his love for Buffy, Season Seven reintroduces a moral vampire into its full-time cast of characters. Although the relationship between Spike and Buffy does not reach romantic love, as Buffy says to Angel when he returns to Sunnydale to offer to fight beside Buffy against The First, "He's not [my boyfriend]. But... he is in my heart" ("Chosen" 7022). When Spike chooses to die in battle, the sunlight that blasts from the amulet on his chest and kills all the Ubervamps may as well be his love for Buffy saving the world.

Episodes Nine ("Never Leave Me" 7009) and Ten ("Bring on the Night" 7010) move the Season Seven story arc into an explicit war narrative, which links Spike's struggle to be moral to a larger fight to save the world. "Never Leave Me" reveals Spike has been acting as a weapon of The First through the use of a musical trigger, which Xander recognizes as a technique the military employs to brainwash operatives. When Spike hears a particular song that reminds him of his mother, he reverts to his evil vampire self and has no memory of doing so. Horrified he has become a weapon of evil, Spike asks Buffy to kill him, and her response and refusal recalls her conversation with Angel in "Amends" and supports her justification for fighting Anya in "Selfless":

SPIKE: Have you ever really asked yourself why you can't do it? Off me? After everything I've done to you, to people around you? It's not love. We both know that.

BUFFY: You fought by my side. You've saved lives. You've helped... You faced the monster inside of you and you fought back. You risked everything to be a better man.... And you can be. You are. You may not see it, but I do. I believe in you, Spike.

Buffy spares Spike's life and more; her belief in his ability to act justly—to be a "better man"—becomes his mantra throughout the rest of the series. Although Buffy may not love Spike, his love for her anchors his actions.

The episode segues from this exchange between Buffy and Spike to an invasion by the Harbingers or Bringers, who smash into Buffy's house and kidnap Spike. Buffy and the Scooby Gang fight back, and Buffy recognizes them as agents of The First. As though naming it brings its force to a head, the scene cuts to the Watchers' Council headquarters in London where the Director addresses the Council:

> Ladies and gentlemen, our fears have been confirmed. The First Evil has declared all-out war on this institution. Their first volleys proved most effective. I, for one, think it's time we struck back. Give me confirmations on all remaining operatives. Visuals and tacticals. Highest alert. Get them here as soon as possible. Begin preparations for mobilization. Once we're accounted for, I want to be ready to move.... We'll be paying a visit to the Hellmouth. My friends, these are the times that define us. Proverbs 24:6. For by wise council you shall make your war.

And with these words, the camera cuts to an exterior shot of the building, which explodes. The ambiguous ideological implications—that these words bring about their very destruction—suggests making war is *not* wise council, or perhaps, the Council itself is not wise.

Regardless, Buffy deploys the very same rhetoric in the next episode when Giles arrives with three potential slayers and the announcement: "We have a slight apocalypse" ("Bring on the Night" 7010). Giles tells Buffy, "you're the only one who has the strength to protect these girls—and the world—against what's coming," but Buffy takes this discourse of protection and expands it to become war. She welcomes the Potentials to the "war room," and after a particularly brutal fight against an Ubervamp she encounters when trying to find one of the potential slayers who runs away, she gives the first of her rousing speeches that pepper the season:

> I'm beyond tired. I'm beyond scared. I'm standing on the mouth of hell, and it is going to swallow me whole. And it'll choke on me. We're not ready? They're not ready. They think we're going to wait for the end to come, like we always do. I'm done waiting. They want an apocalypse? Oh, we'll give them one. Anyone else who wants to run, do it now. Because we just became an army. We just declared war. From now on, we won't just face our worst fears, we will seek them out. We will find them, and cut out their hearts one by one, until The First shows itself for what it really is. And I'll kill it myself. There is only one thing on this earth more powerful than evil, and that's us. Any questions?

This personification of fear into a being with a mouth and a heart equates it to a vampire who bites, but it also points to the heart as a site of weakness—and of strength. Unlike in *The Vampire Diaries*, in which ripping the heart out of a human or a vampire occurs regularly and functions metaphorically and literally, Buffy never cuts or rips the heart out of vampire. She stakes them and beheads them, but this imagery invokes Anya's earlier vengeance, when she summons a Grimslaw Demon to rip the hearts out of the frat boys. Buffy speaks from a place of vengeance here, and suffers for it when their initial offensive act results in immense loss and physical harm. Throughout the rest of the season, she revisits and revises this stance, as she learns how to act justly in a time of war.

Buffy's commitment to a just war—a war waged as resistance against aggression rather than one that includes acts based on personal vengeance—shines through primarily in her defense of Spike as someone valuable to the cause. When the principal of Sunnydale High School, Robin Wood, conspires with Giles to kill Spike because Spike killed his mother, Giles agrees to assist because he believes with Robin that killing Spike is for the "greater good," regardless of Robin's personal motives. Giles and Buffy go patrolling to keep Buffy preoccupied, and Giles attempts to prepare her to accept Spike's death as necessary war collateral:

GILES: We're on the verge of war. It's time you looked at the big picture.
BUFFY: Hello! All I do is look at the big picture. The other day, I gave an inspirational speech to the telephone repair man.

....

GILES: So, you really do understand the difficult decisions you'll have to make? That any one of us is expendable in this war?
BUFFY: Have you heard my speeches?
GILES: That we cannot allow any threat that would jeopardize our chances at winning?
BUFFY: Yes, I get it.
GILES: And yet there is Spike.... Spike's a liability, Buffy. He refuses to see it, and so do you. Angel left here because he realized how harmful your relationship with him was. Spike, on the other hand, lacks such self-awareness.
BUFFY: Spike is here because I want him here. We need him. I'm in the fight of my life.

As I discuss in Chapter 4, Giles sees Angel's departure as right action, and he uses Angel's act as a model for ethical behavior based on reducing harm. Giles errs, however, because he fails to see Spike as valuable to Buffy's flourishing. Buffy defends her actions to keep Spike alive and present by moving between her personal, individual desires—"I want him here"—and group, systemic value—"We need him." Revealingly, Buffy ends this justification by shifting back to the personal rather than saying the collective "we" are in the fight of their lives. Importantly, she retreats to the collective in her final words to Robin after he fails to kill Spike but succeeds in deprogramming Spike's trigger: "Spike is the strongest warrior we have. We are going to need him if we're going to come out of this thing alive. You try anything again, he'll kill you. More importantly, I'll let him. I have a mission to win this war, to save the world. I don't have time for vendettas. The mission is what matters." Buffy repeats her earlier phrase to Giles that the collective needs Spike in order to win the war, and she confirms her commitment to secure and maintain a state of right.

Regardless of her speeches and bravado, Buffy struggles with how to act justly as a leader during war. She expresses her concern in two parallel conversations, one with Robin and the other with Spike. In both dialogues, her concern rests on the deaths for which she feels responsible.

Robin, using the same words as Giles, tries to steer Buffy towards seeing "the big picture" rather than the small details:

ROBIN: You've got things to deal with that are much worse than anything here. Look at the big picture.
BUFFY: Right. The big picture. The one with the big war and the dead little girls.
ROBIN: Not dead. Not dead. Not if you get them ready.
BUFFY: I don't want to lead them into war. It can't be the right thing.
ROBIN: Most wars aren't, you know.

("Dirty Girls" 7018)

This moment is the only time the series acknowledges wars in general are wrong, but given the fate of the world rests upon Buffy and her army defeating the Ubervamps, walking away from this war equates to disregarding her moral responsibility. At the end of this conversation, Robin reminds her of the very words she said to him: "the mission is what matters." The scene then cuts to Spike sitting on his bed, shirtless, a visual metaphor that connects Spike to the mission as a beautiful, vulnerable, moral vampire.

When the Scooby Gang and the Potentials vote for Faith to lead them into war instead of Buffy, Spike's belief in and love for Buffy aids in her flourishing because it returns her to her course of just action. Finding Buffy sleeping in a stranger's house, after people in Sunnydale have started to evacuate the city, Spike tells Buffy they need her and she should not blame herself for deaths that occur as part of war:

SPIKE: There's always casualties in war.
BUFFY: Casualties. It just sounds so... casual. These are girls that I got killed. I cut myself off from them... all of them. I knew I was going to lose some of them and I didn't... You know what? I'm still making excuses. I've always cut myself off. I've always... Being the slayer made me different. But it's my fault I stayed that way. People are always trying to connect to me, and I just slip away. You should know.
SPIKE: I seem to recall a certain amount of connecting.
BUFFY: Oh, please! We were never close. You just wanted me because I was unattainable.

....

SPIKE: You listen to me. I've been alive a bit longer than you, and dead a lot longer than that. I've seen things you couldn't imagine, and done things I prefer you didn't. I don't exactly have a reputation for being a thinker. I follow my blood, which doesn't exactly rush in the direction of my brain. So I make a lot of mistakes, a lot of wrong bloody calls. A hundred plus years and there's only one thing I've ever been

> sure of: you. Hey, look at me. I'm not asking you for anything. When I say, "I love you," it's not because I want you or because I can't have you. It has nothing to do with me. I love what you are, what you do, how you try. I've seen your kindness and your strength. I've seen the best and the worst of you. And I understand with perfect clarity exactly what you are. You're a hell of a woman. You're the one, Buffy. ("Touched" 7020)

Spike comes as close as any character across the three series to articulating in a single moment Murdoch and Nussbaum's definition of love as based on loving imperfection. To recall Murdoch's words, which I quote in the Introduction to this book, "when we try perfectly to love what is imperfect our love goes to its object *via* the Good to be thus purified and made unselfish and just" (100). Spike's love for Buffy—although unrequited—moves both of them towards just action, for after Spike's declaration, Buffy reenters the fray.

If, as Nussbaum claims, the lover sees the beloved as "radiant and wonderful" (*Upheavals* 470), then the series finale ("Chosen" 7022) makes this characterization literal while also connecting love to purification, justice, and unselfishness. The episode begins where the previous episode ended: with a kiss between Angel and Buffy. When Angel says, "Well, I guess that qualifies as 'happy to see me,'" Buffy replies, "Angel, what are you doing... Don't even. I just want to bask. Ok, I'm basked. What are you doing here?" Buffy's response to seeing Angel for the first time in years is to bask in his radiant presence, but she moves very quickly to the practical. Angel hands Buffy a file containing information about The First and an amulet, which is "very powerful and probably very dangerous. It has a purifying power, a cleansing power, possibly scrubbing bubbles. The translation is, uh, anyway, it bestows strength to the right person who wears it.... Someone ensouled, but stronger than human. A champion. As in me." Buffy takes the amulet, but tells Angel she needs him to run the second front in Los Angeles, just in case she loses the fight in Sunnydale. In a very humorous scene in which Angel reveals his jealousy about Spike's place in Buffy's life and about Spike's soul, Angel grumbles, "That's great. Everyone's got a soul now.... You know, I started it. The whole having a soul. Before it was all the cool new thing." Regardless of Angel's initial pettiness, he agrees to run the second front, and thus he leaves Spike as the only vampire with a soul, the only moral vampire, to fight the war alongside Buffy.

More powerful than the radiance in which Buffy basks in Angel's presence, Spike embodies radiance and he radiates. The war ends epically when Spike, now wearing the amulet, channels the sun—a radiant light—that blasts out from the amulet killing the army of Ubervamps. Seeing Spike pinned by the light, Buffy rushes over to him and tries to convince him to retreat from the cavern with the rest of their army.

The epic closes in to the personal when Spike refuses to leave and Buffy interlinks her fingers with his outstretched hand. As their hands burn together, Buffy tearfully whispers, "I love you." Spike replies with a smile, "No you don't. But thanks for saying it." Buffy releases Spike's hand and rushes up the stairs to safety leaving Spike to burn and the cavern to crumble around him.

The *Twilight* saga stages a similar theatre of war to end the series, but instead of going into battle, *Breaking Dawn* concludes by avoiding the confrontation between the Volturi and the Cullens and their allies. The novel presents the resolution as a courtroom battle, with each side presenting evidence to support its claims, but the film, *Breaking Dawn—Part Two* enhances the mostly verbal evidence with a shocking visual spectacle that destabilizes the audience, so they might come closer to feeling the personal grief that accompanies the horrors of war. As with the season finale of *BtVS*, so the final part of the *Twilight* saga conjoins the epic and the personal as the moral vampires fight to protect a state of right against a force that intends harm. I shall discuss the film versions of *Breaking Dawn*, and concentrate primarily on part two, in which the battle occurs, for the audience is called upon to bear witness to war in a way the novel does not.

The title of this chapter quotes Stefan as he reflects in his diary about the distinction between killing and murdering, between engaging in just action and acting upon one's monstrous nature. Edward, too, struggles with this distinction, as he confesses to Bella before their wedding. Early in *Breaking Dawn—Part One*, on the night before their wedding, Edward tells Bella about how in his early days of being a vampire he rebelled against Carlisle and resented him for curbing Edward's appetite. He wanted to know what it felt like to hunt and to taste human blood. As he tells Bella this story, the film cuts to a flashback, in which Edward sits in a movie theatre, watching *The Bride of Frankenstein*. A woman leaves the theatre and Edward follows her. The camera tracks her, and our knowledge of the genre leads us to believe Edward hunts her. Instead, he attacks a man following the woman, and explains in a voiceover to Bella, "All the men I killed were monsters. And so was I." Back in the present, Bella justifies Edward's actions saying, "Edward, they were all murderers. You probably saved more lives than you took." Edward resists her defense: "Bella that's what I told myself. But they were all human beings. I looked into their eyes as they died, and I saw who I was, and what I was capable of." In a similar technique to the first half of Season Seven of *BtVS*, *Breaking Dawn—Part One* presents philosophical questions about just action at the personal level in order to lay the groundwork for an expansion of these dilemmas into the systemic and collective level.

Initially, the collective manifests on a smaller scale when Jacob defies Sam's orders to kill Bella because of her pregnancy. The pack's reaction to her pregnancy anticipates the Volturi's argument about why they should eliminate the threat Bella's fetus presents. Calling the fetus "unnatural," "dangerous," "monstrosity," "an abomination," Sam believes what Bella and Edward "have bred," must be destroyed before it is born in order to protect the pack and humans. Jacob argues that Bella's humanity deserves their protection, and when Leah retorts that Bella is dying anyway, Jacob and Leah fight. Sam intervenes, growling, "We have real enemies to fight tonight." Sam tries to use his power as pack leader to compel Jacob to join their fight, but Jacob resists, citing his birthright—he "wasn't born to follow you or anyone else"—and breaks away from Sam's pack.

Seth shifts the discourse of birthright to right action, when he, too, leaves Sam's pack to join Jacob. Jacob tries to convince Seth to return to Sam and asks Seth, "If Sam comes after Bella, are you really ready to fight your own brothers? Your sister?" Seth does not hesitate before responding simply, "If it's the right thing to do." Jacob invokes family as a line across which Seth would not step, but family reconfigures along love rather than blood connections, which Jacob first realizes when Esme and Carlisle go to him for assistance with securing more blood for Bella. Jacob asks, "You'd risk your lives for her?" To which Esme responds, "Of course we would. Bella's a part of our family now." Jacob reflects, "Yeah. I can see that. This really is a family. As strong as the one I was born into. I know what I have to do." From here onwards, Jacob acts along lines of affiliation rather than filiation, aligning himself with the moral vampires and upholding a state of right.

The protection of an affiliative family functions as a metonym for the state and serves as a stronghold for the attendant action in *Breaking Dawn—Part Two*, which I discuss for the rest of this section. The Volturi stand as the governing body for vampires, and they police vampires to ensure no one breaks any of the few vampire laws in place. Keeping vampire identities a secret is one of the most stringent rules they monitor, which includes forbidding the making of immortal children, that is, turning children into vampires. When Irina—one of the Denali coven—sees Renesmee playing with Jacob and Bella, she believes Renesmee to be an immortal child, so she reports the transgression to the Volturi. In preparation for the Volturi's impending judgment, the Cullens travel the world to gather vampire witnesses, who will testify Renesmee is half-human and half-vampire and not the immortal child Irina believes her to be. The Cullens hope Aro, leader of the Volturi, will see the Cullens have not broken any laws and will leave them in peace. When the Cullens and their allies learn the Volturi will arrive with their own witnesses, they realize Renesmee's origin provides an excuse for a confrontation but is not the primary reason for it. The Volturi thirst for power, which they achieve through the acquisition of gifted vampires. Aro hungers to bring Alice—and her ability to see the future—into the Volturi fold. Fearing for their lives, some of the Cullen's witnesses prepare to depart before the Volturi's arrival.

Edward intervenes and appeals to their sense of justice and right to freedom. In a monologue that draws upon similar rhetorical and filmic techniques to Buffy's "war room" speech to the potential slayers when she rouses them to fight ("Bring on the Night" 7010), Edward addresses the vampires and equates resistance to freedom. The Cullen's living room becomes a war room as members of each coven consider their options. Amun from the Egyptian coven stands first and prepares to leave with the other three members of his coven, including Benjamin who can manipulate the elements. Before he departs, Edward asks,

> And where will you go? What makes you think they'll be satisfied with Alice? What's to stop them from going after Benjamin next? Or Zafrina or Kate or anyone else with a gift? Anyone they want. Their goal isn't punishment, it's power. It's acquisition. Carlisle might not ask you to fight, but I will. For the sake of my family, but also for yours. And for the way you want to live.

Silence fills the room, as the camera pans from one coven to the next, accounting for the individual identity of each vampire, the coven to which they belong, and ultimately the collective as a whole. Jacob stands first and pledges the wolf packs' allegiance to fight. The Denalis stand next. Then Garrett, who says, "This won't be the first time I fought a king's rule." And Benjamin. When Amun tries to stop Benjamin, he says, "I will do the right thing, Amun. You may do as you please." Soon the whole room pledges to fight, and Bella's voiceover makes explicit the potential war to come, "Everyone showed courage, though we knew that Aro's army was moving against us." Garrett and Benjamin, in particular, equate the Volturi's approach with a failure by the state to meet its obligation and, therefore, see their own pledge to fight against the Volturi as just action against an aggressor who threatens their freedom.

The night before the Volturi arrive, the Cullens and their allies exchange war stories around a campfire, and the scene unites the collective around familial and romantic love, and a history of rebellion against an oppressor. As the allies speak, Edward and Carlisle stand slightly away from them all, and Edward reflects, "I can't help thinking, all these people are putting themselves in danger because I fell in love with a human." Carlisle comforts Edward, "You found your mate. You deserve to be happy." When Edward questions, "But at what cost?" Carlisle reassures him, "Everyone here has something to fight for. I certainly do." The camera follows Carlisle's gaze to where Esme smiles back at him and Emmett and Rosalie hold each other. Edward turns his head to look into the tent where Bella sits with Renesmee lying across her lap. The scene ends with a conversation between Bella and Renesmee in which Bella gives

Figure 6.2 Love-based collective face the Volturi.

her daughter a locket, which contains a picture of Edward and Bella and the words, "Plus que ma propre vie." Bella's words—that she loves Renesmee more than her own life—and the locket itself provide a visual metaphor for collective action that originates in romantic love. Edward and Bella's love initiates and justifies killing—and the possibility of being killed—as right action. The battle stories the vampires share around the bonfire reveals their motivation for fighting: some for revenge; some because they enjoy any battle; some because they stand for rebellion; and the Cullens because of their love for each other. Regardless of intention, the vampires unite around a common cause to defend their innate right to freedom, and it originates in love.

The familial, affiliative ties that make up the collective display themselves on the battlefield, as each love-based group stands on the battlefield awaiting the Volturi's arrival. Edward, Bella and Renesmee stand in front and each group emanates out from them: Rosalie and Emmett flank one side; Carlisle and Esme the other; and behind them, Garrett joins the Denali coven visually signalling his future romance with Kate (Figure 6.2). Separate but together, the covens cluster in groups of two, three, four, or five vampires unlike the solid line of the black-robed Volturi guard. As the guard stretches across the horizon, Garrett mutters, "The redcoats are coming. The redcoats are coming," a historical reference that aligns the Volturi with the British and the Cullens and their allies with Americans seeking independence from the British.

Once the Cullens prove no laws have been broken, by showing Aro that Renesmee is not an immortal child, Aro shifts tactics and draws upon now-familiar Bush rhetoric that uses weapons of mass destruction as justification for war. Aro agrees with Carlisle no laws have been broken, and then he continues, "But does it then follow that there is no danger? For the first time in our history, humans pose a threat to our kind. Their modern technology has given birth to weapons that could destroy us. Maintaining our secret has never been more imperative." Aro moves between the Cullen collective and the Volturi guard and addresses his words to both parties. He then stops, and the film breaks the third wall, as Aro looks directly into the camera, and appeals to the viewer in one of the most chilling speeches of the film because it resonates so precisely with American justifications for the War on Terror: "In such perilous time, only the known is safe. Only the known is tolerable." He then shifts his gaze back to the battlefield and continues, "And we know nothing of what this child will become. Can we live with such uncertainty? Spare ourselves a fight today, only to die tomorrow."

As both sides become agitated and it looks like war is inevitable, Alice and Jasper walk onto the battlefield with evidence that Renesmee will not be a risk, that the danger Aro spouts proves irrelevant. Here the film pulls away from the novel, in a clever and shocking translation that suits the adaptation into film seamlessly. Keep in mind the film audience comprises a substantial portion of people who have already read the books, who are deep fans of them. They know at this point in *Breaking Dawn* Alice appears with Nahuel, another child conceived from a human mother and vampire father. She presents Nahuel as physical evidence the Volturi have no reason to fear Renesmee will disclose the vampires' existence. In the film, however, Aro sees her proof in the same way he substantiates all other claims: by holding her hand and seeing what she has seen in the past, present, and future.

Suddenly, however, Alice pulls her hand away, and says, "It doesn't matter what I show you. Even when you see. You still won't change your decision." Alice turns to Bella, tells her to send Renesmee away with Jacob, and then turns and delivers a roundhouse kick to Aro's jaw, which sends him flying through the air. Aro commands the Volturi guard to take Alice away, and as they do, Carlisle yells to let her go and charges towards them. He and Aro leap full speed into the air and grapple with each other midflight. They both land. Aro faces the Cullen collective, the audience, and holds Carlisle's severed head in his hand. The shocked expressions on the faces of Esme, Edward, Bella, and their friends mirrors the horror of the audience. At the screening I attended, an audible gasp filled the theatre. Someone screamed. Conversations broke out in disbelief. This outcome was not part of the novel. Carlisle does not die. People we care about do not die. As the Volturi burn Carlisle's body, the Cullen army attacks, and fierce hand-to-hand combat ensues. Jasper dies. Seth dies. Leah dies. The Volturi guard is decimated, and Aro dies brutally at the hands of Bella and Edward. Bella reaches down to light Aro's decapitated head on fire, the fire reflects in Aro's dead eyes, and fills the screen with flames. The cresting music builds to its crescendo, and then all is silent as the film cuts to Aro still holding Alice's hand. He quickly withdraws his hand and looks into the faces of his enemies. Both sides wait in anticipation. The camera shifts from each familial group, waiting for Aro's decision. Alice says, "Now you know. That's your future. Unless you decide on another course." Alice walks away as Aro hesitates and Caius urges him into battle. The film meets back up with the novel here as Nahuel enters the battlefield, and Aro is spared a decision based only on Alice's vision of his future. The audience exhales. Our beloveds live.

The Vampire Diaries, which concluded its sixth season as I wrote this chapter, changes the syntax of large-scale battles that occur in *Buffy* and the *Twilight* saga to infuse the entire series with war rhetoric and specifically the American Civil War. By setting the story in Virginia in the southern United States, and including a back story in which Damon and Stefan became vampires during the Civil War, the series invites a reflection upon right action that stems from a history of a nation divided against itself in which brother fought against brother. As with *BtVS* and *Breaking Dawn*, the epic couples with the personal when the Salvatore brothers fight and protect each other because of their love for each other and for Elena. This complex triangular relationship between brothers and lovers functions allegorically to represent an emotionally-conflicted America that romanticizes war as protection.

Flashbacks to the Civil War era, present-day classroom lessons about and Mystic Falls commemorations of Civil War battles, Damon's back-story as a soldier who deserted the Confederate Army, and intertextual references to *Gone with the Wind* all lay the groundwork for a reading of the series as an allegory about the shifting nature of war in America's national story. Generally speaking, a rhetoric of war privileges the protection of a nation's citizenry, especially its women and children. In other words, men fight each other to protect women. The brotherhood that develops on the battlefield, however, embeds a fraternal love that may be equally strong or even stronger than romantic love. *The Vampire Diaries* repeatedly poses moral dilemmas which question whether protecting one's lover or one's brother functions as the best action. Damon and Stefan routinely pledge to protect Elena above all else, but more often than not, they end up protecting or saving each other. At an allegorical level, then, the series pits nation against family, public good against personal sacrifice.

The Civil War intertext occurs in the very first episode, when the Mystic Falls High School History class focuses on the 1865 Battle of Willow Creek. The scene segues from the personal to the political with a shift from Stefan holding a picture of Katherine dated 1864 to the inside of a contemporary classroom where the History teacher, Mr. Tanner, stands in front of a blackboard covered in writing, which summarizes the battle. The teacher walks back and forth in front of the blackboard while providing more information and quizzing the students about their knowledge of the battle. He calls upon Bonnie, Matt, and then Elena, asking them how many casualties resulted from this battle. When none of them supply an adequate response and Mr. Tanner humiliates them for their lack of knowledge, Stefan responds with the correct answer:

STEFAN: There were 346 casualties, unless you're counting the local civilians.

MR. TANNER: That's correct. Mr...

STEFAN: Salvatore.

MR. TANNER: Salvatore? Any relation to the original settlers here at Mystic Falls?

STEFAN: Distant.

MR. TANNER: Well, very good. Except of course there were no civilian casualties in this battle.

STEFAN: Actually, there were twenty-seven, sir. Confederate soldiers, they fired on the church believing it to be housing weapons. They were wrong. It was a night of great loss. The founders' archives are stored in Civil Hall, if you'd like to brush up on your facts, Mr. Tanner. ("Pilot" 1001)

This scene establishes both Stefan's connection to that time period via his picture of Katherine and through his impulse to protect Elena. By humiliating Mr. Tanner about his lack of knowledge, Stefan diverts Tanner's verbal fire away from Elena. Furthermore, Stefan's knowledge about the civilian deaths calls attention to distinctions between official and unofficial histories and foreshadows the significance of these twenty-seven civilian deaths. Additionally, the fact it was Confederate—and not Union—soldiers who fired upon the church blurs lines between enemy and hero. Finally, Stefan's wording that the Confederate soldiers fired upon the church because they believed it to be housing weapons borrows from American rhetoric about the War Against Terror being fuelled by a search for weapons of mass destruction, as do Aro's words in *Breaking Dawn*. That the twenty-seven civilians are vampires both supports and challenges these assertions, for these vampires embody both humanity and weaponry, both civilian collateral and domestic enemy.

Elena revisits this first reference to the Battle of Willow Creek and the alternative versions of its history in a later discussion with Damon, when he tells her about the Salvatore brothers being cursed with sibling rivalry ("Family Ties" 1004). In his familiar usage of stories with double meanings, Damon tells Elena a history of the "original" Salvatore brothers, claiming the rivalry he and Stefan enact stems from those first brothers. At this stage, Elena is not aware the 1864 Salvatore brothers *are* the same brothers she knows, so she believes the histories she hears encapsulate the history of their ancestors and not their own personal experiences. When Elena tells Damon she knows about the Battle of Willow Creek, Damon provides even more information than Stefan's earlier intervention with Tanner and connects the tragedy with the Salvatore brothers own personal loss:

DAMON: What the history books left out was that the people that were killed, they weren't there by accident. They were believed to be Union sympathizers, so some of the founders on the Confederacy side back then wanted them rounded up and burned alive. Stefan and Damon had someone they loved very much in that church. And when they went to rescue them, they were shot, murdered in cold blood.
ELENA: Who was in the church that they wanted to save?
DAMON: A woman. I guess. Doesn't it always come down to the love of a woman?
ELENA: Look I'm sorry that you and Stefan have this thing between you, but I can't get in the middle of it, Damon. I just, I hope the two of you can work it out.
DAMON: I hope so too.

("Family Ties" 1004)

Damon's version builds upon Stefan's initial revision of Tanner's misinformed textbook history, and it also begins to reveal some of the ambiguities in how the series negotiates its representation of wartime ethics, including responding to debates about when killing is justified, and who can be killed.

These ambiguities fall into two amorphous formations: the first category contains the multiple referents vampires signify; and the second queries the Civil War as an event that embodies a range of vexing ethical dilemmas pertaining to wars both past and present. As vampires, Damon and Stefan exist on the margins of the mostly-human town, but as members of one of the founding families of Mystic Falls, Damon and Stefan belong to the elite inner circle of the Founders Council. Generally speaking, the Council—past and present—casts vampires as evil incarnate and a danger to the community, but time and time again, Stefan and Damon protect the people of Mystic Falls from outside forces. More specifically, Damon occupies a liminal space between insider and outsider, rebel and sympathizer. Damon, and not Stefan, fights in the Confederate Army and then later deserts the Cause, raising the ire of his father. Damon, and not Stefan, joins the Founders Council working from within the system to learn the Council's secrets, but inevitably also supports their cause to protect their community. Union sympathizers equate to vampire sympathizers, an enemy within.

Both these constructions rely on the interactions between the four species that coexist in *TVD* storyworld: humans, vampires, witches, and werewolves. Season One focuses primarily on the relationship between humans, vampires, and witches, and Season Two, introduces werewolves and Klaus—a unique vampire/werewolf hybrid, who intends to create a race of hybrids. Until Katherine returns and Caroline becomes a vampire in Season Two, Stefan and Damon are the only vampires dwelling in Mystic Falls and therein become the primary means to characterize vampires. Initially, they represent a range of meanings because, seemingly, they occupy opposite ends of a personality spectrum: Stefan's compassion, control, and reason counteracts Damon's disregard for human life, impulsiveness, and passion.

As Season Two progresses, however, flashbacks to Stefan and Damon in their early days as vampires during the Civil War reveal Damon to be the sensitive, loving brother—open to Katherine's love and devastated by her apparent death—whereas Stefan loses himself in the debauchery of killing, caring nothing for the lives of the people he ravages. This reversal diminishes the significance of this brotherly dialectic and suggests right and wrong, good and evil may exist in everyone. In other words, apparently good people act badly and seemingly bad people perform right actions.

A reference to the American Civil War occurs in the first episode of *TVD*, but the connection between *vampires* and the Civil War is made explicit exactly halfway through the first season, when Elena's brother Jeremy researches the Civil War for one of his high school History papers ("Bloodlines" 1011). In the library, he meets Anna, who, unbeknownst to Jeremy, is a vampire who lived during the Civil War. Their resulting debate ping pongs back and forth between Jeremy's position that "vampires are metaphors for the demons of the day" and Anna's contention that vampires really exist. When Anna asks who those demons represent, Jeremy answers without hesitation that they symbolize the Union soldiers, the demons who attacked at night. Anna rebuts, "That sounds like vampires to me," and Jeremy responds, "*Allegorical* vampires, which is what it is: creative expression during a very volatile time. I mean a country at war doesn't want realism. They want fantasy. Thus vampire fiction." While *The Vampire Diaries* carefully couches its war history within the context of the Civil War, a metanarrative moment such as this one, invites an analysis of how the series positions itself in relation to contemporary wartime politics. For instance, *The Vampire Diaries* first aired in 2009, the year President Obama announced a plan to pull American soldiers out of Iraq and committed to sending over 20,000 American troops to Afghanistan. In other words, 2009 may be considered a "volatile time" for America, "a country at war."

Five episodes later, Jeremy picks up this conversation thread again with Anna in an attempt to express solidarity with vampires. He says, "Maybe vampires aren't how we thought.... Maybe they're normal. And good. Just outsiders. Misunderstood" ("There Goes the Neighbourhood" 1016). The title of this episode and the fact Anna and her mother Pearl are Asian-American call attention to the demonization of people of colour, both in the Civil War era and as Bush's 2001–2009 so-called "War Against Terror" comes to an end. The show both problematizes this demonization through the romantic relationship between Jeremy and Anna, and then upholds it when Anna and her mother and several African-American characters die in the first season. If Anna and her mother are metaphors for racialized others, then the show hedges its bets to satisfy both political sides: vampires embody both evil outsider and alienated beloved.

It is important not to push an allegorical reading too far, however, for as Ken Gelder says in his 2012 book *New Vampire Cinema*, "vampire films can often invest themselves with some level of national or political representation—or citation—even as they might dissolve those connections away; which means that the (national) allegorising impulse of film commentators, and even film directors, can often be frustrated" (vii–viii). This dissolution of the national or political representation may occur more frequently in vampire *films*, but in this long-running television series, *The Vampire Diaries* repeated representations or citations backward to the Civil War and forward to commemoration invite deeper consideration.

An allegorizing impulse, however, does not align easily with one interpretation. It is tempting to say about Season One, for instance, that Stefan functions as the righteous North and Damon as the rebellious South, both brothers vehemently defending their ideals for the same reason, to protect Elena. But then Stefan falls off the blood wagon, his addiction to human blood reveals him to be not-so-ideal, and Damon steps into the role of the dependable brother, a gentleman suitor who stands by Elena's side. Then, in Season Two, werewolves stalk onto the scene, and the rhetoric switches to species against species rather than brother against brother. Instead, the brothers must unite in order to fight a common enemy, and herein arises the possibility of another allegory: a united America against an enemy from another race. This interpretation dissolves, however, when a vampire-werewolf hybrid—Klaus—appears as the enemy, which unites werewolves and vampires to stop his attempts to create an even more powerful race of hybrids.

Perhaps, then, vampires function not so much as metaphors for the demons of the day, than as figures who *reveal* the demons of the day. Although Jeremy says during the Civil War vampires symbolized the Union soldiers, the show never represents vampires this way. Instead, the series uses flashbacks to expose the founding families—and mainly the founding *fathers*—to be the most evil figures. Although vampires in 1861 Mystic Falls blend in seamlessly to the fabric of the town's structure, the founding fathers fight to rid the town of vampires because they believe vampires are evil creatures. Damon and Stefan's father leads the charge against vampires, to the extent that he kills his own sons—which contributes to their transformation into vampires—because, as he says, "he would rather they be dead than to exist as evil creatures." He then records their deaths as innocent victims of the Battle of Willow Creek rather than as shameful vampire sympathizers. Similarly, in Season Two, neither vampire nor werewolf emerges as more demonic than the other. Instead, the demon of the day—or at least of the season—seems to be the ideological differences that place them at war with each other.

The Vampire Diaries does not stand alone in its use of the American Civil War to raise contemporary issues. Other small and large screen examples of contemporary popular culture that dig the Civil War from its shallow grave include *Homeland*, and in the vampire genre *True Blood*, *Eclipse* from the *Twilight* Saga, and *Abraham Lincoln: Vampire Hunter.* Whereas *Homeland*, rather predictably, cites Chamberlain's actions for the Union at the Battle of Gettysburg as a model for the lone heroic soldier, Civil War *vampires* align with the Confederate rebel soldiers of the South. Vampires Bill Compton in *True Blood* and Jasper Hale in the *Twilight* Saga both fought for the South before being turned into vampires, as did Damon in *The Vampire Diaries. Abraham Lincoln: Vampire Hunter* shifts the perspective by situating itself historically during the Civil War rather than using the Civil War as an historical background for a contemporary narrative.

Regardless, in these cases of vampire narratives, one might ask, why do 21st-century vampires align with and fight for the South? In *Abraham Lincoln: Vampire Hunter*, Confederate soldiers employ the vampires to help defeat the North, so Abraham Lincoln must fight not only the rebel Confederates, but also their blood-sucking counterparts. These vampires, in other words, serve a mainstream narrative about the North being on the right side of history. But what about the vampires we love and with whom we sympathize? How could Bill, Jasper, and Damon all fight for the evil South? Damon receives an ideological pardon because he deserted the Confederate army, but, overall, *True Blood*, *Twilight*, and *The Vampire Diaries* reanimate the South not as an evil entity that will suck the life blood out of the nation, but as a rebel force that opposes an authoritarian ruler who seeks to rip the heart out of marginalized peoples. By this line of thought, *True Blood* uses the Southern vampires as metaphors for people oppressed due to their sexuality and/or race, as many commentators note and as the opening credits make overt with their explicit reference to the Westboro Baptist Church homophobic religious leader, Fred Phelps, who protested that "God Hates Fags," which becomes "God Hates Fangs" in *True Blood*.

Furthermore, Season Seven—the final season of *True Blood*—goes to great lengths to revisit Bill Compton's Civil War life and to call into question previous assumptions about him as a Confederate soldier and slave owner. In Episode Five, for instance, tellingly titled "Lost Cause," Bill remembers a series of events that culminate in his decision to join the Confederate army. Through flashbacks interspersed throughout the episode, it becomes apparent Bill opposes the Civil War and calls it a lost cause. Behind his public claim, however, sits the deeper ideological position that he opposes slavery. When he and his family try to escape to the North with an African-American family, who may once have been slaves but are now free, they are discovered, and the African-American man is shot and killed, as a warning to Bill that whoever deserts the army will be similarly killed, regardless of color. Bill's final flashback shows him dressed in a Confederate uniform telling his wife their family is in danger if he does not join.

The Vampire Diaries racial politics, however, remain shadowy, as several academic bloggers bring to light. For instance, in a 20th January 2012 post on the blog *Racialicious*, just before Season Three aired, Kendra James and Jordan St. John discuss the Civil War aspects of *The Vampire Diaries*. Kendra James states,

> I wish I could understand why everyone's decided vampires are all Southern these days, but that's where we are, and *TVD* will always, to me, be a younger and better version of *True Blood*. But it's not perfect. The show's writers could have easily acknowledged the racial and social issues that come with placing yourself within the context of war and tackled the issues head on, instead of dancing around as *True Blood* tends to do.... Romanticizing and whitewashing the African-American experience isn't a new occurrence (see: *Gone With The Wind* or Douglas Sirk's remake of *Imitation of Life,* to name a few), and it's troubling to see the trend surface again in 2012.... Elena is clearly supposed to be the Scarlett O'Hara of the Civil War-obsessed Mystic Falls. They're positioned next to each other in the season two finale: two dark haired, strong, southern women of different periods. As the season two finale progresses into chaos, so does Scarlett's world on the screen in the town center. At one point Elena is literally shown as Scarlett, with the crumbling Mystic Falls taking the place of Scarlett's burning Atlanta. The writers had to know what they were doing. I understand that they were trying to highlight the idea of Elena being a strong female character, but was that really the message conveyed through Scarlett? A woman who (forgetting her numerous other flaws), is in the end left crying over a man on a staircase? It seems to go against the character Elena's been built to be so far, and drags her back into Bella territory.

This post and others like it, rightly point to problematic absences and elisions in the representation of racialized characters and histories. In this article, James aligns the whitewashing of a Civil War history with the weakening of an arguably strong female character. I take this idea one step further, or perhaps one step sideways, to look more closely at how the series aligns its Civil War history with *Gone with the Wind* in order to reveal the personal tragedies that lie beneath epic, heroic narratives. I disagree, however, with James about Elena's character; the images do not show Scarlett or Elena crying on a staircase. They show Elena assisting Damon, himself cast as a wounded soldier, seemingly about to die, while Atlanta burns behind them.

Ambiguous responses to the race politics in *The Vampire Diaries* eerily mirror early reviews of *Gone with the Wind*. In his essay "A Boy on the Train, or Bad Symphonies and Good Movies," Peter Franklin discusses the politics of reading film and music, and he quotes the following two reviews in order to distinguish between reading practices. A review from the *Hollywood Spectator* in 1939 sings the praises of the film: "There is no flag-waving in the picture. It takes no sides in the controversies it records, preaches no sermons, points no morals—just lets us see humanity in action and uses a little group of wholly unimportant people as the symbols of what it wishes to express" (qtd. in Franklin 20). Alternatively, in early 1940, the black writer and dramatist Carlton Moss published the following open letter in the *New York Daily Worker*:

> Whereas *The Birth of a Nation* was a frontal attack on American history and the Negro people, *Gone with the Wind*, arriving 20 years later, is a rear attack on the same. Sugar-smeared and blurred by a boresome Hollywood love-story and under the guise of presenting the South as it is "in the eyes of the Southerners," the message of *Gone with the Wind* emerges in its final entity as a nostalgic plea for sympathy for a still living cause of Southern reaction.
>
> The Civil War is by no means ended in the South, Mr Selznick. It lives on and will live on until the Negro people are completely free.
>
> (qtd. in Franklin 20)

When we see Elena and Damon against the backdrop of the famous Atlanta burning scene, they, too, might be read as either unimportant people symbolizing humanity in action or some "boresome Hollywood love-story." My impulse combines these two options to barrack for a story that tells us about the importance of romantic love to right action.

The Vampire Diaries returns repeatedly to Mystic Falls' Civil War history and holds several commemorative events in which the townspeople frock up in crinoline gowns or Confederate uniforms. The most extended *Gone with the Wind* intertextual moment—and the one to which Kendra James refers above—occurs in the final episode of Season Two ("As I Lay Dying" 2022) when Mystic Falls holds an outdoor screening of the film in a park that features a memorial on which the following words appear, "Who gave their lives in the defense of our country," thus uniting the Civil War with all wars in which Americans fought and continue to fight. No one mentions, however, a reference to the novel that appears a full ten episodes earlier ("The Descent" 2012) in one of the most emotionally-moving/affective episodes, when Damon kills another vampire, Rose, as an act of mercy after she becomes the perhaps-not-quite-innocent victim of a battle between the werewolves and vampires in Mystic Falls.

At this stage, the series has spent the first season and a half (33 episodes) developing Stefan as the good vampire brother, Elena and Stefan as the romantic couple whose epic love will conquer all, and Damon as the passionate, impulsive vampire who loves his brother's girlfriend but who has little regard for other people's (or vampire's) lives. When Stefan falls off the wagon and starts drinking human blood again (from a blood bank, not from human flesh), however, Damon steps in to replace him by Elena's side at the Founder's Ball and begins to display publicly his ability to care for people beyond his own circle of interest.

At this point in the series, Damon's capability for compassion becomes most apparent in his relationship with Rose. As a 500-year old vampire who sacrifices romantic for platonic love, she—and her five-episode story arc—function as a cautionary tale about the cost of shutting off one's emotions. Rose enters the narrative when she kidnaps Elena in order to negotiate a pardon for her friend Trevor. When her plan fails and Trevor is killed, she seeks shelter with Damon and Stefan and a friends-with-benefits relationship develops between Damon and Rose. Rose says to Damon, "I don't love men who love other women, I think more of myself than that. But it doesn't mean I can't be your special friend," ("By the Light of the Moon" 2011). All too soon, Rose becomes the victim of a werewolf attack and because a werewolf bite can kill a vampire, Rose begins to suffer a painful descent towards death.

While Damon tries to track down a cure for Rose's werewolf bite, Elena nurses Rose in Damon's bedroom. As Elena helps Rose into bed, her gaze moves around the room, stopping on a painting, a large elegant bathtub, and then a stack of books. She picks up the top book and the camera closes in on the title, *Gone with the Wind*. Elena scoffs, puts the book down, and Rose says, "You've never been in Damon's room before have you? Not what you expected…" The conversation that follows uses Elena's response to the novel as an opening into Rose's thoughts about love and family:

ROSE: You're lucky you know. No one's ever loved me the way you're loved.

ELENA: I doubt that.

ROSE: Trevor was my best friend. Nothing more…. I just never thought it was a good idea to set up roots. The whole idea of family, it's not exactly compatible with being a vampire…. When you live long enough, everything disappears. So much time wasted. I just wish I hadn't been so afraid.

This conversation continues later in the episode after the venom spreads through Rose's body and causes hallucinations, madness, and excruciating pain. Damon finds Rose in town, delirious and in anguish after she has killed a man. Damon brings Rose back to his bed, and in her final conversation with Elena, she reflects, "Damon's a lot like me. He wants to care and when he does, he runs away from it. I'm sorry for what I've done today. And you need to fight. I know you're scared, but you have to do it anyway." This extended exchange between Rose and Elena uses *Gone with the Wind* as insight into Damon's ability to feel love and loss and in order to make the point that every day contains a fight to make a life well lived, a point Buffy makes to Angel, too.

When Damon finally succumbs to Rose's pleas to make her pain stop, he uses his mind control to make her dream of home. Her death scene fluctuates between Rose smiling and joyous in the summer sunny fields of her home and her lying suffering and pale in the dark somber space of Damon's bedroom. When Damon finally presses the stake into her heart, he does so while she dreams of home, so the tears flowing down his cheek symbolize not her pain but his. Damon's pain reaches through the screen as the camera closes in on his face, pulling the viewer into the intimacy of his grief. Importantly—and a technique the series frequently employs—no one but the viewer witnesses this scene, and indeed not until the end of the next season does Elena discover this example of Damon's compassion, which leads to one of their most passionate kisses, as I discuss in Chapter 3 (Figure 6.3).

This episode pairs with the Season Two finale when Damon lies dying in his bed also suffering from a werewolf bite that occurs two episodes earlier when Damon protects Caroline and Matt from Tyler Lockwood as he changes from human to werewolf under the full moon ("The Last Day" 2020). Both of these werewolf bites dig into my central argument about how the series uses the vampire who does not bite to kill as a metaphor for right action. Both Rose and Damon fall as victims in a war in which

Figure 6.3 Damon presses a stake into Rose's heart.

they did not choose to participate, bitten by the enemy. *TVD* repeatedly uses parallel moments such as this one to create an affective response, to set up the viewer to anticipate one outcome—Damon's death in this instance—and then to thwart this outcome, in order to experience the fearful anticipation of Damon's death, and the death of a potential love.

In this scene, Elena holds a dying Damon in her arms, and in this intimate embrace, she forgives him for his past wrongful actions, and bestows upon him a kiss, the first—but not the last—they will share. This almost-ending posits a bittersweet *Romeo and Juliet*-type closure, but then refuses it when Katherine—Elena's doppelgänger—arrives with the cure for Damon, secured by Stefan, who makes a deal with Klaus to do everything Klaus asks in exchange for a vial of his blood, which will stop the werewolf venom from killing Damon. The ultimate gesture of love is a brotherly sacrifice made by Stefan, who gives himself over to the enemy, a willing hostage, in order to save his brother. Once he learns Damon will live, he agrees to become the very monster he so long despised. The second season ends, then, not with a woman crying on the stairs or with a civil war. Instead, one brother sacrifices his life to give his brother life. And somehow that feels like love—but with too great a cost.

Each series represents love—romantic that expands to include the familial and communal—as worth protecting from an outside force that threatens to annihilate this love. Romantic love does not exist for itself only, however. Rather, it represents a way of life worth defending. Angel and Buffy save the world from the Mayor and then reunite briefly in order to avert another apocalypse. The Cullens and their allies flank Edward and Bella to stave off the Volturi. *The Vampire Diaries* pulls the American Civil War into the present as a backdrop for Damon and Stefan's love for Elena to show that fraternal love can be as powerful as and can exist in tandem with romantic love. Petty jealousies are cast aside as Spike and Jacob join their respective frays, and Stefan and Damon sacrifice themselves so their brother can flourish. An answer to Stefan's question, "But how do I stop a monster without becoming one?" might well be, "Act from a base of love and not hate or fear or from a desire for power." These three series suggest the most monstrous acts occur when one shuts oneself off from emotions, from love, and even from the pain that often accompanies love. While they all represent war and killing as an aspect of life, they stop short of glorifying it. Instead, they try to show that the deaths sustained in such wars touch individuals; lives lost are loves lost as romance becomes tragedy, even for an immortal.

Works Cited

Abraham Lincoln: Vampire Hunter. Dir. Timur Bekmambetov. Abraham Productions, 2012. Film.

"Amends." *Buffy the Vampire Slayer: The Complete Third Season on DVD*. Writ. and Dir. Joss Whedon. Twentieth Century Fox, 2002. DVD.

"As I Lay Dying." *The Vampire Diaries.* Writ. Turi Meyer, Al Septien, and Michael Narducci. Dir. John Behring. CWTV. 12 May 2011. Television

"Bloodlines." *The Vampire Diaries.* Writ. Kevin Williamson and Julie Plec. Dir. David Barrett. CWTV. 21 January 2010. Television.

"Bring on the Night." *Buffy the Vampire Slayer: Season Seven Collector's Edition.* Writ. Marti Noxon and Douglas Petrie. Dir. David Grossman. Twentieth Century Fox, 2002. DVD.

"By the Light of the Moon." *The Vampire Diaries.* Writ. Kevin Williamson and Julie Plec. Dir. Elizabeth Allen. CWTV. 9 December 2010. Television.

"Chosen." *Buffy the Vampire Slayer: Season Seven Collector's Edition.* Writ. and Dir. Joss Whedon. Twentieth Century Fox, 2002. DVD.

"The Descent." *The Vampire Diaries.* Writ. Sarah Fain and Elizabeth Craft. Dir. Marcos Siega. CWTV. 27 January 2011. Television.

"Dirty Girls." *Buffy the Vampire Slayer: Season Seven Collector's Edition.* Writ. Drew Goddard. Dir. Michael Gershman. Twentieth Century Fox, 2002. DVD.

"Family Ties." *The Vampire Diaries.* Writ. Kevin Williamson and Julie Plec. Dir. David Barrett. CWTV. 21 January 2010. Television.

Franklin, Peter. "The Boy on the Train, or Bad Symphonies and Good Movies: The Revealing Error of the 'Symphonic Score.'" *Beyond the Soundtrack: Representing Music in Cinema.* Eds. Daniel, Goldmark, Lawrence Kramer, and Richard D. Leppert. Berkeley: U of California P, 2007. 13–26. Print.

Gelder, Ken. *New Vampire Cinema.* London: British Film Institute, 2012. Print.

"Graduation Day: Part 1." *Buffy the Vampire Slayer: The Complete Third Season on DVD.* Writ. and Dir. Joss Whedon. Twentieth Century Fox, 2002. DVD.

"Graduation Day: Part 2." *Buffy the Vampire Slayer: The Complete Third Season on DVD.* Writ. and Dir. Joss Whedon. Twentieth Century Fox, 2002. DVD.

"Grave." *Buffy the Vampire Slayer: Season Six.* Writ. David Fury. Dir. James Contner. Twentieth Century Fox, 2002. DVD.

"Help." *Buffy the Vampire Slayer: Season Seven Collector's Edition.* Writ. Rebecca Sinclair. Dir. Rick Rosenthal. Twentieth Century Fox, 2002. DVD.

"Him." *Buffy the Vampire Slayer: Season Seven Collector's Edition.* Writ. Drew Z. Greenberg. Dir. Michael Gershman. Twentieth Century Fox, 2002. DVD.

Homeland. Creators Alex Gansa and Howard Gordon. Teakwood Lane. 2011-. TV Series.

James, Kendra. "Table for Two: Kendra and Jordan Break Down the Vampire Diaries." 20 January 2012. http://archive.feedblitz.com/99002/~4129874#99002_1

Kant, Immanuel. *The Metaphysics of Morals.* Trans. and Ed. Mary Gregor. Cambridge: Cambridge UP, 1996. Print.

"The Killer in Me." *Buffy the Vampire Slayer: Season Seven Collector's Edition.* Writ. Drew Z. Greenberg. Dir. David Solomon. Twentieth Century Fox, 2002. DVD.

Korsmeyer, Carolyn. "Passion and Action: In and Out of Control." *Buffy the Vampire Slayer and Philosophy: Fear and Trembling in Sunnydale.* Ed. James B. South. Chicago: Open Court Publishing, 2003. 160–172. Print.

Meyer, Stephenie. *Breaking Dawn.* New York: Little Brown, 2008. Print.

Milavec, Melissa M. and Sharon M. Kaye. "Buffy in the Buff: A Slayer's Solution to Aristotle's Love Paradox." *Buffy the Vampire Slayer and Philosophy:*

Fear and Trembling in Sunnydale. Ed. James B. South. Chicago: Open Court Publishing, 2003. 173–184. Print.

Murdoch, Iris. *The Sovereignty of Good.* 1970. New York: Routledge, 2013. Print.

"Never Leave Me." *Buffy the Vampire Slayer: Season Seven Collector's Edition.* Writ. Drew Godard. Dir. David Solomon. Twentieth Century Fox, 2002. DVD.

"Pilot." *The Vampire Diaries.* Writ. Kevin Williamson and Julie Plec. Dir. Marcos Siega. CWTV. 10 September 2009. Television.

"Selfless." *Buffy the Vampire Slayer: Season Seven Collector's Edition.* Writ. Drew Godard. Dir. David Solomon. Twentieth Century Fox, 2002. DVD.

"Storyteller." *Buffy the Vampire Slayer: Season Seven Collector's Edition.* Writ. Jane Espenson. Dir. Marita Grabiak. Twentieth Century Fox, 2002. DVD.

Stroud, Scott R. "A Kantian Analysis of Moral Judgment in *Buffy the Vampire Slayer. Buffy the Vampire Slayer and Philosophy: Fear and Trembling in Sunnydale.* Ed. James B. South. Chicago: Open Court Publishing, 2003. 185–194. Print.

"There Goes The Neighbourhood." *The Vampire Diaries.* Writ. Bryan Oh and Andrew Chambliss. Dir. Kevin Bray. CWTV. 1 April 2010. Television.

True Blood. Creator Alan Ball. HBO. 2008–2014. TV Series.

Twilight. Writ. Melissa Rosenberg. Dir. Catherine Hardwicke, 2008. DVD.

The Twilight Saga: Breaking Dawn—Part 1. Writ. Melissa Rosenberg. Dir. Bill Condon, 2011. DVD.

The Twilight Saga: Breaking Dawn—Part 2. Writ. Melissa Rosenberg. Dir. Bill Condon, 2012. DVD.

"The Wish." *Buffy the Vampire Slayer: The Complete Third Season on DVD.* Writ. Marti Noxon. Dir. David Greenwalt. Twentieth Century Fox, 2002. DVD.

Zanger, Jules. "Metaphor into Metonymy: The Vampire Next Door." *Blood Read: The Vampire as Metaphor in Contemporary Culture.* Ed. Joan Gordon and Veronica Hollinger. Philadephia: UPenn, 1997. 17–26. Print.

Conclusion

"If We Cease to Believe in Love, Why Would We Want to Live?": Fallen Angels, Emotional Zombies, and other Rebel Lovers

When I first started thinking about this book, I conceived of it as an inquiry into paranormal romances featuring interspecies love between humans and their beloved vampires, fallen angels, zombies, werewolves, faeries, or pixies. The more reading and thinking I did, however, the more I realized such a book would either be far too long to be publishable in one volume or far too vague to be of value. Then, I began to wonder about the popularity of all these series and about where such interest in these romances originated. Such questions led me to ruminate on my own pleasure in watching *Buffy*, to read the *Twilight* saga novels and later watch the films, and to notice the rising popularity of *The Vampire Diaries* television series. I started to track the characteristics that moved across the series and as I did so, a pattern emerged. *The Beloved Does Not Bite* puts flesh on the bones of that pattern to animate an argument about sustained romantic love between a human and a vampire as the imperative to act justly.

In the quotation from *The Vampire Diaries* that serves as the title for this conclusion, the human Katerina Petrova speaks to her potential vampire beloved, Elijah, one of the Original vampires, in response to him telling her he does not believe in love. She responds by saying, "That is too sad for me to accept. Life is too cruel. If we cease to believe in love, why would we want to live?" ("Klaus" 2019). Her question suggests love to be the main reason for life, and, as *The Beloved Does Not Bite* posits, for living well. By Katerina's reasoning, love serves as an antidote to a cruel world, and as a reason for working towards a just world. Elijah's brother, Klaus, however, warns Elijah against love, for it is a vampire's greatest weakness: "We do not love and we do not feel," Klaus cautions Elijah. Both Klaus and Elijah cannot stop themselves from loving, however, and, indeed, their struggle to resist and embrace love spins-off in to their own series *The Originals*. Given these exchanges take place in a flashback to England in 1492, Katerina's words also suggest this lesson about love is one to be learned over and over again.

Love as a starting point for questions about identity can be traced across a range of YA series, as has been noted by other critics. For instance, in his co-edited collection *Open Graves, Open Minds*, Bill Hughes links the teen zombies of Daniel Water's *Generation Dead*—the novel from which the collection's title was taken—to the figure of the sympathetic vampire (245). Furthermore, in his discussion of *Generation Dead*, he makes explicit the connection between the three series with which *The Beloved Does Not Bite* engages:

> With *Generation Dead*, we are back on the same high school terrain that *Buffy*, and, more recently, L.J. Smith's The Vampire Diaries and Meyer's Twilight series explore. The setting allows the usual (here, very effective) exploration of the issues of becoming a young adult: love and sexuality (thus sharing concerns with the adult 'paranormal romance' genre); looming adult responsibility; and developing a sense of who one is, where one belongs—identity, in other words. (251)

Hughes does not expand in detail upon this point, but he directs attention to future work that might be done on the intersection between love, responsibility, and identity.

Although the *Generation Dead* zombie novels invite a closer analysis of love and morality, the trilogies and sagas that feature a romantic relationship between a human and a fallen angel seem to align most closely with the conventions of the vampire sub-genre. Between 2007 and 2014, no fewer than twenty YA novels—at least ten different series—about fallen angels were published primarily in the United States and Australia. Cassandra Clare's immensely popular *Mortal Instruments* trilogy and Melissa de La Cruz's *Blue Blood* series began the trend in 2007, but most of the first novels in the subsequent series have been published since 2010. Arguably, the most well-known of these series is Lauren Kate's *Fallen* saga, which includes *Fallen* (2010), *Torment* (2011), *Passion* (2011), *Rapture* (2012). The following analysis focuses on this saga as an exemplar of the genre and as a way of providing a brief analysis of the saga itself.

Drawing on the success of the *Twilight* series, most of the fallen angel series adhere to many of the generic conventions outlined throughout *The Beloved Does Not Bite*, including a central plot line that follows the tormented romance between a human (or part-human) female and a monster male. What distinguishes the fallen angel narratives from vampire narratives—such as *Buffy*, *Twilight*, and the *Vampire Diaries*—is the fallen angel narratives rely on the bible and on *Paradise Lost* as overt intertextual references. While the details of the story change—in some cases the female protagonist is at least part angel, for example—in each case, the angel figure has challenged God and been sentenced to eternal damnation. In the *Fallen* saga, for instance, God has cursed the angel Daniel to live forever and to fall in love with his human beloved, Luce, over and over again in different lifetimes. Up until the life chronicled in

Fallen, each time Daniel and Luce fall in love, Luce spontaneously combusts and then returns 17 years later, only to repeat the same pattern of falling in love and dying.

If you know the story of Romeo and Juliet, of Buffy and Angel, of Bella and Edward, of Damon and Elena, then you know the bones of the story of Luce and Daniel and of many other star-crossed and death-marked lovers throughout fallen angel narratives, including Clary and Jace in the *Mortal Instruments*; Nora and Patch in the *Hush, Hush* saga; Clara and Christian in *Unearthly*; and Mercy and Luc/Ryan in *Mercy*. Each of the stories relies on generic conventions of the romance, in which two seemingly incompatible people—or in this case beings—overcome all odds in order to be together. Love conquers all. They sacrifice all for love. Their attraction is undeniable yet unexplainable. Their love is forever. Or as the promotional poster for *Passion* states, "Defy Time. Defy History. Defy God. Risk it all for love."

The defiance in the *Fallen* saga is a defiance against the curse God has placed on Daniel and Luce when Daniel refuses to choose sides between God and Lucifer at the time of the Fall, which readers do not discover until book three. Daniel and Luce's love is thus always already informed by rebellion and is repeatedly connected to fighting a battle. Book one ends with Luce having to leave her school in order to be protected from whatever as yet unknown forces are trying either to kill or capture her. As she flies away, she reflects on her commitment to Daniel in a passage that makes overt a link between love and war:

> No one had come right out and told her that there were more battles to be fought, but Luce felt the truth inside her, that they were at the start of something long and significant and hard.
>
> Together.
>
> And whether the battles were gruesome or redemptive or both, Luce didn't want to be a pawn any longer. A strange feeling was working its way through her body—one steeped in all her past lives, all the love she'd felt for Daniel that had been extinguished too many times before.
>
> It made Luce want to stand up next to him and fight. Fight to stay alive long enough to live out her life next to him. Fight for the only thing she knew that was good enough, noble enough, powerful enough to be worth risking everything.
>
> Love.
>
> (448)

Luce's "strange feeling" forges an affective and semantic link between love and war, and will drive her in *Passion* to exert her free will, visiting some of her past lives and deaths with Daniel in order to find a way to end their curse.

These fallen angel books are marketed to the same audience that consume the *Twilight* series. The series follow similar generic conventions, but they also refer directly to *Twilight* paratextually and intertextually. On the back cover of *Hush, Hush*, for example, one of the accolades for the book is from bellaandedward.com, a *Twilight* fansite, which calls *Hush, Hush* "absolutely brilliant." Similarly, twilight.org asks the question, "Will *Fallen* be the next *Twilight*?" Finally, the second *Fallen* book, *Torment*, directly draws upon massive fansites dedicated to Twihards divided between Team Edward and Team Jacob. Luce finds herself attracted to the "normal" Nephilim—human and angel—boy, Miles, who seems more appealing than the mostly absent and often brooding Daniel. When two of Luce's friends are divided about who Luce should date, Luce says, "'why didn't you guys come down in your Team Daniel and Team Miles T-shirts?'" to which Shelby replies, "'We should order those.'"

One of the most significant ways the fallen angel series draw and expand upon the vampire sub-genre is through their focus upon a world at war. While vampire narratives' issues of responsibility primarily circulate around the vulnerability of an individual, fallen angel narratives place the future of the world at stake, although its safety may hinge on the actions of an individual or a couple, who have been cursed by a higher power. This trope of a hero or heroine, such as a Slayer, saving the world is nothing new, but in fallen angel narratives, the actual war between the forces of good and evil hovers in the margins of the narrative, even as the fallen angel hero represents both guardian angel and angel of death. The *Paradise Lost* intertextual back story casts the fallen angel as always already a rebel warrior, so the female protagonist loves but also fears her fallen angel beloved and fears *for* the safety of her beloved, herself, and the world at large.

As I discussed in Chapter 6, the vampire series all contain or reference battles during which the beloveds must defend their communities from an enemy who threatens to destroy them, and in *The Vampire Diaries*, references to the American Civil War infiltrate the series and inform its politics. Similarly, in the first book in the *Fallen* saga, war is related to this Civil War, and much is made about Luce being from Georgia, in America's South. Readers are repeatedly reminded that Sword and Cross, the school where Luce meets Daniel, used to be a military base and that the cemetery on the school grounds includes the graves of fallen soldiers. Additionally, in one scene, Daniel takes part in a Civil War re-enactment, so when he comes to "save" Luce from Cam—a fallen angel who sided with Satan and is therefore known as a demon—he arrives wearing a Civil War uniform. *Fallen* ends and *Torment* begins with Daniel and Cam negotiating a truce in their current battle, which is ominously referred to as the End Times. Book three, *Passion*, however, is premised on the idea that Luce needs to travel back to her past lives in order to determine how to change the cycle of her life, love, and death. In this book, the horrors of war are more explicit, as Luce enters first, Moscow in 1941 in the midst of WWII, and then Milan in 1918, where she meets Daniel as a WWI soldier.

As in the vampire series (*Buffy* in particular), the fallen angel series negotiate between staging battles between good and evil and suggesting only certain types of wars are worth fighting. For example, *Passion* concludes with Daniel travelling back to the moment when Lucifer and God are taking roll call about which angels are siding with whom. When it comes to Daniel's turn, he says,

> "With respect, I will not do this. I will not choose Lucifer's side, and I will not choose the side of Heaven."
>
> A roar went up from the camp of angels, from Lucifer, and from the Throne.
>
> "Instead, I choose love—the thing you have all forgotten. I choose love and leave you to your war. You're wrong to bring this upon us," Daniel said evenly to Lucifer. Then, turning, he addressed the Throne. "All that is good in Heaven and on Earth is born of love. This war is not just. This war is not good. Love is the only thing worth fighting for."
>
> (403)

Daniel's speaking back to God and Lucifer—to higher authorities—functions in at least three ways: as criticism of the meaninglessness of wars based on a desire for power for the few at the expense of the many; as a way of empowering young people, who embody hope for a better future; and as an acknowledgment it is often young people—and particularly young men—who die and/or suffer from participating in wars.

Paranormal romances, and especially romances featuring fallen angels, call attention to how young people exist as war fodder in adult bids for power and to how young lovers rebel against and overthrow power structures. Similarly, several YA dystopias published at the same time as these paranormal romances focus on romantic love as rebellion. In two of the most popular of these trilogies, The Hunger Games (Collins 2009–2011) and Divergent (Roth 2011–2013) series, the romance between the female protagonists, Katniss and Tris respectively, and their male comrades advances the narratives. For instance, although it is Katniss's love for her sister that initiates her participation in the annual Hunger Games, once she enters the Games, her ostensible romance with Peeta increases her appeal to the audience, saves both of them from death, and forces the Capitol to change the rules of the Game. Similarly, in Roth's series, Tobias's love for Tris enables Tobias to break through the mind control that turns him into a pawn of the authorities (*Divergent* 244–249); Tris realizes her love for Tobias makes her a better person (*Allegiant* 389); and, ultimately, Tris sacrifices her life to save the people she loves (*Allegiant* 441).

Both The Hunger Games and Divergent trilogies focus primarily on the fight against the authorities, and the romance serves as a subplot that nevertheless functions to undermine the power structure. This idea of love as rebellion, however, underpins numerous post-2010 YA dystopias, in which an alternative community protests against either a corrupt king or an invisible ruling party. Several series published during approximately the same period as Divergent (2010–2014) use love as a starting point for rebellion, rather than rebellion as the setting for a love story. Two of these series—the *Eve* books and *The Selection* series—depict how love restores justice to a corrupt kingdom. Promoted on the front cover as a "fresh look at what it means to love," the *Eve* books by Anna Carey—*Eve* (2011); *Once* (2012); and *Rise* (2013)—tell a story about how girls in New America are selected, without their knowledge, as breeders to repopulate the kingdom. The main character, Eve, escapes the night before her so-called 'graduation' as a breeder, and escapes into the wild, where she meets Caleb, the man who becomes her beloved. In *Once*, Eve discovers she is actually the king's daughter, so she is kidnapped and taken to the palace. Instead of fighting the rebellion with Caleb outside the palace walls, she joins forces with the subversives inside the palace to dismantle the system.

The Selection series by Kiera Cass—*The Selection* (2012); *The Elite* (2013); and *The One* (2014); and two more novels that follow the Selection of the main characters' daughter—tells the story of America Singer and centers on her entrance into The Selection, a matchmaking contest to see who will marry the prince. The king created a caste system and The Selection as a way of strengthening the popularity of the royal family by offering the winner and her family a chance to rise within a caste system that most of the populace accepts without question. When America starts to fall in love with the Prince and begins to learn more about the system his father and father's ancestors created, she rebels against it and advocates to dismantle the caste system.

Two other trilogies focus on how an invisible system, rather than a corrupt king, seeks to control the emotional impulse to love, by controlling how they love and who they love. In the Matched series—*Matched* (2010); *Crossed* (2011); and *Reached* (2012)—the governing Society dictates people must be classified as Matched, Single, Aberration, and Anomaly. Most people elect to be Matched rather than Single because the Officials groom the populace to believe the healthiest citizens are those who live in well-matched marriages. In order to achieve such a healthy citizenry, in each person's 17th year, the Society selects a partner for those individuals who choose to be Matched. By contrast, in the Delirium trilogy—*Delirium* (2011); *Pandemonium* (2012); and *Requiem* (2013)—love has been declared a dangerous disease that threatens the safety of the population. In order to alleviate the threat, the government forces every eighteen-year-old to undergo a procedure that cures them of love.

The authorities in these two series justify their actions either by circulating propaganda that cites the dangers of love to the peace and security of the city (Delirium) or by erasing the memories of people who witness conflict (Matched). With the cure and the matching system, everyone seems happy, divorce has basically been eradicated, and people live in a state of passivity and mediocrity, free from passions—or deep emotions—of any kind. Neither of the ruling bodies in Matched and Delirium, however, admit they *are* in fact fighting wars and killing people who threaten to overturn the system. Cassia in Matched and Lena in Delirium know nothing about these wars, nothing about ways of living that challenge the status quo, until they fall in love with Ky and Alex, respectively. Cassia and Lena fall in love with people who the state rules they cannot love, and both beloveds become soldiers in the states wars against an unnamed enemy. Whether love be the cure or the disease, in these two trilogies, love functions as the ideological origin for government control and as the emotional impetus for collective rebellion.

Each of these paranormal romances and futuristic dystopian series could be analyzed using the framework *The Beloved Does Not Bite* develops. In each series, love moves the female protagonist to rebel against an authoritative structure that seeks to control the general population under the guise of protection and the betterment of a society. In this process of rebellion, love initiates just action in the defense of freedom. When people ask me what this book is about, I frequently answer, "vampires and love," but perhaps a better response would be to say this book presents a thought experiment about whether or not romantic/erotic love moves people to act justly. If monster stories provide imaginary answers to real problems, as Richard Kearney argues, then perhaps it behooves us to imagine acting with love as an answer to those problems we face as we move through life. Love can have moral weight, and it can do some heavy lifting. Perhaps when these burdens feel too heavy, we might return to those monster stories or futuristic dystopias to provide a safe space to test our potential responses to the challenges we face every day.

Works Cited

Adornetto, Alexandra. *Hades*. New York: Macmillan, 2011. Print.
———. *Halo*. New York: Macmillan, 2010. Print.
———. *Heaven*. New York: Macmillan, 2012. Print.
Carey, Anna. *Eve*. Sydney: HarperCollins, 2011. Print.
———. *Once*. Sydney: HarperCollins, 2012. Print.
———. *Rise*. Sydney: HarperCollins, 2013. Print.
Cass, Kiera. *The Elite*. Sydney: HarperCollins, 2014. Print.
———. *The One*. Sydney: HarperCollins, 2014. Print.

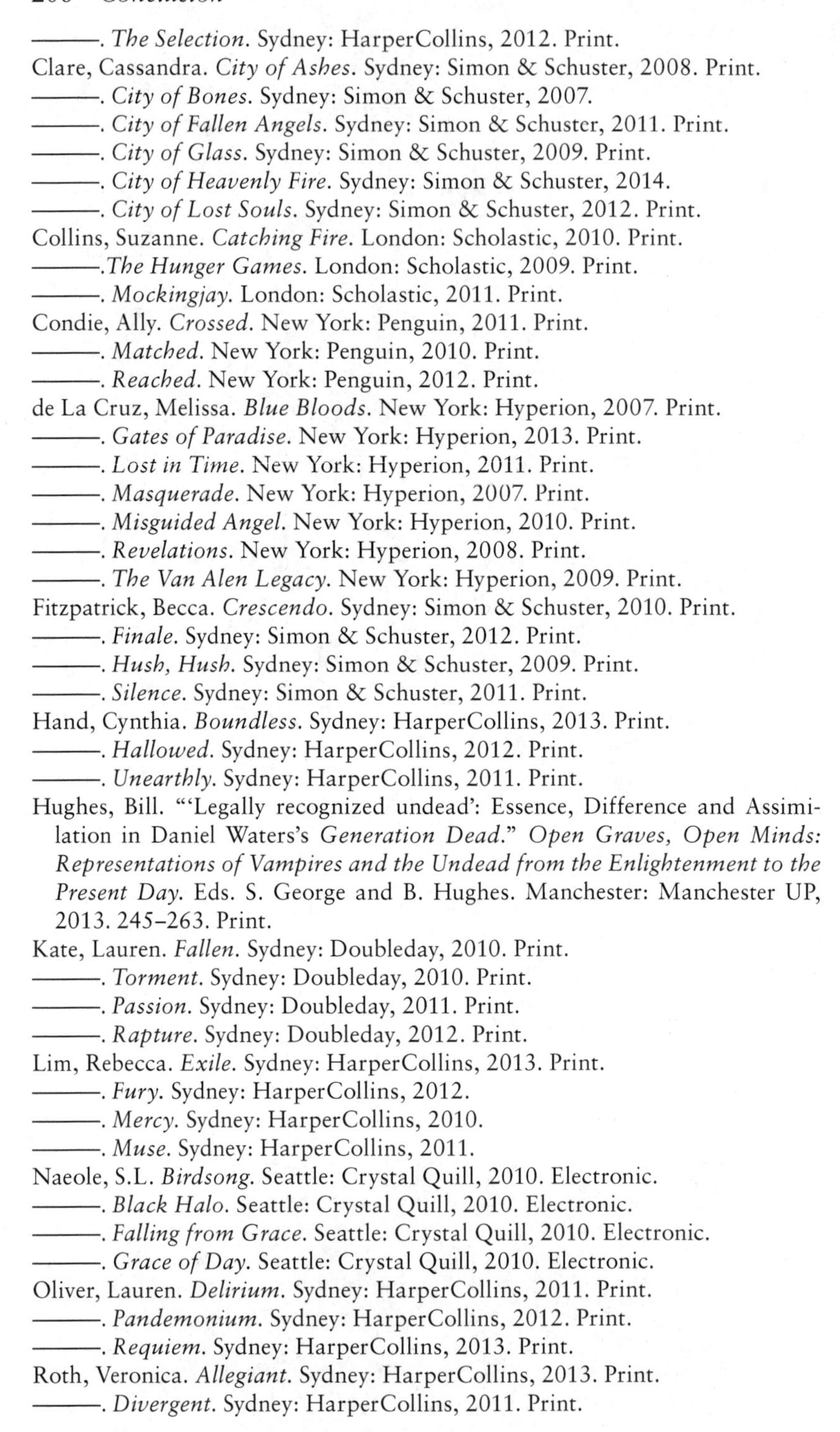

———. *The Selection*. Sydney: HarperCollins, 2012. Print.
Clare, Cassandra. *City of Ashes*. Sydney: Simon & Schuster, 2008. Print.
———. *City of Bones*. Sydney: Simon & Schuster, 2007.
———. *City of Fallen Angels*. Sydney: Simon & Schuster, 2011. Print.
———. *City of Glass*. Sydney: Simon & Schuster, 2009. Print.
———. *City of Heavenly Fire*. Sydney: Simon & Schuster, 2014.
———. *City of Lost Souls*. Sydney: Simon & Schuster, 2012. Print.
Collins, Suzanne. *Catching Fire*. London: Scholastic, 2010. Print.
———.*The Hunger Games*. London: Scholastic, 2009. Print.
———. *Mockingjay*. London: Scholastic, 2011. Print.
Condie, Ally. *Crossed*. New York: Penguin, 2011. Print.
———. *Matched*. New York: Penguin, 2010. Print.
———. *Reached*. New York: Penguin, 2012. Print.
de La Cruz, Melissa. *Blue Bloods*. New York: Hyperion, 2007. Print.
———. *Gates of Paradise*. New York: Hyperion, 2013. Print.
———. *Lost in Time*. New York: Hyperion, 2011. Print.
———. *Masquerade*. New York: Hyperion, 2007. Print.
———. *Misguided Angel*. New York: Hyperion, 2010. Print.
———. *Revelations*. New York: Hyperion, 2008. Print.
———. *The Van Alen Legacy*. New York: Hyperion, 2009. Print.
Fitzpatrick, Becca. *Crescendo*. Sydney: Simon & Schuster, 2010. Print.
———. *Finale*. Sydney: Simon & Schuster, 2012. Print.
———. *Hush, Hush*. Sydney: Simon & Schuster, 2009. Print.
———. *Silence*. Sydney: Simon & Schuster, 2011. Print.
Hand, Cynthia. *Boundless*. Sydney: HarperCollins, 2013. Print.
———. *Hallowed*. Sydney: HarperCollins, 2012. Print.
———. *Unearthly*. Sydney: HarperCollins, 2011. Print.
Hughes, Bill. "'Legally recognized undead': Essence, Difference and Assimilation in Daniel Waters's *Generation Dead*." *Open Graves, Open Minds: Representations of Vampires and the Undead from the Enlightenment to the Present Day*. Eds. S. George and B. Hughes. Manchester: Manchester UP, 2013. 245–263. Print.
Kate, Lauren. *Fallen*. Sydney: Doubleday, 2010. Print.
———. *Torment*. Sydney: Doubleday, 2010. Print.
———. *Passion*. Sydney: Doubleday, 2011. Print.
———. *Rapture*. Sydney: Doubleday, 2012. Print.
Lim, Rebecca. *Exile*. Sydney: HarperCollins, 2013. Print.
———. *Fury*. Sydney: HarperCollins, 2012.
———. *Mercy*. Sydney: HarperCollins, 2010.
———. *Muse*. Sydney: HarperCollins, 2011.
Naeole, S.L. *Birdsong*. Seattle: Crystal Quill, 2010. Electronic.
———. *Black Halo*. Seattle: Crystal Quill, 2010. Electronic.
———. *Falling from Grace*. Seattle: Crystal Quill, 2010. Electronic.
———. *Grace of Day*. Seattle: Crystal Quill, 2010. Electronic.
Oliver, Lauren. *Delirium*. Sydney: HarperCollins, 2011. Print.
———. *Pandemonium*. Sydney: HarperCollins, 2012. Print.
———. *Requiem*. Sydney: HarperCollins, 2013. Print.
Roth, Veronica. *Allegiant*. Sydney: HarperCollins, 2013. Print.
———. *Divergent*. Sydney: HarperCollins, 2011. Print.

———. *Insurgent*. Sydney: HarperCollins, 2012. Print.
Shirvington, Jessica. *Emblaze*. Melbourne: Hachette, 2011. Print.
———. *Embrace*. Melbourne: Hachette, 2010. Print.
———. *Empower*. Melbourne: Hachette, 2013. Print.
———. *Endless*. Melbourne: Hachette, 2012. Print.
———. *Entice*. Melbourne: Hachette, 2012. Print.
Sniegoski, Thomas E. *The Fallen 1*. Sydney: Simon & Schuster, 2010.
———. *The Fallen 2*. Sydney: Simon & Schuster, 2010.
———. *The Fallen 3*. Sydney: Simon & Schuster, 2011.
———. *The Fallen 4*. Sydney: Simon & Schuster, 2012.
———. *The Fallen 5*. Sydney: Simon & Schuster, 2013.
Terrell, Heather. *Eternity*. New York: HarperTeens, 2011.
———. *Fallen Angel*. New York: HarperTeens, 2010.
Waters, Daniel. *Generation Dead*. New York: Hyperion, 2008. Print.
———. *Kiss of Life*. New York: Hyperion, 2009. Print.
———. *My Friends are Dead*. OMZ, 2016. Print.
———. *Passing Strange*. New York: Hyperion, 2010. Print.

Index